ABOVE THE FOLD

ABOVE THE FOLD

A Personal History of the *Toronto Star*

John Honderich

SIGNAL

MCCLELLAND
& STEWART

Library and Archives Canada Cataloguing in Publication
Title: Above the fold : a personal history of the Toronto Star / John Honderich.
Names: Honderich, John, 1946- author.
Identifiers: Canadiana (print) 20220189129 | Canadiana (ebook) 20220189188 |
ISBN 9780771000201 (hardcover) | ISBN 9780771000218 (EPUB)
Subjects: LCSH: Honderich, John, 1946- | LCSH: Toronto Star (Firm) | LCSH:
    Canadian newspapers—Ontario—Toronto—History. | LCSH: Newspaper
    publishing—Ontario—Toronto—History. | LCSH: Journalism—Ontario—
    Toronto—History. | CSH: Canadian newspapers (English)—Ontario—Toronto—
    History | LCGFT: Autobiographies.
Classification: LCC PN4913.H66 A3 2022 | DDC 070.4/1092—dc23

Jacket design by Matthew Flute
Jacket art: (front) Matthew Flute; (back) John Honderich and his father, Beland, on the grounds of Rideau Hall in 2004. (Tobin Grimshaw/The *Toronto Star*)
Author photograph by Rene Johnston
Typeset by M&S, Toronto
Printed in Canada

Published by Signal,
an imprint of McClelland & Stewart,
a division of Penguin Random House Canada Limited,
a Penguin Random House Company
www.penguinrandomhouse.ca

1   2   3   4   5   26   25   24   23   22

Penguin
Random House
Canada

To the loyal legions of *Star* staff who, over time,
have epitomized the finest in Canadian newspapering

CONTENTS

John Allen Honderich, 1946–2022 (Courtesy of the Honderich Family)

FOREWORD

by Robin Honderich

"A Paper for the People"—that's what a small group of disgruntled printers and apprentices set out as the vision for the *Evening Star* when they launched it in 1892, the newspaper that eventually would become the *Toronto Star*. It was a powerful and enduring slogan that both my father and grandfather lived by, although in very different ways.

This book is an inside look at the journey of the *Toronto Star*, Canada's largest and most successful newspaper, based in Canada's largest city. It is also the tale of the father and son who were at the heart of its operations for just shy of half a century and, in so doing, helped shape a city, a province, and a nation.

It's a story that will appeal to journalists and non-journalists alike, as well as newspaper lovers in general.

My father John Honderich possessed not only a larger-than-life personality, equipped with a belly laugh and smile that few will ever forget, but also a drive and determination that appeared to have no limit. From where I stood, it was the combination of the person he was, the values he held dear, and the engine that drove him that ultimately led to his success in life. In his early seventies, Dad was still chair of the board of Torstar, the parent company of the Toronto Star, and intimately wrapped up in the boardroom dramas that came with the position. For much of his late career, he was still out most nights of the week, often asked to attend event after event as the public face of the *Star*—the person everyone wanted to see. As his son, and someone who wanted him to be with us for a while, the questions for me in the last decade were: Does this incredible engine have a best-before date? What will happen when he does finally slow down, whether by choice or circumstance?

Sadly, we now have the answer. My dad died the morning of February 5, 2022, of an apparent heart attack. My wife Becky, our two boys—his only grandchildren, Sebastian (six) and George (four)—and I had dinner with him the night before. In no way did any of us see this coming.

As it turns out, Dad lived less than two years after he left Torstar. The sale of the company was finalized in the first few months after the COVID-19 pandemic began and he was intimately involved in the transaction right up to the end. In fact, he often referred to that last year leading up to the sale as one of the busiest of his life, certainly from a corporate perspective, at least. It was also clearly very difficult for him to be shepherding through the sale of the company he loved and had put so much of his life into, while at the same time trying to ensure it landed in good hands. He rarely complained about the responsibility, but I could see and feel the weight it put on him. In just a few pages you will come to understand that burden even more.

It felt very cruel to have "retired" during the pandemic. It must have been the same for many others. For Dad, it was a sudden pivot from being a corporate executive driving a complex sale to being stuck at home with little to do and few people to see. Now, "little" is definitely a relative term because for Dad, "little" meant being active on three boards of directors. And I should clarify that he never once actually used the "R" word with us to describe his situation. Despite direct inquiries on the matter, Dad insisted he was "interregnum," which I came to learn meant "between kingdoms." He didn't know where his next "kingdom" was going to come from, but he was certain there was going to be one.

It was also during that year and a half following the sale of the company, and his subsequent departure from Torstar, that Dad sat down to write this book. He had spoken of doing so for a long time. He had taken trips to Germany and Kitchener-Waterloo years before to do research on the family roots but although he truly appeared to want to write this book, he couldn't quite seem to bring himself to do it. I think perhaps he was waiting to see if there was another chapter for the *Star* still to come. After the Torstar sale, that possibility ended and this book became Dad's primary focus. He attacked it as he would any other task in front of him—with a vengeance! He delighted in being well ahead of every single deadline set by his publisher. Once a newspaperman . . .

This book, however, isn't just about Dad, but also about his dad, Beland Honderich. The man I knew as "Grandpa Bee," but others knew by a few less-flattering nicknames. Bringing to light Grandpa's story and his rise to the top at the *Star* was, I believe, one of Dad's motivating factors in putting pen to paper. He is very honest in these pages about his relationship with his father. It was fascinating for me to read about it, but it also made me reflect on my own relationship and experience with my father. And I could not help but note that while Dad had clearly worked through his own father-son experience, at least as he describes it here, he had yet to recognize some of the parallels of his own experience of being a father to me and my sister Emily.

So, you may be wondering, just how do I fit in? Well, I am John's son and the third Honderich in three consecutive generations to work at the *Star*. I did not contribute to the forty-nine consecutive years where either my father or grandfather was in charge, but I had a front row seat like few others, especially during the last two decades, and I feel very much a part of the journey.

In fact, due to the *Star's* unique share structure, I had an even more in-depth view through the Torstar Voting Trust, which controlled the company. Not only did I hear many stories at the dinner table, I

actually joined our family board and trust in my early 20s. From that
point on, alongside the rest of my family, I would receive a formal
Torstar update, initially from Grandpa, and then soon after from
Dad. In the last few years, it became a particular highlight when Dad
had started turning to me to aid in the formal Torstar update, as the
"boots-on-the-ground" employee who could speak to the digital space
a little more eloquently than my technologically challenged father.

Although my father wore many hats in the end—among them,
Honderich family representative on the Voting Trust, chair of the
Voting Trust, and chair of Torstar—what many readers may not
know is that these positions were ultimately conditional on the support of his family. Like all other Voting Trust families, we elected a
representative for both the Voting Trust and the Torstar board. In
theory, that representation was up for review and approval every year
at our family board meeting. Given Dad's role in the company, it was
most often a no-brainer that our family would reappoint him, but
it's an element of Dad's story that is not fully spelled out here. Not
only was he running a newsroom or a company or a board, he was
also always having to report back to his family and keep us all
onside—even during the difficult years in the late stages of his
tenure, when the family was taking large personal financial hits due
to the industry's struggles.

It's one reason why I think the entire Honderich family is owed
some credit in whatever due one might prescribe to the *Star* and its
journalism. This is especially true for Dad's two siblings Mary and
David, who never worked for the paper, but who bought into its underlying principles and mission, remaining steadfast in support of Dad
and his efforts throughout difficult times. As someone said to me
recently, Dad "wasn't a bean counter." Rather, he was a newspaperman.
Someone who believed deeply in the value of journalism and what it
means for a healthy democracy and society—and we were behind him.

I followed a winding road, as my father did, to end up working at
the *Star*. I always credit him, as he did his father, for putting no

significant pressure on me to join the company. The choice was my own. And after six years at the Canadian sports network TSN, and completing a master's degree abroad, I eventually applied for a job in the *Star's* digital department, focusing on video.

I joined the company in January 2014 and, as I write this in May 2022, I am still at the *Star*, now as a director focusing on digital subscriptions. That has kept alive a streak of seventy-nine consecutive years with at least one Honderich working at the newspaper.

After I joined the *Star*, there was no question that Dad and I became closer than we had ever been. In a recent lunch with my mother, Katherine Govier, who was married to Dad for eighteen years, we discussed the avalanche of love and affection for him after his death. Two straight days on the front page of the *Star*, above the fold, no less, and a special section the following weekend! My goodness! Even he might have thought that was too much. But he would also have been touched beyond imagination.

As my mother reflected on their lives together, she recalled a conversation she had with him in the late stages of their marriage. She said, "You know, the paper is not a person. It's not going to love you the way I do." She added with a laugh, "I guess I was wrong!" I had to concur.

The tributes and heartfelt messages we received didn't come just from journalists and former colleagues at the *Star*, but also from senior politicians from coast to coast, from top business and community leaders, and from everyday readers of the paper. I was amazed at how many people spoke to the quiet gestures he made to help people out. He truly had a huge heart and extended it to many.

In my eulogy for Dad, I joked that after he and my mother got divorced, he "made it official" and married the *Star* as his second wife. Except, it wasn't really a joke, as that's what it felt like for his immediate family as he put most of his time, energy, and love into the paper. There were and are costs to those choices. But, after seeing the outpouring he received upon his death, both my mother and I felt we gained a little more understanding of just what he got back from all that he gave to "the paper for the people" and the people with whom he worked.

As one of the fortunate few to read an early draft of this book, I noted that it did not truly convey just how beloved Dad was at the *Star*. When I raised this with him several months before his death, he said to me, "Well, I can't say any of that." But I can.

Given the unique and bittersweet opportunity here to add a small piece to his work, I want to convey just how much love there was for my father. He was a complex person privately, but to the public and his colleagues, he was a unique bundle of energy, passion, and enthusiasm that endeared him to many. He was just as likely to be debating policy with the premier or the mayor as he was to be talking up his favourite server at Biff's Bistro, one of his most-favoured Toronto restaurants, or the gas pump kid at the marina near his cottage. That was especially true at the *Star* where Dad befriended and earned the trust and respect of so many, at all levels of the organization.

This was no more evident than at the celebration of life my sister Emily and I organized. COVID-19 rules meant that we had to host a very small and private funeral, but a few months later we were able to throw a party for dad that he would have been proud of. We pulled together a wonderful combination of *Star* editors and writers, past and present, combined with friends and family. We were honoured to have the prime minister come and pay his respects and were blown away when Mayor John Tory presented the keys to the City of Toronto to Dad, posthumously. But for me, the best part of the night was the feeling in the room. Having so many people that Dad had touched in some way, from all walks of his life, together in one room, swapping stories and laughs over a glass was something I won't ever forget. In a way, I felt like I got to walk, at least for one night, in his shoes.

I had become somewhat immune to people stopping Dad on the street or getting giddy once they heard my last name and relation to him. But not completely. For example, as I was buying a new suit for his celebration of life, the salesperson at the store, upon learning that I was John Honderich's son, became overwhelmed with emotion. He spoke about Dad's contribution to the city and how he came to admire him. He was, however, also a Ryerson journalism graduate who had left the field after a number of years of trying to make a living—a sad but indicative sign of the current state of the industry that concerned Dad so much.

My father wasn't perfect by any means. While he had many friends and fans, there is also a pretty long list of people he had run-ins with over the years, many of whom you will read about in the following pages. Dad was extremely principled, not to mention stubborn, which led to some bitter disputes with even the best of friends. I often heard him shrug off those disputes, which I thought painful, as a sort of "cost of doing business." What really mattered, he would say, was that he and the *Star* remain focused on the bigger picture.

This book is many things but it is ultimately about that bigger picture. And there is no one better at capturing it than Dad. So, over to you . . .

Toronto

May 2022

PREFACE

They would be the last words my father ever spoke to me. Uttered within the sterile anonymity of a shared hospital room on the fifth floor of Vancouver's St. Paul's Hospital, they struck as a thunderbolt. It had been two weeks since a crippling stroke had left his right side virtually paralyzed, his speech cruelly impaired, and his indomitable spirit crushed. I had been the first of the three siblings on the scene. Yet to this point, any meaningful exchange had not unfolded. Another in a series of family disputes—this one over my revulsion at his needless yet calculated evisceration of my brother's pride and his role in the family trust—had rendered recent contact almost non-existent. So when I first saw him in that room, his only mission trying to escape, I was not surprised by either his froideur or his steely glares. But two weeks later, that mood had evolved, with the inevitability of the medical outcome now clear. He waited for the moment when we were alone, then curled his left finger in that oh-so-familiar "come hither" gesture. And then, summoning every ounce of remaining strength, he rasped out the words: "Don't . . . let them . . . ruin . . . the paper. . . ."

"Of course," I replied hastily, the sheer emotion of making that proclamation welling up inside. "I won't. . . ."

Our eyes fixed, the closure was complete. In that one electric instant, the sheer enormity and intensity of our lifetime bond crystallized.

What we shared was, of course, an unbridled passion for "the paper," the *Toronto Star*. Not just any paper—but Canada's largest and arguably most successful newspaper. It is the paper whose more than century-long crusade for a kinder and fairer society has had an indisputably profound effect on Canadians. Many of this country's basic social welfare programs—pensions, unemployment insurance, medicare, minimum wage, workmen's compensation—were championed first, early, and hard by the *Star*. It has been, at different times, home base to the likes of Ernest Hemingway, Morley Callaghan, Ralph Allen, Nathan Cohen, Pierre Berton, Lotta Dempsey, Milt Dunnell, Charles Templeton, June Callwood, Duncan Macpherson, Peter Newman, Gary Lautens, Jocko Thomas, Doris Anderson, Boris Spremo, Robert Fulford, Richard Gwyn, Dalton Camp, Michele Landsberg, George Bain, Christie Blatchford, Joey Slinger, Rosie DiManno, and Chantal Hébert.

It is also the newspaper that brandishes a corporate history unlike any other. In an extraordinary exercise of arbitrary power, the Ontario government of George Drew made illegal—*retroactively*—the will of the *Star*'s great spiritual founder, Joseph E. Atkinson, in which he sought to leave the paper to the foundation that bears his name. Following a decade in which that government had virtual veto power over all the *Star*'s operations, control of the paper eventually devolved to the five families of the Torstar voting trust, one of which was the Honderichs. And in the process, those families committed before an Ontario court to observe and promote the Atkinson Principles, the intellectual and spiritual basis on which the *Star* has always been operated. That promise still exists. And through this serendipity of historical circumstance, my father and I had the privilege of serving as the second- and third-longest-seated publishers respectively—Mr. Atkinson being the longest.

Little wonder, then, that such a tradition and legacy would envelop, if not sometimes overwhelm, our relationship. We could always discuss news coverage or Toronto's competitive newspaper market. Editorial endorsements would often be dinnertime fare. Yet we also never underestimated how tenuous the paper's future could be—thus his deathbed plea. That plea was not directed at anyone in particular; rather, it was an impassioned call to all involved to remain constantly vigilant about the quality of the paper *and* the commitment to maintain the Atkinson Principles. It had been his life's work, his monumental legacy. He surely did not want it all to go for naught. Nor, surely, did I.

This is certainly not the stuff of traditional father–son relationships, and indeed ours was anything but. There was love between us, yet it was rarely expressed. I had stood at his side for two of his three weddings—the first being appropriately impossible—but my sister Mary was clearly his favourite. Our fights were occasional but sometimes very hurtful. During his career, my father garnered the provocative epithet of "the Beast," and I was often the victim of his infamous wrath. Expressing open pride in what I had accomplished was simply not done, until the *very* end. Yet we also did so many things together. I was exposed to so much and only now have begun to appreciate fully the breadth of his paternal influence. Most important of all, we shared the same passion.

As I left St. Paul's Hospital that October day in 2005, my mind wandered back to a glorious day the year prior when I had received the Order of Canada. It was one of those translucent June days that shows Ottawa's Rideau Hall at its finest. Up to a few days before, it had been unclear whether my father would even bother to make the trip from Vancouver. Once he decided to attend, he first rejected the invitation to dinner. Then, just as abruptly, he accepted it. There was a bit of a stir, for we were supposedly only the third or fourth father-son combination to have both received the honour. But it was the moment prior to the ceremony in the majestic gardens that will be forever etched in my mind.

There was a freelance photographer who had been specially assigned to capture the occasion—promotion of *Star* bosses always being an unstated must at the paper. He lined up the shot, both of us resplendent in dark blue suits. Then, to make conversation as photogs often do, he posed a seemingly innocuous question: "So, how long *did* you guys run the place?"

Neither of us knew, nor had we ever thought to do the calculation. So we did. My father was appointed editor-in-chief in 1955 and then publisher in 1966. He was at the helm for twenty-two years until 1988, when he stepped down. At that very same time, I was appointed editor. Six years later I became publisher, a role I remained in for a decade until 2004.

"That would make forty-nine years," I finally replied.

"Not bad," quipped the photog.

And indeed it isn't. For almost half a century, ultimate editorial responsibility for the *Star* rested continuously with either Beland or John Honderich. We certainly never spoke of it in such terms. Yet, on reflection, there is a curious historical anomaly to the number forty-nine. The *Star*'s first great publisher, Joseph Atkinson, also served for forty-nine years, from 1899 to his death in 1948. Half-century bookends, one might say, for ninety-eight years of historic newspapering.

It was precisely this unique legacy that prompted me to nudge my father often, after his retirement, to write his autobiography. But he would have none of it. "It wouldn't be the truth," he would usually retort. To which I would just as usually reply, "But it will be your truth and your story. That's what autobiographies are." Even the gentler suasions of his beloved third wife Rina had little effect. "Bee, you have such an important story to tell," she would say. Instead, "Bee" spent much of his time researching and investigating the circumstances around and the reaction to the Ontario government's unprecedented move against Atkinson's will. Indeed, he wrote a booklet about it, which I have incorporated in this story. He also did an exhaustive study of the forty-nine years Atkinson served as publisher, seeking out consistencies and editorial patterns. They would not be as ideologically consistent as he would have preferred; yet he still wrote an analysis of that period that is invaluable reading.

Then there is "The Book," the authorized history of the *Star* that was commissioned by my father for the paper's centennial in 1992. Two gritty veteran newshounds, Jack Brehl and David Macdonald, spent a couple of years interviewing as many *Star* players as they could, compiling several cabinets full of files. It is a virtual treasure trove of material—a bonanza for any recounting of the forty-nine Honderich years. "The Book" was completed but my father refused to allow its publication. "It would make things more difficult within the voting trust," he told me several times. Having not read it then, I couldn't make an independent judgment. Now that I have, I can, and I'm still not sure of the real reason for his refusal. Whether it was the vivid recountings of the razzle-dazzle go-get-'em journalism of the *Star* in the '50s, the assessment of earlier leadership at the paper, the insights on Bee himself, the byzantine yet intense battles within the voting trust, or a combination of some or all of the above, is still not clear to me. That said, the manuscript is rich in information and anecdotes, much of which I have incorporated here.

Perhaps the most complicated and difficult decision in launching this project was whether I would be prepared to write about my father, my own career, and the relationship between us. The first part of this challenge was not difficult. As Canada's largest newspaper, the *Star* surely deserves to have its story told. In 1962, *Star* journalist Ross Harkness wrote a book entitled *J.E. Atkinson of the "Star"*, which has become the definitive source for the first half century of the paper. With the exception of "The Book," sitting on that dusty shelf, no subsequent biography or treatise on the paper itself has been published. While I am certainly biased, I have always felt my father's story must be told. When receiving his Order of Canada, he was celebrated as "one of the finest journalists ever produced in Canada." His impact on the *Star*, not to mention on Canadian journalism and Canadian society, was profound.

Writing about my own story and my relationship with my father was an entirely different matter. Certainly, the circumstance of a son succeeding his father as boss at a public company is not unique. How that process unfolded, whether the son succeeded, and whether the silver spoon of nepotism reared its ugly head undoubtedly make the tale that much more tantalizing. Add to these the interplay of emotions, pride, and dismay that mould any father–son relationship and the tale beckons even more. It is well known in *Star* circles that my father and I did not have an easy relationship. On the other hand, flowing from his nickname, gossip mags later pinned on me the corresponding moniker Beast *Jr.* On his passing in 2005, I was surprised, if not taken aback, to find among his possessions a file with every piece of correspondence we had ever exchanged. Reading through those memories was at times reassuring, at times infuriating, and at times embarrassing. Yet the framework for our relationship sat there in a crumpled pile of mostly old letters.

Ultimately, I decided the challenge was too enticing and the subject of the *Star* too significant for me not to forge ahead. That decision has led to a journey of discovery as I have tracked down the family roots in Hesse, Germany, unearthed countless tidbits about my father's early years in Baden, rummaged through the files of the *Kitchener Daily Record* to read his early stories, read for the first time his early work at the *Star*, and contemplated the saga of our time together at the paper, as witnesses to a half century of both Canadian history and newspapering. As with any self-respecting journalist, my aim has been to be both fair and accurate. But, as I kept saying to my father when urging him to write his own story, it is inevitably my version of events, my version as a son. In that sense, the perspective of a scholarly critic or journalistic savant is necessarily lessened. Yet, in my research and countless interviews, my aim has been to seek out as much commentary and independent perspective as possible—if only to verify my own take on events.

Thus what emerges in the pages ahead is my story of a father and son: our respective early years in journalism; our spats, foibles, and successes; our entirely different paths to the same unique chair of publisher; our efforts to shape debate, be it local or national; and our struggle to maintain and enhance the stature of Canada's largest newspaper. The task has been daunting, but the rewards and discoveries bountiful. For me, it has turned out to be a story well worth recounting. My sincere hope is that readers agree.

PART I

1

MENNONITE BADEN

Throughout his entire early life, my father Beland struggled to overcome adversity. Be it poverty, partial deafness, the shunning by his own Mennonite community, high school failure, losing the family home, joblessness, or the Great Depression, he survived it all. Yet giving up or feeling sorry for himself was never part of his emotional wiring. Ultimately, he lived life at both extremes—first in deep poverty and then, as one of Canada's most renowned journalists and newspaper proprietors, in very comfortable wealth. Never, however, did he forget his beginnings or his heritage. They shaped him, forging him into a driving, single-minded, obsessive individual who strove for perfection in all he did. The impact of the humiliation of a down-and-out family losing its home through foreclosure or the ignominy of failing at high school is challenging to gauge. But his is certainly not the usual Horatio Alger rags-to-riches story. While there are elements of such stories in his lifeline, it was his particular pioneer Mennonite history that shaped him perhaps more than anything else.

He was immensely proud of his heritage, although he spoke rarely of it outside the family. One notable exception came in 1965 when he returned to his Ontario hometown village of Baden, just west of Waterloo, to speak to the local historical society. How emotional it must have been for him to return as "local boy made good" to that high school gym, just a short hike down Snyder's Road from where he first grew up. It hadn't been his high school. That was sixteen kilometres away in Kitchener, the source of much academic heartache. That night, however, the soon-to-be publisher of Canada's largest newspaper spoke of his childhood in terms I'd rarely heard.

"As a young lad, I can recall my grandfather telling me stories about the early settlers and their struggle to clear the land and build their cabins," he recounted. "It seemed to me then, as it does today, that it must have taken a great deal of courage to come to a new country and start, with little more than your hands, to push back the frontier. Perhaps I am a romanticist at heart, but it gives me strength in facing problems I encounter, to look back and recall what my forbears and the early settlers accomplished in the face of such odds. The problems we face in our daily lives today are vastly different, but nothing we have to do requires more courage and strength of character than they displayed."

So the story of Beland and, by extension, me, must necessarily begin with Christian Honderich, Beland's grandfather, who first arrived in Canada in 1825. The exact point of departure for the thirty-six-year-old Christian and his new wife Margaret has been a matter of considerable and persistent family conjecture. Germany has always been accepted as the country of origin. But was it more specifically Alsace-Lorraine, Bavaria, or Hesse? Each had its history of Mennonites seeking out religious freedom and free land in the New World.

The doyenne of local Mennonite history for Baden's Wilmot Township, Lorraine Roth, has done extensive genealogical histories on all 130 settlers who claimed lots in the "German Block" around Baden. Her research is by far the most authoritative. She writes that Christian, Margaret, and Margaret's brother Jacob Gingerich probably left from Waldeck, a small principality in modern day Hesse. Unfortunately, while the usually fastidious Germans kept meticulous records for most citizens, such was not the case for the reviled and religiously rejected Mennonites. As Lutheran orthodoxy held greater and greater sway, there was little tolerance for a heretical sect that had a deep aversion to infant baptism, the Anabaptists believing "religion is not to be child's play."

Sure enough, however, in the bosom of a stone museum in Kassel—perhaps best known as home of the Brothers Grimm—I discovered documents sketching out the existence of a small Mennonite farming community in nearby Waldeck. It seems the principality's prince took a different view and offered a place for the "*Schweizer*" to work on his farms. The literal translation of *Schweizer* is Swiss, and it is thought the Honderichs were originally of Swiss origin, with a town near Bern indeed boasting the family name. These same Swiss gained a reputation as superior farmers and honest workers. Though the law of the time deemed them outcasts and forbade their owning land, the prince was able, through his position, to offer them leases to farm parts of his large estate. So long as they paid their rent, handed over a designated portion of their crops, and tended his animals, they were free to build their own herds and farm as they wished.

The records indicate the particular *Schweizer* farm was near Berich, a village directly beneath the towering turrets of the prince's stone castle, which still looms over the Eder River valley. It is spectacular country, with large rolling hills and verdant thick forests. The river, however, has since been dammed up to form the Edersee reservoir, thus placing the old Berich farm under water. But the records clearly show details of both the Honderich and Gingerich families.

Enter Christian Nafziger, an enterprising Mennonite from Munich, who came to Upper Canada in 1822 seeking land for his religious compatriots. Legend has it he was led to the highest point in the western-most wedge of Waterloo County, Baden Hill, by an Indigenous guide and shown a great swath of forested terrain to the west. With the assistance of nearby Mennonites, Nafziger then petitioned the government to buy a section. Though he received encouragement, he was told nothing could be guaranteed without royal assent. On his return to Bavaria in 1822, he stopped off in London to secure just that. In a subsequent letter, he proclaimed success, saying consent was provided "by His Royal Highness." Whether this was actually King George IV himself or a designate is not clear, but family lore inevitably insists on the former. Following that, Nafziger spread the word among the various German Mennonite communities, extolling this new opportunity.

One can only imagine how unexpected and dramatic this offer would appear to Christian Honderich. Certainly the reclusive life required to avoid religious persecution had its limitations, and there was no guarantee the prince would continue to show his kindness. Furthermore, on most farms, three to four Mennonite families would be housed in very close quarters. The prospect of two hundred acres of land (fifty of them free provided certain conditions were met), combined with the prospect of religious freedom, must have appeared irresistible. Thus Christian and Margaret, along with her brother Jacob, set out for a new life.

Ultimately, the two men secured directly adjacent lots on what is now Bleams Road, just south of Baden. Christian Honderich was intent on one day building a water mill, so he carefully selected the lot through which a sparkling brook still runs. Jacob Gingerich was a wagoneer who preferred the sturdy oaks on the lot directly to the east. For the front fifty acres, each paid a five-pound survey fee, and eventually more than one hundred pounds (or four hundred dollars) for the entire lot.

Beland would later recount how he would often sit at night in rapt fascination as his grandfather recounted the struggles of those early pioneer days. The Honderichs have always been immensely proud that the first white settler born in Wilmot was John Honderich, Christian and Margaret's first son. Through eight generations, our family branch has also maintained the tradition, one variation notwithstanding, of alternating the name of the first son born between "Christian" and "John."

When Christian arrived by horseback at his chosen lot, his first tasks were to create a small clearing beside the brook and build a basic log cabin. He was said to have found remnants of a beaver dam on the creek, but the greatest menace by far came from growling wolves and bears. To keep them at bay, he kept fires burning throughout the night, and to get provisions he would trek the sixteen kilometres to Waterloo and then return, the sacks strapped to his back. Told and retold is the story of how Christian would stack piles of brushwood in front of the door and windows of the cabin before his occasional trips to Waterloo. If he did not return by nightfall, a solitary Margaret would light the wood to frighten off the animals. Not unexpectedly, the Mennonites of the area also strove to protect and comfort each other. For example, a swath of forest was cleared so Margaret and her brother's family could signal to each other.

Clearing the land, however, was the obsession. It was also the prerequisite for securing a deed to the land. Pumpkins were the favourite crop as they adapted well to the virgin soil between stumps. Trees were felled on top of each other wherever possible and burned. Wood had no value. The greatest amusement was to prepare a gusher of trees for felling to the point where a single axe stroke would precipitate a domino-like collapse. A man to each tree, on a given signal, would take his final swing and the resulting boom could be heard for miles. To heighten the dramatic effect, this was usually done at daybreak. For Beland, these tales had so much meaning, for he came to know the farm intimately, tapping its maples, digging out old tree roots, and working its fields.

In fact, his whole life might have centred on this farm were it not for the religious cataclysm that suddenly befell both his father and grandfather. For each and every Honderich, worshipping as a member of the ultra-conservative Amish Mennonite congregation was simply a given. Deviation in the slightest was taken as heresy. Indeed Jacob Amman, spiritual founder of this particular branch, railed against other Mennonites for becoming too worldly, adopting new styles of clothing, and not conforming to the apostolic doctrines of faith. One of the most contentious practices at that time became the use of buttons. Not godly, was the verdict. Thus emerged the use of hooks and eyes for fastening clothes and replacing "barn-door britches" with hook flies on men's trousers. Years later, there would be a similar debate over the tolerance of any chrome on cars. Better to paint all fenders black was the usual answer.

In such a world, the very thought of being exposed to "false doctrine"—that is, attending a different religious service—was simply anathema. Yet Beland's grandfather Christian had the audacity to go along with his son John to a revivalist session, perhaps Baptist, in Niagara. The retribution was swift and brutal. Christian and family were immediately excommunicated from the church. From that day forward, none of his younger brothers who had also come to Canada would ever again shake his hand—grabbing his elbow being the sole form of allowed greeting. His family would never again be invited to the farm for dinner. And when Christian died at age seventy-four and his body was laid out in the parlour of the family homestead, his brothers dared not enter. Instead, they prayed for his soul from the bedroom directly above, with cotton in their ears, lest they hear any "false doctrine."

This event changed forever the lives of Christian, his children, and ultimately his grandchildren, Beland included. The family had to move to Baden, where their story was, of course, well known. Living somewhere betwixt and between—neither as Mennonites nor as part of the village's establishment—they were apart, a family shunned. Unlike all his farm cousins, Beland would never learn German, as was the Mennonite tradition. While he certainly spent some time with his cousins, their lives would be separate—different schooling, lifestyle, socializing, and religious upbringing.

Yet for our family, Christian's "bold streak of independence"—as I heard it called often—was a singular badge of honour. Beland revered his grandfather. Indeed, his older sister Ruth would often say, "Bee was most like him." From this trauma was forever etched in his mind a respect for rebellion, the right to differ, and the right to decide how to worship. In that society, the Honderichs lived the life of the black sheep of the family. So young Beland knew what it meant to be born on the wrong side of the tracks, for he lived that experience every day. It gave him a life view he never lost. But he always remained tremendously proud of his grandfather's rebellious-ness, despite the hardship it inevitably brought to the family.

Beland was born November 25, 1918, in Kitchener, the third of six children and the second boy. His father named him after a Montreal doctor he had come to admire, opting curiously to adopt the man's last name. During the prior several years, Beland's father John and mother Rae had moved house multiple times between Baden and Kitchener in constant search of work and sustenance. Sadly, John never seemed able to make his mark, hindered greatly by a profound deafness. Sign language was his only means of communication. Supporting his family, let alone finding his niche, also became a never-ending challenge. He did everything from keeping bees to selling honey, to making soap, picking fruit, and gathering coal along the railroad track, to publishing a village newspaper or pamphlets on religious freedom. Everyone in the village viewed him as a proud man. Urie Bender, for one, remembers particularly how John always rode his bike "with dignity, as straight as a ramrod." His youngest son Ted, however, later described his father as a "hapless man, who could not support his family and tended to live in a world of his own." Asking for help was not easy for John. And for his wife to work outside the home was simply not acceptable. Nor did the times or social conditions allow for any support of the deaf.

It was religion that first brought John and Rae together, having met on a train en route to a religious gathering. Raised a Methodist in

Bruce County, Rae first steered the family to Baden's Presbyterian church before turning Pentecostal. All remember her as warm, with an infectious laugh and a deep caring for her six children. Practical and resourceful, Rae was the glue that held the family together. All her children adored her. Daughter Ruth also remembers her as the family source for ambition, noting, "I clearly recall her challenge that to achieve our goals, we must put into them both heart and energy."

Around Baden, the family kept very much to itself. Everyone in town would have known the family had been shunned, which would inevitably have added to their sense of alienation. And they were clearly outside the intense social whirl that so often characterizes small-town life. "The family was very poor," recalled neighbour Harold Schmidt, "but no one remembers they were poor for everyone was poor." Another neighbour, Ernie Ritz, remembered the family as "reserved and respected, people whose handshake was a good as gold." Another Badenite, Shirley Koenig, recalled that reserve but added "there was always some sort of competition going on between the kids."

Beland later recounted tales of a somewhat raucous household, where discipline was meted out regularly as the various siblings fought for recognition and respect within always cramped quarters. Older sister Ruth never wavered in her quest for success and career, coupled with an acute desire to escape village life. Later it would be Ruth who benefitted from the family's scarce resources by going to Ottawa to work in a bank, an act of gender equality not common for the times. Older brother Loine—whose extraordinary name supposedly has Gaelic roots—was both headstrong and unpredictable. He later became a Pentecostal preacher, spending many of his later years spreading the faith along the craggy coast of Newfoundland. Pentecostal missionary work in New Zealand also lured younger sister Mary, always spoken of as sweet and accommodating. Younger brother Robert is usually remembered as the black sheep of the family, having run afoul of the law and been often up to no good.

The youngest of the brood, brother Ted, who soared to great heights as a world-renowned philosopher, was never really part of the family mix, having been born fifteen years after Beland. Indeed, he was one year in age closer to me than to his older brother.

It was into this unpredictable world, within an impoverished and shunned family living in a struggling village, that a young Beland learned to survive and compete. Life in Baden was simple, and quiet. In this village of three hundred or so, young kids were left mostly to create their own excitement and mischief. Beland certainly dabbled in both. Sliding down that same Baden Hill on cardboard sheets was a favourite pastime. And when the holes in the soles of your shoes went right through, you'd cut that cardboard to plug them. In spring or summer, boys would likely go barefoot to school. In winter, the sight of a snowplow was a cause for village celebration. The village's main roadway, Snyder's Road, wasn't paved 'til Beland was four. The volunteer fire brigade was established when he was eight, and the hydro was upgraded when he was nine. "Going to town" meant travelling the ten kilometres down Snyder's Road to New Hamburg, where the women would go to the ladies' shop and do their visiting while the men played horseshoes behind the New Hamburg Hotel.

Baden was very proud of its elementary school, a four-room structure with belvedere built right beside the railway tracks. And when that whistle blew, signalling an approaching train, everything had to pause because of the noise. Discipline was strict and permission was always required to leave one's seat. Each day started with a prayer and Bible reading, and ended with a prayer. The curriculum was basic, fitting the times: writing, arithmetic, art, music ("vocal and otherwise"), literature composition, hygiene, and nature study. The two annual highlights were the Christmas carol concert and Arbour Day in May, when each class had a specific task around town. The meticulous attendance records show that Beland was an assiduous student. In his final year, he was one of only eight eligible to attend high school in Kitchener.

Doing odd jobs from an early age was just expected, given the times. For Beland, one of his earliest occupations was helping his father gather material for his publishing ventures. Since John was deaf, he counted on his second son to accompany him to village meetings and the like to take notes. It turned out Beland became fanatical about accuracy and good spelling, traits that never abandoned him. Whether those reportorial habits were drummed in or naturally developed ultimately doesn't matter. The journalism bug was caught early on.

When Beland was ten, life for the entire family brightened dramatically, if briefly. With the unexpected death of grandfather Christian, John was able to move his family into "the Big House." The building, which still stands as a handsome, three-storey, off-white brick structure right on Snyder's Road, was unlike any place they had ever lived before. Built by Christian in the early 1900s, it is Victorian in style with pine floors, oak trim and newels, transom windows in each of the six bedrooms, and wooden handles on the doors. A back stairway snakes its way up to the third floor. For most of his formative years, I was told, Beland shared a small second-floor bedroom with his older brother Loine that looked out on Castle Kilbride, the stately home just to the east. Even today, one cannot help but be struck by this impressive, proud Victorian home, with its towering enclosed belvedere. It was home to the Livingstone family, often referred to as Baden's royal family. Village lore has it that a succession of family heads would sit under the cupola and keep an eye on their flax fields to the north while watching the comings and goings of their mill to the south.

The next few years would be the happiest for Beland. He was doing well at school, he had a crush on one of the Livingstone daughters, and he kept helping his father with his "reporting." His siblings remember well Beland wanting to be a preacher. He would stand on soapboxes in the back yard, giving voice to his oratorical aspirations. Urie Bender remembers him as a stocky teenager who was a real "go-getter." He was always called Beland, the more familiar "Bee" coming much later, and he never would tell an off-colour joke. "My image is of a teenage gentleman," he recalls. His younger siblings remember a more dominant, if not overbearing, older brother.

It was about this time that Beland started developing quite serious ear problems, particularly in his left ear, completely unrelated to his father's deafness. There were constant infections and discharges, so much so that his father sought out a reputed specialist. "He threw some kind of hot liquid on my ear," Beland would often recall. Whatever the intent, the remedy proved to be an unmitigated disaster. For the rest of his life, Beland had to endure a significant and permanent loss of hearing in his left ear, along with constant infections and discharge problems. It is how I always remember him. He would, as a matter of course, insist you sit on his right so he could hear you better.

When the time came for him to go to high school, the security of village life, however challenging, evaporated quickly. The prospect of Kitchener-Waterloo Collegiate and Vocational Institute had to be daunting, if not downright terrifying for Beland. After all, his entire schooling experience had been limited to four rooms where everyone knew each other. KCI, on the other hand, was an imposing, three-storey brick neo-classical structure on the city's main street, best known as the alma mater of Canada's longest-serving prime minister, William Lyon Mackenzie King. Founded in 1855, it was the only high school in Waterloo County and it took its teaching very seriously. There were standards to be met, and certainly the area's disparate Mennonite and Scots communities would heartily endorse its traditions of discipline and hard work. For Beland the first hurdle was getting there. There was no such thing as a school bus, so he would have to either hitch-hike the sixteen kilometres or splurge the ten cents—if he had it—to take a freight train. The latter, it turned out, would be the exception.

No doubt his emotions were running high that first September day in '31 as he climbed up the rather steep steps to the wooden centre doors and turned right to the cavernous auditorium for the traditional first assembly. A fellow student and one-room-school-house veteran, Dorothy Newbury, later marvelled at the huge auditorium curtains, wondering "who had the nerve to climb up to such heights and hang them."

Asked about his time at KCI, Beland would invariably mention debating and then mutter about having difficulty with "technical courses." That he engaged in debating was certainly true. In each of his three years, he entered the boys' debating contest, whose results were dutifully reported by the *Kitchener Daily Record*. His nemesis turned out to be one Armand Klinck, who managed to win all three debates. In the first, Beland gave a speech on aviator Charles Lindbergh while Klinck spoke on pets. "So close was the competition between the two that only one point was Armand Klinck's margin of victory," declared the breathless *Record* story. The following year, Beland spoke on "pioneer life in the locality in which we live," and in his final year, on "electricity." His sole victory came in a pairs debate with older sister Ruth, a source of lifetime pride for both.

On the academic side, it seems it was an entirely different story— one I had never known. When visiting KCI decades later on a research mission, I wasn't sure what to expect. After sorting through boxes of yellowed memorabilia, I asked my kindly host if there was any record of marks. "We don't usually show it, but I'll see what I can do," she replied. Moments later, she returned from the bowels with a musty, dusty "marks book." In it were painstakingly recorded the individual marks of every student who attended KCI in the '20s and '30s. I leafed through impatiently. And suddenly, there in black and white, an untold family secret was laid bare.

In his first year, Beland failed four of his seven subjects, ending up with a paltry average of 35.9 per cent. The 0 in Art and 5 in Algebra defy rational explanation, except perhaps he missed exams or was forced to stay home to work. Nevertheless, his low ranking meant he was forced to repeat grade nine, doing so the following year in the "tech" stream. While his record improved, he still managed to fail four courses and was "passed conditionally" with a barebones average of 50.1 per cent. On a positive note, his best mark was in English, but his struggles had clearly not abated. The last entry in the book stated dryly "Left in March." That would be the finale of Beland's entire educational career. He would never return.

For someone whose intelligence and insight were seen later as formidable, if not downright impressive, the tale of the "marks book" is hard to fathom. In later years, Beland was certainly forthright about his forced departure from KCI to work to support his family. Failing a year, however, was never mentioned, let alone three years of grim academic struggle. I remember well his predilection for viewing anyone with a post-graduate degree, particularly a Ph.D., with an awe bordering on reverence. To him, education became an "inalienable right" and he always preached to his children the absolute necessity of higher education and "learning about the world."

In retrospect, one can only speculate on the cultural and experiential gaps that made the transition from village life in Baden to a city high school so traumatic for him. Surely Beland is not the first to have such problems and then go on to succeed. But his scholastic record in elementary school did not foreshadow failing, nor did his already visible attributes of resolve and determination. There was admittedly the constant challenge of transit to and from Baden. And there is no doubt his family was struggling desperately to make ends meet and avoid foreclosure on their beloved "Big House." Yet the experience of failing was, without question, forever etched on Beland's psyche. He would often recall his mother's words to him at the time. "You can do better," she'd say. "You can be better." His prodigious diligence, his constant drive to always work harder than others, his striving for perfection, and his acceptance that nothing could ever be taken for granted all make greater sense within the context of his high school struggles.

During this same three-year period, the impact on Beland of his family's futile efforts to save their home from the clutches of the Waterloo Trust and Savings Co. cannot be underestimated. In 1930, father John had taken out a $1,500 mortgage to be repaid in full in three years. From subsequent documents, it appears John was unable to pay back even one cent of the principal, let alone the interest or property taxes. The Great Depression was surely exacting its toll, but so too was his inability ever to secure a long-term job or successfully launch a business. And his attempts were numerous, with forays into selling honey, cheese, and even candy. "They all failed quickly," remembers Ruth. "Unfortunately, and to my terrible dismay, I was on occasion taken out of collegiate to serve customers of which there were very, very few." One of father John's more successful undertakings was making a salve-type workman's soap, said to be excellent. John would then take to his bicycle and try to sell the soap around the village. However, once again, supporting a family of six children demanded more income than he ever made at this. It seems that as long as his father Christian had been alive, John and his family had received the necessary support. But without it, their financial survival was problematic.

The constant threats from the trust company and the prospect of losing such a fine home brought terror to the Honderichs. "Waterloo Trust—how we hated them!" recalls Ruth. "Daddy circulated a petition against the foreclosure among the villagers, but nothing came of it." He also editorialized against it in his paper, *Village Item*. When the foreclosure and formal notice of sale were posted in twenty-five area locations in early 1934—the exact time Beland left KCI—it marked the onset of much tougher times for the entire family. The "Big House" was gone, income was scarce, and the prospects were downright disastrous. The cruel irony came when the house, once valued at $4,000, sold for only $1,900.

For Beland, now a fifteen-year-old high school dropout without formal training, and in an era when full-time work was virtually non-existent, the next three years would be his life's worst. It would be a time to scrape, sweep, borrow, or dig to earn precious pennies to help support the family. He would do anything, right down to scavenging along the rail lines for errant pieces of coal to heat their home. His cousin, Cameron, who lived on the family farm, remembers the time vividly: "We had no money, but I didn't know we were poor. Living on a farm, we had food, fuel and homemade or handed-down clothing. But for those living in town, it was hand-to-mouth existence."

For the Honderichs, the first order of business was finding a place to live. The solution came in a cramped apartment above what was affectionately, if pretentiously, called the "Opera House." Opened in the '30s, the building housed a stage on the second floor and boasted "beautiful curtains and dressing rooms." Occasionally there would be week-long performances of plays such as *Uncle Tom's Cabin*. More often it was used for school, community, and political events. On the ground floor were a dry goods store and a liquor store. "I hated it," recalls Ruth, "as did mother."

A life-changing breakthrough came a few months later when the Wilmot Telephone Co. unexpectedly offered Rae the position of operator, which included the residence in which the exchange was housed. Up to that point, John had been most reluctant to allow his wife to work outside the home, that not being the tradition. Circumstances, however, dictated a change of heart, and the family now had a stable residence and a steady, albeit modest, income. Rae became not only the breadwinner but also the voice of Baden as a kind and caring chief operator. "She was so well liked, always polite and helpful," says cousin Cameron. And according to Shirley Koenig, who quit school at age sixteen to work for ten cents an hour at the exchange, "She was so good to work for, but very much in charge." Shirley also remembers the many Pentecostal-style prayer meetings Rae held at the exchange.

For Beland, the immediate challenge became finding work wherever and whenever he could. One of his occasional stints was working as an irregular farmhand for cousin Delford Honderich, whose farm was kitty-corner to the original Honderich homestead. By the early '30s, a farmhand would be lucky to earn $15 a month for work that a decade earlier would have garnered double that amount. The work was what one would expect—tough and menial. Indeed, a happenstance photo in the *Kitchener Daily Record* shows a farm team working as "the sap runs in any maple bush." In the lower photo is a stooped capless teenager—Beland Honderich—sawing wood. The other three workers are all sporting caps, reflecting their status as good practising Mennonites. Delford kept a daily diary chronicling farm life in the tersest of forms. So for March 16, 1934, it reads "Roy, Oll & Beland—tapped trees—got meat over." Then there is April 5: "Beland to Baden for bran—boiled all day." Or April 24: "Beland spread manure—I went to Hamburg." Or finally April 30: "Beland took pails home." It seems that once the sap stopped running, so did Beland's work there—until the next time.

Another job he had collared was delivering the *Record*, a post handed down by his mother. It paid little but offered what turned out to be a glorious opportunity for exploitation. First, however, he was to learn his first lesson in responsibility. "I got behind in my bills and was told by Joe Fehrenbach that if I didn't get caught up quickly, he would take away my bicycle," Beland recalled later. He didn't make good, and Fehrenbach, the then circulation manager, drove into town, picked up the bike, and kept it for three weeks. "Honderich was dashing around town on his bike instead of minding his business," Fehrenbach said. "His mother had difficulty controlling him. I felt good about helping her out." Beland recalled, "It taught me a damn good lesson."

The headstrong teenager learned another lesson when he took a job as a water boy on a railroad repair and construction gang. Horse race betting was popular, and the crews liked to bet. Beland became the runner, picking up all the bets and dropping the money with the bookie in Strathroy. The next day he'd pick up the winnings and distribute them down the line. He noticed after a while that he never brought back as much money as he picked up, so he decided to go into business for himself. The problem was the very day he became a bookmaker, everyone in the gang hit the same winner and he didn't have enough funds to pay them all. So he told the station master, who decided to bail him out provided he'd work the rest of the summer for free.

Among the odd jobs and shifts, he took it upon himself to organize local sports teams from Baden to play against neighbouring teams. Baseball and hockey were the two principal sports, with hockey played on the iced-over village tennis court. For the baseball team, curiously called the Baden Pirates, he recruited heavily from his farming cousins. They would all gather beside the Baden Inn and then be trucked to play in communities nearby. The Honderich boys, Beland included, turned out along with others to be a formidable team. Indeed, the *New Hamburg Independent* noted in its Baden news, "The local boys have made quite a showing of themselves since they entered the league by winning three of four games." Beland would then dutifully report the scores for the *Record* at ten cents an inch, meticulously including as many names as possible. It was a formula he would never forget, and it would apply to hockey as well.

All in all, these were quite desperate times. Dad later told me it was the "darkest period" of his life. I always had the sense he and his siblings would do their damnedest to try to forget this time. His sense of near despair was captured powerfully in a one-page letter sent to his three children much later in life. It set out his wishes regarding what should be done—and not done—on his passing. In it, he recalled his frequent lonely treks by foot to work on Delford Honderich's farm and how he would pass the hillside cemetery where his Grandpa Christian was buried. "My school days were over; I was starting out on a new life with little idea of how it would unfold. But looking up at the cemetery where my grandfather was buried seemed to give me hope. For this reason it seems like a fitting place for my ashes."

It was a memory none of us had known, let alone appreciated. Yet its impact on Beland was unquestionably lifelong and profound. I have never sensed he gave up, stopped trying—or worse, felt sorry for himself. Those feelings simply were not part of him. Like most others at the time, he was caught in the same trap. Jobs, money, and opportunities were all scarce. He could use all his ingenuity and work harder than anyone else but still end up caught in the same vicious cycle. By now, he was dead set on becoming a reporter. He'd file his short briefs and sports stories to the *Record* as often as he could. He was certainly trying to impress anyone who would listen. But ultimately, he was an inexperienced village stringer, a teenager, and a high school dropout.

2

OFF TO KITCHENER

Beland's breakthrough came suddenly and unexpectedly when two barn fires ignited on successive nights, each involving a property of the richest man in town, with the whiff of arson ripe in the air. It would be one of the most dramatic moments in Baden's history. For the village stringer, this was as good as it got. As any journalist knows, luck, happenstance, being in the right place at the right time—call it what you may—often play a critical point in a budding career. The reporting landscape is rife with stories of reporters and photographers being serendipitously at the right spot as a big story or catastrophe breaks. Nowhere is this more important for newspapers than in breaking news—fires, grisly crimes, explosions, multi-vehicle highway accidents. So it was for my father.

On a late Monday night in early February 1937, one of the Livingstone barns on the edge of the village shot up in flames. Housed inside were the family's prized Holsteins. Thirty-one cattle along with several horses died in the blaze. The story from the *Record*'s "correspondent" in Baden ran big on page three the next day with the headline "Livingstone Barn at Baden Gutted by Fire with $12,000 Loss." It was written in the classic inverted pyramid style, presenting the big news off the top. Nothing fancy, just the facts—and lots of them. Beland had everything from the dimensions of the barn, to the number of cattle burned, to eyewitness reports, to even an interview with the manager of the barn. There, at the bottom of the story, was the only hint something might be awry. The manager had noticed a car outside the barn as he was leaving two hours before the fire broke out.

The headline topping the *Record* the following day left no doubt arson was involved. "See Incendiarism in Second Baden Fire" it thundered. This time the young correspondent let the words flow more evocatively as he tried to capture the scene. "With the embers of Monday night's disastrous barn fire on the J.P. Livingstone farm still smoldering, the second barn on the property fell prey to flames this morning." Beland interviewed the two guards who had been posted to protect the barn and got first-hand reports of both of them seeing a man mysteriously fleeing into the bush in the early-morning hours. The loss was estimated to be $25,000, with thirty-seven purebred Shorthorn cattle, five purebred horses, and almost a hundred turkeys lost in the blaze. Beland even managed to get the names of the three village lads who rescued about fifty turkeys from the inferno. It was always suspected, yet never proven, that Livingstone's half brother was the culprit.

For Beland, however, these stories turned out to be far more valuable than the slightly more than $2 he received in freelance fees—for both stories. He had proven to editors back at the *Record* that he could deliver on a big story when it counted. So, a few weeks later, when city editor Art Lowe was looking for a full-time reporter, he called the same circulation manager, Joe Fehrenbach, who had so famously abducted Beland's bicycle when he fell behind with his bills. Fehrenbach had now come to admire the diligence and potential of the eighteen-year-old. It would be somewhat of a gamble, he is reputed to have told Lowe, but Beland's work had impressed him, particularly his reporting on the fires. Lowe took the advice and offered the enterprising teenager a full-time reporter's job at the princely rate of $15 a week. Life would never be the same. My father packed together his few belongings and moved to Kitchener, where he boarded with his sister Ruth. As it turned out, he would never look back. As he later recalled, "I left Baden with a strong sense that I had something to prove—a need to make good."

The *Record*, which the young and energetic neophyte now called home, had a stellar reputation as a solid, well-edited mid-size paper. Indeed, its editorial tradition was strikingly similar to that of Joseph Atkinson's *Toronto Star*, standing for many of the same economic, social, and equity issues. Not surprisingly, *Record* publisher William J. Motz also considered fellow Kitchener native and now prime minister Mackenzie King a trusted personal friend—as did Atkinson. Indeed, under the Motz family, the *Record* endorsed the federal Liberals from King to Pierre Trudeau.

The editorial department of the *Record* in the '30s was also organized much like the *Star*'s, albeit on a considerably smaller scale. There were individual departments (e.g., sports, world, women's), each with its own editor, and the paper had a rewrite desk. The *Record*'s front page reflected the paper's self-defined mandate of covering the major news of the world. Page three, for which Beland wrote most of the time during his six-and-a-half-year stint, was reserved for local and regional stories. But unheard of and unimaginable was a news formula that would later see papers such as the *Record* focus their coverage almost exclusively on local issues. There was a world out there to cover—and damnit, the *Record* would endeavour to do just that for its twelve thousand or so subscribers.

It was also a traditional if not hidebound newsroom that Beland entered in the spring of '37. This was a paper that wanted stories written the old-fashioned way—straight up and according to that style. Writing was all about precision. There was a right way and a wrong way. In many respects, Waterloo County's deep rural roots and German Mennonite heritage were reflected in how the paper was run. Reporters were expected to wear a shirt and jacket if they were going out "into the community." The paper's policy on paying freelancers was frugal and lean—a dime an inch. Bylines were rarely if ever given. Indeed, my search of the *Record*'s archives did not produce a single story with the byline "Beland Honderich" on it. Pay and promotions were also done the old-fashioned way. After six months, every reporter would be called in for a review. Across the table, a senior editor would sift through a file containing every spelling mistake and every story requiring re-editing. There would be a terse discussion and then the editor would write down the amount of any raise on a slip of paper. Nothing would be said. Rather, this slip would be shoved across the table with the verdict on it. This culture of restraint even extended up to the Motz family, which produced several publishers. Each would make it a point to drive "ordinary" cars and live in "respectable" housing. Even the architecture of the *Record*'s Queen Street building in downtown Kitchener reflected this plain and simple approach. About the only frivolity was the "thank God" American Hotel across the street—thank God, for you only had to cross the street to get a beer.

As a young, green reporter, Beland would have been left very much to his own devices. No one would have sat down with him—as a modern-day mentor would—to discuss the basic elements of story writing. Furthermore, he would be expected to develop his own contacts. It was sink or swim, as he would have known. On the other hand, Beland's sheer determination and tenacious work habits were now firmly engrained. He also had an uncanny knack for reaching out and engaging others, often relying on a heavy dose of charm. For the rest of his life, he always took it as a given that he would have to work harder than anyone else. Here he was—a high school dropout with no formal journalism training, and a hick from Baden to boot—with a sought-after position at a newspaper. As it turned out, his worst fears were realized only one week into the job.

Word filtered down from publisher W.J. Motz that Beland would "never amount to much" as a newspaperman. In a hierarchical place such as the *Record*, that would normally have been the end of it. Indeed, city editor Lowe advised the fledgling staffer, "Keep out of sight as much as you can." However, Lowe also decided to take Beland under his wing and loaded him with assignments, as many as three a day. "I will never forget that Art Lowe showed a great deal of confidence in me," my father would say later.

Perhaps the most critical influence on the young reporter, though, was legendary *Record* editor Cully "Iron Duke" Schmidt. This was a man who hated to waste words, whether by type or tonsil. And his no-nonsense approach won him his sobriquet, bestowed in recognition of traits shared with the Duke of Wellington. But for all his bluster, Schmidt also had a soft touch. He forever had a penchant for the underdog and an unfailing urge to help any novice who exhibited his prime virtue—a willingness to work.

The two of them developed their own game. Beland would bet Cully an ice cream cone that he could write a story that required zero editing or shortening. "I bought a lot of ice cream cones," Bee remembered later, always relishing telling the tale. "He was a great editor. We would argue about stories and what needed changing and I never won those arguments." Cully recalled the bets "as a little game between us. I think he enjoyed seeing what I could do with copy to shorten it. It was part of his training." This drive to perfection would become one of Beland's trademark manias. Later, he would acknowledge his standards were "hard to meet." Indeed, he went one step further, admitting, "I find it difficult to satisfy myself." Younger brother Ted would later write, "He was as severe a man as I have ever met, taking perfection by his heights to be the only tolerable option."

With his first paycheque in hand, Beland set out to change his image as a country bumpkin. He went to one of Kitchener's more fashionable men's shops and bought a fancy suit. Finely tailored suits, crisp shirts, and a preference for the best in men's wear in general would be the rule for the rest of his life. While Beland was ferociously proud of his roots, he had lived through poverty and wanted no more part of it. His roots might be Mennonite, but his sartorial custom from now on would be upscale, if not eventually Saville Row. One has only to look at the front-page photo of the *Record* on the day of the royal visit to Kitchener in June 1939. There in front, publisher Motz is seen smiling in a somewhat rumpled jacket. But standing partially obscured in the third row, in an obviously finely tailored double-breasted pin-stripe suit, a tightly knotted tie with gold tiepin on a white shirt, and slicked-down black hair, stands the twenty-year-old reporter. It's not often a fledgling reporter looks more elegant than his employer.

The acute desire to escape his image as a yokel manifested itself another way too. Beland had a tendency of not very consciously letting his mouth hang open. It is not an uncommon trait, but one suggesting perhaps a less than proper upbringing. He later recounted how early on an editor mocked him on the floor of the newsroom for his gaping mouth, adding he was not fit for the job. Acutely sensitive of how he might appear to others, the young reporter remembered being mortified. From then on, he did everything to remember to keep his mouth shut, although it must be said he never lost the trait entirely.

It would be during that royal visit, on the eve of World War II, that Beland was able to shine. The paper pulled out all the stops for the ever-so-brief visit of the King and Queen as they steam-whistled their way through southwestern Ontario. Thousands of onlookers lined the railway line and even more jammed the tracks around the Kitchener station as the flag-draped train stopped for just fifteen minutes. But in breathless prose the next day, the paper chronicled the exploits of Dorothy Russell and her two sons, who watched the train approach Kitchener and then hired a taxi to track it all the way to Hamilton and then down to Niagara Falls. There was no such thing as overplaying a royal visit, a lesson Beland would take to heart, although he was the furthest thing from a royalist imaginable.

The one ongoing story Beland always covered was the status of Waterloo's Mennonites, particularly their military obligations in wartime. While he and his family had long since "strayed from the fold," Beland always felt the group's deeply held religious beliefs must be respected. I can remember travelling with him many times to see the original deed at the family farm in which King George IV had granted military exemption to Christian Honderich. It had been part of the bargain, there in black and white. Indeed, the pacifism that is so deeply engrained in the Mennonite faith had for centuries been a point of friction in Europe and then in North America. During World War I, Waterloo County gained national attention and infamy as local Mennonites noisily rejected any call to serve. Berlin changed its name to Kitchener and the county's German heritage induced both suspicion and distrust.

When Canada declared war in 1939, the *Record* editorialized that the conflict was "about fighting evil things." The next day the paper reported "all known local Nazis will be rounded up right away." All railway bridges went under military guard and three Kitchener German clubs were set to close their doors. It also became somewhat of a local crusade that Waterloo County would do its supportive Canadian bit this time around. Indeed in 1940, the county approved a national plan to dispatch ten million pounds of surplus Canadian bacon to Britain.

As part of this spirit, local Mennonites came to realize they would not get the complete exemption from military service that had been granted in WWI. However, Beland's stories chronicled these communities' desire to avoid any type of military service. Instead, they came up with the compromise to work as farmers or foresters under civilian control. At a showdown meeting in Ottawa, Major General LaFlèche unwisely threatened the Mennonites present, to which Waterloo Mennonite Jacob Janzen shot back, "Listen, Major General, I want to tell you something. You can't scare us like that. I've looked down too many rifle barrels in my time to be scared that way. This thing's in our blood for 400 years and you can't take it away from us like you'd crack a piece of kindling over your knee. I was before a firing squad twice. We believe in this. It's deep in our blood." Ultimately, in late '40, Minister of National War Services Jimmy Gardiner ruled that Canada's Mennonites would be allowed to choose among non-combatant training, first-aid training, and civilian labour service. As the on-scene reporter, Beland would later call this a very reasonable compromise.

While the ongoing Mennonite story was vital, it was the turbulent Kitchener labour scene that became Beland's dominant beat. "He was a tremendous reporter who studied the labour movement and felt labour was not being treated fairly," remembers fellow reporter Francis Denney Sutton. "He covered all those strikes. He really knew labour." Indeed, Beland started at the *Record* just days after the city's first major strike concluded at the B.F. Goodrich rubber plant. The fledgling Canadian rubber workers' union claimed a moral victory, for while no formal agreement was signed, the company did agree to a few concessions. A few months later, an un-bylined front-page story highlighted the need for protection of unions. "Unions have meant much to the workmen in Kitchener factories and must be protected," the story began. The choice of lede is telling. It has all the earmarks of a Beland Honderich story.

Beland's experience growing up and his never-failing empathy for the underdog fuelled a lifelong belief in unionism and the rights of workers to be dealt with fairly. He had seen workers poorly paid. He had been underpaid and living on the edge himself in Baden. Like others of his age, the searing poverty and wrenching mass unemployment of the Great Depression had left a huge mark on his psyche. He always took it as a fundamental given that people should be treated decently. Those beliefs would be severely tested much later at the *Star*. Nevertheless, his underlying values never changed, and his strong convictions about workers' rights would lead him in a very short time to form the first newspaper reporters' union in Canada.

As the labour reporter, Beland chronicled the dramatic turnabout in the labour market during the war. As late as the summer of 1939, more than nine hundred unemployed workers in Kitchener were still applying for the fewer than one hundred open jobs. A year later, unemployment was virtually non-existent. In the first five years of the war, the labour force jumped by a staggering 60 per cent, including replacements for those 3,300 who had enlisted. This acute labour shortage also handed the unions a powerful tool in their attempt to attain both recognition and higher wages. It all came to a climax in early summer 1941, when ten strikes had already been fought at the button, shirt, rubber, meat packing, and truck manufacturing plants. And the labour reporter's stories blanketed the front page on almost a daily basis.

About this time, Beland also started covering the colourful, if not pugilistic, Mayor Joe Meinzinger. An orphan who quit grade school to work in Kitchener's factories, Meinzinger was a former boxer who ran for mayor on the slogan of "Vote for Joe, the man you know." In that campaign, he fussed about possible communist influences in the labour movement. But that sentiment quickly shifted to reflect the general pro-labour mood in the city. The *Record* gave great play to his later comment "The sooner the manufacturers come to their senses and admit the working man is a cog in the wheel, the better for them." Meinzinger would often interject himself into labour disputes, more often than not to little effect. But for the aspiring Beland, it was nothing short of a bonanza. The stories were plentiful, the disputes high profile, and the experience invaluable. Of note, both the mayor and city council were so impressed with Beland's work, they passed a special motion of commendation when he left the *Record*.

Though Beland was decidedly dedicated to his job, he still found time in off hours to carry on his tried-and-true tradition of organizing sports teams—and then, of course, writing about their exploits. Kitchener was certainly as hockey mad as any other small city, and it boasted a storied record of strong Junior A teams. After all, this was the city that had just produced the memorable Kraut Line for the

Boston Bruins, which saw Hall of Famer Milt Schmidt united with his Kitchener childhood buddies Woody Dumart and Bobby Bauer, also Hall of Famers. All three had their rights acquired by the Bruins in '35 and would eventually lead the team to two Stanley Cups.

But it was another local Hall of Famer, Howie Meeker, whom Beland came to know very well. Beland, who was team secretary of the Waterloo Siskins at the time, used to drive the young Meeker, who would later become a Toronto Maple Leafs great, coach, member of Parliament, and TV commentator, around town to hockey practice all the time. "He was a great hockey enthusiast, very energetic, just a great guy," Meeker remembers. "And whenever he made a commitment, you could count on it." That trait came into play in a Junior B squabble between the teams from Stratford and Waterloo, Beland being club secretary for the Waterloo Siskins. The prize was the playing rights to the promising puckster Meeker, whose razzle-dazzle had already caught the eye of both teams. The deciding rule then was residential—which team was closer to Meeker's New Hamburg home. Stratford had already signed Meeker, and his preference was to stay there. But Waterloo was measured as closer, and so the Siskins had a right to draft him. The Stratford coach was so determined not to lose, he had already guaranteed Meeker a job as a machinist's apprentice. "That was the way things were done those days," says Meeker. In fact, in order to seal the deal, the coach also physically moved the "Welcome to Stratford" highway sign one mile closer to New Hamburg. Bee, on the other hand, proposed that Meeker take two weeks to think about it and promised he would let him go to Stratford if that was what he decided. In the end, Meeker opted to stay where he was and Bee kept his promise. Watching all this unfold was the *Stratford Beacon Herald*'s sports editor, Milt Dunnell, who would eventually become one of Beland's closest, lifelong friends.

By 1943, with hundreds of stories under his belt and a reputation for all-around dependability, Beland had begun attracting notice elsewhere. Down the road at the *Toronto Star*, editor Jim Kingsbury was looking for experienced reporters, his editorial ranks having been significantly depleted by the demands of the Canadian military for overseas duty. He couldn't offer a full-time position, for those were deservedly reserved for staffers serving abroad. Even so, it would be a glorious opportunity for an aspiring reporter to work in Canada's largest newsroom. Among others, Kingsbury asked, of all people, his new sportswriter Milt Dunnell, recently arrived from Stratford, if he could recommend his old hockey reporting buddy. "I was covering junior hockey and I ran into Bee, who was covering the Kitchener Dutchmen," Dunnell recalled later. "I approached Bee, but he said 'I don't want to leave Kitchener.' I told him to give it some thought. Next time I was back in Kitchener, he'd had some kind of run-in with his paper and asked if the position at the *Star* was still open."

In telling me the story, Dad never mentioned a "run-in." Instead, he stressed the opportunity to "move up" and expand his horizons. From the very beginning, it was clear he never lacked ambition or feared taking a chance. With considerable satisfaction, he would always recount how he moved to the *Star* as a "wartime replacement," adding, "There were no guarantees." He was very proud of that. Not that it was an easy decision. "I agonized for weeks about going to Toronto, and even after joining the *Star* I thought of coming back to Kitchener because my roots were there," he said later. But while his loyalty to the *Record* never flagged—indeed he always referred to it as "the finest provincial daily in Canada"—he felt the chance to work in Toronto represented a rare opportunity to work for a newspaper he'd always respected and, just as importantly, one that reflected his core values.

There was another major change in his life around this time. He was about to propose to his sweetheart of almost a year, Florence Wilkinson. They had met on Chapel Street, where he had an apartment and where Florence lived nearby with her great aunt and uncle, known innocently enough as "Auntie" and "Uncle." Florence was a flaxen-haired beauty who had gone to Waterloo College for a year and was now working for an investment broker. Theirs was a whirlwind romance, or at least as whirlwind as romances were in wartime years. She would accompany him everywhere—on assignments, to hockey games, and on frequent visits back to Baden. He would often pick her up for strolls at night in the neighbourhood, and his brief love notes she kept to her death. She was "always warm and reassuring," remembers future brother-in-law Ted. "I have nothing but pleasant memories of her then." Yet her early life in Saskatchewan had been anything but idyllic. Her mother had died suddenly, along with her younger brother, and her father, a CPR station manager in Rose Valley, Saskatchewan, shortly thereafter dispatched her to Victoria to live with his aunt Eunice. A happy and comforting time there was soon severed when Florence's father remarried and reunited his daughter with his new wife and stepdaughter on a farm in western Ontario. It was a disaster from the outset, with Florence miserable and constantly picked on. "It was one of the worst periods of my life," she would say later.

Then she moved to Kitchener to live with her father's aunt and uncle, who became the rock and foundation of her life. Not surprisingly, as her great aunt and uncle they represented the values and ethics of their age, two generations older than Florence. The Methodist tradition ran strong in the household, and a high premium was placed on hard work and frugality. Frivolity or frippery were rarely displayed, a deeply ingrained habit that would later come back to haunt the young Florence. Uncle had come close to hitting the jackpot with a shopping store development in Edmonton, and he would often question Beland on business affairs.

To me, they were my real grandparents, the elders whom I always revered. Despite the huge age gap, Uncle was still playful when a decade later we would come to visit as a family. One of my greatest childhood memories was going with him, hand in hand, to watch the trains pass at the end of the street and gaze in amazement as they would flatten nickels, sometimes even quarters. The first train trip my sister and I ever made alone was to visit Auntie and Uncle and skate on the neighbour's backyard rink. Auntie was a paragon of love and devotion. Many an hour was spent with her on the back-porch steps, particularly after Uncle's passing, chatting about anything and everything. The rules were strict, but the feelings, while unexpressed, ran deep.

On reflection, I came to understand how absolute their concern and love were for my mother. It was never clear, for example, if they fully approved of the nattily dressed, intrusive yet ambitious reporter. After all, it was said he was coming off a long relationship and journalism was hardly a career that promised financial security. There was also no doubt that once their charge made a commitment to someone, it would be lifelong. Her religious faith was constant and she aspired to raising a family and supporting her husband. That she would do just that for the seventeen-plus years of their marriage was never later questioned by Beland. Her open, warm personality, her generosity of spirit and total acceptance of his family, along with her willingness to venture out, very much appealed to him. While the potential move to Toronto, quite frankly, made her feel "apprehensive," she was more than prepared to overcome any misgivings and embark on a new life. A wedding date was set for October 15, 1943.

Before giving notice to the *Record*, Beland had one more journalistic flourish to complete. It involved perhaps the most unlikely of heroines, Mary Churchill, the twenty-year-old daughter of British prime minister Winston Churchill. Quite unexpectedly, Mary expressed a desire to visit a Canadian army training base for women—which just happened to be in Kitchener. So a plane was quickly commandeered and a whirlwind trip to the Canadian Women's Army Corps camp at Knollwood Park whipped up. For war-weary Kitchener, this was about as close to a second royal visit as one could imagine. For the *Record*, the three-hour late-afternoon visit was to receive the full court journalistic push, with Beland playing the leading role. Every detail of this engaging young woman's visit was lovingly chronicled by the *Record*.

Blanket coverage. Strike coverage. Political coverage. Sports coverage. Crime coverage. Beland had now seen and been part of it all. In fact, he could say with some confidence that he had received a varied and thorough training in the basics of good reporting. Indeed, his advice later to aspiring reporters was always the same: seek out a smaller city newspaper, where the experience is invariably wider and the opportunities greater. It was a lesson I would take very much to heart exactly three decades later.

After more than six years of reporting with absolutely no by-lines, for Beland a journalistic irony came on his wedding day, twelve days after he left the paper. There in the upper corner of the daily "Women's Activities" page of the paper ran the headline: "Miss Florence Wilkinson Bride of Beland Honderich." Whether it was churlishness or not, the story failed to mention that the groom was a freshly departed *Record* reporter. Certainly, regular readers would have had no reason to recognize the name. Thus, he was simply described as "formerly of this city but now of Toronto." From the account, and from stories later told, the ceremony certainly appeared to be as written—"a pretty autumn wedding." The groom's sister sang and the bride's best friend played the organ of Trinity United Church, the site having been chosen by the bride. With period journalistic flourish, the bride's gown was described as "white faille cut on princess linen and made with a sweetheart neckline, long lily-pointed sleeves, and a full skirt, ruffled at the hemline to match similar ruffling on the bodice. It was complemented with a halo headdress of white ostrich feathers surrounding a three-quarter length veil, and with a cascade of Better Times roses and bouvardia centered with a gardenia." The groom, though not described in the story, not unexpectedly wore a finely tailored suit.

3

A STAR IS BORN

I t is almost impossible to imagine Beland's first reaction as he crossed the threshold of the old *Toronto Star* building. Not only was he entering the home of country's largest newspaper, but the pure grandeur and power of the edifice was simply overwhelming. 80 King Street West. Built in 1929, this twenty-two-storey art deco tower near the corner of King and Bay Streets was a marvel of its time and a testament to the stature of the newspaper. The building had its own power station in the basement plus two plumbing systems, one for water and one for ink. A state-of-the-art newsroom was connected to the floor below by two fire poles. One could just imagine a young reporter being ordered to slide down and "stop the presses!" Two brass sconces graced the outside wall welcoming one and all to an ornate marble lobby, with white-gloved attendants operating the brass elevators. A felt-covered commemorative booklet produced for the opening somewhat breathlessly declared the building "a symphony of vertical lines that recede and fade into the sky . . . like a mountain top."

This was also the building that inspired *Superman*. The co-creator of the comic strip hero was Toronto-born Joe Shuster, who, it should be noted, used to hawk copies of the *Star* in downtown Toronto. He was so clearly dazzled by the magic of the place, it became the model for his *Daily Planet* building. That magic also percolated through to

Star editors, who, in 1939, became obsessed with thought of the King and Queen staring up at the enormous photo of themselves on the building's ornate façade as they passed by in a planned motorcade. It turned out the driver of the royal car was a personal friend of one editor. So a deal was struck to have the driver suddenly point to the photo as they drove by. The ruse worked and three photographers, all strategically placed, captured the moment for posterity.

The newsroom—the heart of any newspaper—was then a clamour of typewriters, teletype machines, and the more than occasional barking of orders. To one side was the main news desk, where men, mostly in jackets and ties, were editing paper copy. Editing and re-editing were the hallmark and tradition of the *Star*, both then and now. Once a story was deemed publishable, shorn of any extra verbiage but rarely short of pizzazz, it would be inserted into pneumatic tubes and sent down to be set into type. On the other side of the room, reporters were huddled at desks. The walls were bare, but the electricity and buzz at deadline were a constant. Ever-squawking police radios were out in the open, as was a bank of clattering teletype machines near the foreign desk, which was alerted to bulletins by a ringing bell. The air was always replete with the pungent scent of printer's ink. This was certainly not a place for the faint of heart, especially since the operating mantra for the paper was then unambiguous: "Get it first, sew it up, then play it big."

While Beland had earned his reportorial stripes at the *Record*, which fashioned itself after the *Star*, this was clearly the big time. There were more reporters fighting for editors' attention, more competition to get a story on page one, and, perhaps most importantly, more snarling editors to placate. Figuring out what was wanted and what pleased the bosses would take Beland some time. And quite soon, everyone was calling him Bee, a tradition that never changed. The new recruit always remembered he was at 80 King West on spec. Forty-five *Star* journalists had enlisted in the war effort, forcing the paper to constantly seek reinforcements. In fact, Bee had also tried to enlist in both the army and the merchant marine at the outset of the war, but his poor eyesight made that impossible. His younger brother Robert would join the air force. Bee's abortive enlistment attempt, however, allowed him to be available as one of the *Star*'s highly disparate recruits. This group included Ray Munro, an ex-Spitfire pilot and later professional mind-reader, a Russian-born copy editor who always claimed he was being watched by the secret police, the husband of a strip-tease artist, and, of course, the slightly myopic and hard-of-hearing reporter from Baden.

What no one doubted then was the stark reality that the *Star* was Joseph Atkinson's paper. He embodied what it stood for, what it fought for, and what it meant at its core. When Bee walked in the door, Atkinson—known as "the Chief"—was in his forty-fourth year as proprietor and was indisputably the driving force of the paper. He had taken over in 1899 when the *Star* was struggling as the smallest in a crowded market of six. By '43, the *Star* had the largest circulation of any paper in the land, its history of espousing "radical liberal" causes firmly embedded and its place in the political and intellectual firmament of Canada unquestioned.

Right from the outset, Bee revered "Mr. Atkinson." He completely accepted his boss's crusading tradition, his concern for the little guy, and his signature approach to newspapering. In many respects, they were kindred spirits, shaped by eerily similar upbringings. Joe Atkinson was born into near poverty in 1865 in Newcastle, Ontario, the youngest of eight children. His father was killed by a passing train while walking on the tracks when Atkinson was a mere six months old. His mother was forced to support her family by opening up a boarding house for mill workers in town. At the communal supper table, Atkinson would hear first-hand the workers' grievances and their complaints about the lack of any social safety net, particularly when the mill burnt down. His mother died when he was fourteen, forcing him to seek work in the woollen mill and forever ending his formal schooling.

It would be a chance ad in the *Port Hope Times* that changed Atkinson's life. The paper was offering $6 a week for someone with a bicycle to collect accounts. He had no bike, but he applied anyway, and within an amazingly short time he was running the day-to-day office business of the *Times*. His life was austere, with most of his spare time devoted to his church and to reading books. Alcohol was never to be touched. When the paper changed from a weekly to a daily, Atkinson became a local reporter, earning a $1 a week bump in pay. His career was set.

Atkinson's move to the big time came shortly thereafter, when he was offered a job by the *Toronto World*, a conservative newspaper that nonetheless espoused public ownership. Several months later, he was hired away by the more liberal *Globe*, then the only high-quality paper in town. Atkinson's reputation took off and he travelled widely as well, becoming the *Globe*'s correspondent in Ottawa, where he developed a close relationship with Sir Wilfrid Laurier. After eight years with the *Globe*, he was recruited by the *Montreal Herald* for his first management-level job as managing editor.

Meanwhile, back in Toronto, the *Evening Star* was struggling financially. Established in 1892 by printers locked out by the *News*, the *Star* aspired from its first issue to be a "paper for the people," espousing and championing working-class issues. However, a succession of owners had failed to turn the paper into a money maker. In those days, it wasn't uncommon for newspapers to be financed by political parties. Thus came Atkinson's big break when a group of Liberal supporters came scouting for someone to run an afternoon newspaper that would support Laurier. Atkinson negotiated an agreement to run the *Star* as editorially independent of any political party yet dedicated to liberal causes. His annual salary was $5,000, of which $2,000 was dedicated to buying shares in the company.

When he took over, he discovered the paper's paltry circulation of seven thousand had been inflated, a not uncommon practice at the time. So, he set out to differentiate the *Star* from the others, espousing causes and reforms not popular with the establishment. The list of editorial causes reads like a social reform agenda for the twentieth century: abolition of public hanging, workmen's compensation, unemployment insurance, welfare, old-age pensions, union rights, mother's allowance, women's suffrage, universal medicare, compulsory school attendance, and public ownership of utilities. While each of these gains is now taken for granted, Atkinson was virtually alone at the time in his relentless advocacy for them. Although never codified in precise terms, this collective set of editorial positions and the world view that informs them have come to be known as the "Atkinson Principles." In many ways, they defined the *Star*—both then and now. This was a paper that stood for something. You knew what you were getting, and the values were clear.

On the content side, Atkinson was equally radical. Ads were wiped off page one to provide more news coverage. Sports and women's issues were given greater play. He also had the paper redesigned to offer free classified ads and sponsor countless contests and promotions. While reporters were routinely dispatched across the globe, there was no such thing as underplaying a local crime story. Coverage of local human-interest stories was massive, if not overblown. The operating principle was clear: beat the competition—and don't hold back. Heaven help the reporter who got scooped by an exclusive interview or juicy detail in one of the competitors. Some of the headlines tell the story: "Man She Adored Left Her To Drown" or "She Loved Him Naught, His Life Was Insured."

A decade later, the result of Atkinson's strategy spoke for itself. The *Star* had catapulted into first place in Toronto's crowded newspaper market with a circulation of fifty-seven thousand. By 1913, Atkinson had acquired a majority of shares in the paper, and over time he gradually secured them all. His wholehearted espousal of "liberal" causes, while then vehemently opposed by many, ultimately turned out to be very good for business. It is a *Star* lesson that has never been forgotten.

The other major force Bee had to contend with was Harry Comfort Hindmarsh, or HCH, as he was always called. A giant at the paper for more than four decades, his influence was second only to the Chief's. The son of a long line of sea captains, he served as editor of the student newspaper *Varsity* at the University of Toronto, where his penchant for jazziness and hyperbole first surfaced. He too was a "radical liberal" who shared entirely Atkinson's reform agenda. He was a self-styled "rebel" who saw everywhere inequalities demanding rectification. He was first hired almost by chance as a reporter in 1911 by Colin Campbell, a city editor in urgent need of a replacement for a staffer too inebriated even to show up. The teetotaling HCH was the answer.

His big break came with the sinking of the *Titanic* in 1912. As was the custom, the paper dispatched a crew of reporters and photographers under Lou Marsh, the legendary sports reporter after whom the trophy for Canada's outstanding athlete was eventually named. Other papers were replete with stories of panicking male passengers pushing women and children out of the way to get into lifeboats. After interviewing a host of passengers, HCH wrote that these stories were completely untrue. Instead, he recounted how male passengers were ordered into lifeboats by the ship's crew to provide necessary oarsmen. On his return to Toronto, HCH was summoned into Atkinson's office, where the Chief declared, "I hope you can substantiate your story," to which HCH retorted, "I can," instantly producing from his waistcoat pocket written statements from ship's officers. From that point on, the Chief had his eye on HCH, and his rise in the newsroom became rapid.

Indeed, Atkinson became so intrigued with his new recruit that he decided he might make an ideal partner for his precocious and dazzling daughter Ruth. "I'm going to introduce you to a real man, my girl," he told his daughter, whereupon HCH was invited to the Atkinson home for dinner on more than one occasion. The first time, however, Ruth went out with girlfriends, simply to make a point of her independence. HCH persisted and eventually won

Ruth's heart. Atkinson's first act after the marriage was to fire HCH, insisting his new son-in-law "should make his own way." He then had second thoughts, musing that having close relatives working at competing papers "might not be practical." Thus emerged a dynamic newspapering duo for whom the *Star* was a passion if not an obsession. But unforeseen were the intense intra-family disputes that would later tip the fate of the *Star*.

When Bee showed up for work his first day, he reported to city editor Jim Kingsbury, a moustachioed man who resembled a riverboat gambler. After directing the new hire to a vacant desk, he ignored him for weeks. That time was very hard on Bee. He and his new bride were living in a boarding house on Spadina Road, having exhausted most of their meagre savings in making the move from Kitchener. Indeed, he remembers not eating much that first week while awaiting his paycheque. It was the height of wartime, so it was no surprise that some of Bee's first assignments were covering troop trains passing through Toronto. The war also touched him personally that year as his brother Robert, training as a gunner, was killed in a plane crash in South Africa.

His first big story came when Kingsbury sent him to catch the next train for Kingston, where he was to interview a RCAF pilot who had bailed out of a plywood Mosquito bomber and survived. Bee ran to the station but missed the train. So he hopped an inter-city bus, caught up with the flier, and got his story. His boss was impressed. Shortly thereafter, he learned his first newsroom lesson while finishing up a feature story Kingsbury had assigned him. He was putting on the final touches when he learned another rookie had just finished the same job. Angry, he tore the paper from his typewriter and tossed it away. Right beside him, another "temp," Fred Bodsworth, retrieved it from the floor. "That's one of their games," he said, pointing to the city desk. "They like stirring up rivalry, to see who'll do best." Bee then calmed down, pored over his copy, and submitted his version, which ultimately made it into the paper.

His reputation on the rise, Bee then proved his versatility by reporting on a major strike, the growth of Hutterite farms in Alberta, and the funeral of Franklin D. Roosevelt. In the *Star Weekly*, he wrote on Reno's divorce industry, health insurance, and juvenile crime. He always kept his eye out for those social experiments, particularly in health, that he knew intrigued Atkinson. One of his first was a front-page feature on a small community in northern Ontario, Richard's Landing on St. Joseph Island, that established its own unique healthcare system.

The series, however, that really caught Atkinson's attention centred on the 1944 election of North America's first socialist government in Saskatchewan. Bee spent weeks afterwards travelling around the province, striking up a close relationship with Premier Tommy Douglas and making little secret of his admiration for the string of groundbreaking laws and experiments that emerged. While his story prose might have been straightforward, the headlines were anything but: "Drought or Depression, Act Saves Farmers"; "[Medicare] Lifts Worry from Mothers, Aged and Helpless"; "Saskatchewan Succeeding Where Big Business Failed"; "Bomber Crew of 10 to Run Saskatchewan Co-Op Farm"; and "Civil Servants on Prairie Protected from Politics." Douglas was so impressed, his government published Bee's stories in a special glossy booklet. Shortly thereafter, Atkinson appointed Bee a part-time editorial writer.

With his time now split between writing editorials and covering big stories, Bee was really beginning to understand the *Star*'s inner workings. One lesson came when a dozen staffers were sent to Windsor to cover a long strike at a Ford plant. During their stay, an alleged murderer broke out of jail and Bee was dispatched to find his mother. Instead, he ended up with the fugitive himself and an exclusive first-person story. He was so excited, a veteran had to help him write his lede. "Tonight I walked the streets of Windsor with a wanted criminal, while police cars passed us on the street. . . ." The next day, word came that HCH was putting the story on page one.

Minutes later, revised word came that the Chief had killed the story on the grounds *Star* reporters should not consort with known felons. "Hindmarsh was the heart of the paper, always pumping out fresh ideas," Bee would say later. "But Atkinson was the soul, the conscience that kept us from going too far out of line."

It was HCH's penchant for the unusual, however, that led to an unexpected promotion for Bee. It began with a brief item about a Belgian girl who had stowed away on a ship to New York and then travelled north to Canada. Stopped at the Ontario border, she insisted she was heading to Kirkland Lake to marry a soldier named George. Acting on one of his famous hunches, HCH dispatched Bee "to see if George doesn't have a wife already." Indeed, he did, and Bee was the one to tell Alice. She then recounted how she'd sent numerous food parcels to George, especially tinned sardines. "He just loved sardines," she said. "But when I think of it now, that he was making love to that woman with the sardines and food I sent, it really makes me boil." Written in dead-pan style, it made for a memorable page one story headlined "George Won Marcelle with My Sardines—Alice."

Upon Bee's return, HCH praised the piece and then proposed one of the most unusual occupational non sequiturs. He offered Bee the position of financial editor, knowing his *Star* reporter barely knew the difference between a stock and a bond. Unknown, of course, was Bee's somewhat checkered high school record. My father always loved telling the story that he quickly replied, "But if it doesn't work out, I can always go back to feature writing," to which HCH responded, "No, you can only go out the door."

Thrown into his new position, Bee remembered he had no time whatsoever to bone up on financial affairs. But he sensibly decided to pitch his pages to ordinary readers: "Across from my office I could see a tailor working above a clothing store. So I always wrote with him in mind." It became an approach to writing complicated stories that he never tired of recounting, particularly to family. He would

also recall how he wrote about various business issues, barely keeping one step ahead of his readers. His first by-lined story as editor
involved the pulp and paper giant Abitibi coming out of receiver-
ship. What followed were primers on margin buying of stocks, the
hotel boom, how to sell short, and the future of the logging industry.
He also prided himself on accuracy, citing his earlier experience of
writing obituaries at the *Record*. "Make one mistake in a small-town
obit and there's hell to pay," he later told a journalism class.

As time passed, Bee relished tackling complicated and controversial stories. He riled the financial community by exposing shady
stock deals, urging Ottawa to tax capital gains, and promoting credit
unions as "people's banks." But his constant fear of being pushed
"out the door" also meant he was all business. After flying to San
Francisco to interview the president of the Bank of America, he was
asked by reporter Ned Belliveau how he enjoyed the city. "All Bee
saw was the airport, the banker's office and his own hotel," Belliveau
later told a colleague.

In a newsroom where standing up to the bosses was far from recommended, Bee also flashed his trademark resoluteness at an early
stage. After writing a piece about a small mining company, he
received a visit in his cubbyhole from none other than the Chief.
Atkinson rebuked him for writing a speculative piece about such a
small company and, by inference, touting its shares. Politely but
firmly, the freshman editor argued that penny stocks were a postwar
fact of life that couldn't rightly be ignored. Seemingly mollified, the
Chief left. Soon after, HCH lumbered in. "I hear you had a visitor,"
he said. "He just told me to give you a raise."

A mere few months into his new job, Bee's family life also changed
dramatically. Both he and Florence had always wanted children, and
their efforts in that regard started immediately after their wedding.
However, their first child, a son expected in 1944, was stillborn.
I would successfully make my way into the world at Toronto's
Western Hospital on July 6, 1946. As Bee would unfailingly tell me

every birthday, it was the same day the Canadian dollar was devalued. Never quite sure what to make of my emergence linked to a currency fluctuation—and not a particularly joyous one—I would later prefer to say, albeit almost as reluctantly, I was born the same day as U.S. president George W. Bush. Or, as I would later joke with my mother, "Just think, you and Barbara [always bepearled] Bush were on the birthing table at exactly the same time. But only one of you was wearing pearls."

I was given the first name John, my father intent on re-establishing the five-generation Honderich tradition of the first son naming his first son either John or Christian. Bee's older brother Loine had broken that tradition, so as second son, Bee reinstituted it. Parenthetically, it is a tradition I and my son Robin Christian have carried on into the eighth generation, his son being Sebastian John. My second name is Allen, that being the family name of my maternal grandmother.

My emergence, it seems, was a joyous event fulfilling my parents' fervent desire for a child. All old photos show doting parents enraptured by their new son. It seems I was quite jolly and that I easily adapted to life in my new home at 343½ Belsize Drive, just off Yonge Street. This was not an era when fathers were much involved in child rearing. Bee was not present for the birth—the dollar having fatefully intervened—and six weeks after my birth, he launched out on an extended tour of western provincial capitals. Yet mother was very happy, ecstatic in her new home and blessed on both sides by supportive and caring neighbours. My earliest memories were of my prized toy train set, much tricycle and wagon riding, wading in the backyard plastic pool, and running through hoses. And less than two years later, my sister Mary arrived. Life was relatively simple, if not austere—with only a couch and chair in the living room—but seemingly content.

Later I would become aware of my father's very frequent absence, but not in these early days. A check of his travels as business editor reveals financial dispatches coming out of Vancouver, Calgary, Edmonton,

Regina, Winnipeg, and Ottawa on a regular basis. In many cases, those breaks from his family would be extended. But the *Star*'s expectation that reporters and editors be ready and willing at shortest notice for out-of-town assignments was a given, one not even questioned by my parents. In less than three years, Bee had risen quite dramatically through the ranks. There was no doubt his career was paramount. His family was important, yet the call of editorial duty would always prevail. It was a pattern that never changed, sometimes for the better, sometimes for the worse.

Throughout the winter of '47–48, Atkinson's health really began to deteriorate. His workday usually ended by 1 p.m. and was followed by a solo lunch at the National Club. His doctor had warned both son Joe Jr. and daughter Ruth about symptoms of "indigestion," which could mask a heart attack. In December '47, he chaired his forty-eighth and last annual meeting, able to boast of a Canadian record circulation of 360,000 and revenues of almost $14 million.

The following month he turned his attention to his will. He had intended on leaving most of his wealth to his grandchildren, but Ruth and HCH objected to their four children being potentially spoiled. Atkinson's lawyers had also warned that succession taxes on such a large bequest could be so stiff that the heirs might be forced to sell the *Star* to pay them. So he opted for an unusual, albeit legal, mechanism that forever changed both the paper's and Bee's future. He chose to bequeath all his shares to the Atkinson Charitable Foundation, a charity he had created in 1942 with a token gift of $5,000.

As he wrote in his final will, his primary purpose was to ensure his beloved *Star* would continue forever to be run as a public trust by those imbued with his "doctrines and beliefs." And he specifically directed this to happen "for the benefit of the public in the continued frank and full dissemination of news and opinions, with the profit motive, while still important, subsidiary to what I consider to be the chief functions of a metropolitan newspaper." Furthermore, a certain percentage of profits was to be given to charities "for the promotion of social, scientific and economic reform." These were not the wishes of a proprietor content to let his successors carry on after him. He had fought extraordinarily hard to make the *Star* the progressive paper it was, and he wanted to enshrine that legacy. Nothing less. His controversial declaration that the profit motive should be "subsidiary" to the goal of running a great newspaper would later be viewed as capitalistic heresy. To the Chief, it was a journalistic credo.

The one vital question left unanswered was who should succeed him as president—his son or son-in-law. Atkinson had walked this family tightrope by putting HCH in charge of all editorial while Joe Jr. oversaw circulation, advertising, production, and the business office. The personal chemistry between the two men was non-existent. Though Joe Jr. rarely showed any animosity, HCH often ridiculed him to his face or behind his back. Later Joe Jr. confided that he spoke often with his father about the paper's future and his own. "He assured me that there was nothing to worry about," Joe Jr. wrote in '64. "I would naturally assume his position as president."

In this, he was simply outfoxed by HCH. Sensing the will would be silent on succession, HCH secretly convened a meeting with three other directors—Alex Stark, Fred Tate, and editor-in-chief George Maitland. In the absence of Joe Jr., who conveniently wasn't invited, HCH was elected president, with his brother-in-law set to be vice president. Later HCH would tell Joe Jr., "Since I am seventeen years older, this is my only chance to become president. You'll get another chance."

That Atkinson failed to designate his successor, when all other details were meticulously addressed, remains a mystery. It does not seem plausible that he forgot. Was he trying to set up a showdown between the two aspirants, a tactic he'd often used with lesser executives? Or was he deliberately leaving that decision to the Foundation's trustees, forcing them to choose their new leader? This seems more plausible. Whatever the case, the behind-the-scenes machinations of HCH and the other directors launched a period of high-level intrigue that plagued the company for the next decade.

By April '48, Atkinson's doctor told family members his heart condition was worse. In early May, on hearing the news, Prime Minister Mackenzie King wrote to Atkinson, recalling happy times together and expressing hope his old friend would enjoy another summer in Muskoka. "I shall miss him dearly," King wrote in his diary. A few weeks later, the Chief died of heart failure in his Warren Road home.

As would be expected, Atkinson's obituary had long been written and set in type. It described in glowing prose the rags-to-riches story of how he had turned Toronto's poorest newspaper into one of North America's richest, partly through "blanket" coverage of big news. And HCH was determined to do the same on the death of his father-in-law. Every reporter in the newsroom was assigned to the story. More than twenty reporters kept phoning around the globe, amassing tributes to their boss. The eventual list of 232, every one of them dutifully reported, ranged from the prime minister to actress Mary Pickford. All told, almost ten full pages were dedicated to the Chief—blanket coverage by any definition.

Nor was Bee excluded from the mix, receiving the prize assignment of writing a detailed description of the funeral a day in advance. After inspecting the church and sifting through a sheaf of prepared texts, he sat down to write, a Bible at his elbow. "Representing the Dominion government, with the prime minister, were Hon. Paul Martin, minister of health and welfare; Hon. Humphrey Mitchell, minister of labour. . . ." As soon as he finished, Bee was dispatched to the Atkinson home to help tend to the prime minister's needs. It is highly unlikely anyone realized these two had attended the same high school, albeit with contrasting academic records. Yet there he was, the twenty-nine-year-old upstart from Baden, opening the front door for the prime minister and then showing him upstairs into a guest room for a nap.

The funeral was solemn but simple. In the vast church named for his old friend Timothy Eaton, the Chief was eulogized as Canada's most successful newspaper publisher and lauded as a political reformer. Bee's pre-written account had been out since noon. He would not have been pleased, however, with the one typographical glitch: "As crows lined the streets. . . ."

Interestingly, the same day a small *Globe and Mail* story speculated that even though all Atkinson's shares were to be transferred to a charity, they might still be subject to provincial death duties of $8 million. A day or so later, lawyer Alex Stark called on Joe Jr. to break the news that HCH had been secretly voted in as president. The two had a heated exchange, but the deed was done. However, a bitter Joe Jr. ultimately agreed to fill the new position of board chair, using his father's old office. While the title seemed grand, there was no doubt who was in charge.

Sensing the need to act swiftly to ensure compliance with Atkinson's will, the board moved to have the Atkinson Foundation officially recognized as a charity, both federally and provincially. This was essential if death duties were to be avoided. Atkinson's executor, National Trust, put forth a value of $8.76 million. Curiously, if not ominously, the rival *Telegram* opined in its pages that the *Star* was worth "at least $25 million" and subject to at least $10 million in death duties. That another paper saw fit to question the valuation of an established valuator seemed odd, to say the very least. So did the provincial government's protracted refusal to provide a ruling on the charity issue. Not surprisingly, the Liberal federal government certi-fied the Atkinson Foundation as a legitimate charity, free from fed-eral tax. But death duties were a provincial matter. The province eventually settled on a valuation of $10.5 million for the estate. But despite repeated efforts, Queen's Park remained defiantly mum on the charity issue.

After forty-nine years, Atkinson's era had come to an end, but still hanging precariously in the balance was the fate of his legacy.

4

ONTARIO STEPS IN

It would be a short ten months after Atkinson's death when the course of history for his beloved paper would be forever changed. In fact, the corporate fundamentals of who would run, own, or control the *Star*—decisions effectively laid to rest in his will—would dramatically and unexpectedly catapult back into play. The change came without warning, save a few errant rumblings that filtered into the *Star*'s executive offices.

On the afternoon of March 25, 1949, with the spring session of the Ontario Legislature drawing nigh, treasurer Leslie Frost rose from his seat. He sought special permission to introduce important legislation "respecting certain charitable and other gifts." What made the announcement so unusual was the fact the government of the day had no leader. Former premier George Drew had been defeated in the 1948 provincial election by CCF crusader "Temperance Willie" Temple. As a result, no major legislation was expected until the ruling Conservatives chose another leader. Another anomaly pertained to the treasurer introducing legislation on charities. Normally, this would come under the purview of the attorney general.

Before entering politics, Frost was a small-town lawyer from Lindsay, Ontario. He reflected the conservative views of the rural wing of his party and would become known as "Old Man Ontario" for his preservation of these values. He first entered politics in 1924 and worked through the ranks until Drew appointed him treasurer in 1943. A kindly, soft-spoken man, he was admired in the legislature for his friendly, folksy manner, normally preferring compromise to conflict. This day, however, he was about to introduce a bill that would cast him in an entirely different light and embroil him intimately in the future of the *Star* for the next decade.

The legislation, called the *Charitable Gifts Act*, stated that henceforth no charitable foundation would be allowed to own more than 10 per cent of the shares of an active business. Any foundation in violation of this new rule would have three years to comply, the deadline being April Fool's Day 1952. Furthermore, any foundation owning more than 50 per cent of an active business would have to provide an annual accounting of operations to a new super-oversight bureaucrat, the public trustee. Finally, the act was retroactive. There would be no exemption for any foundation that the day before had been the legal owner of a business—say for example, the recent new owner of the largest newspaper in Ontario.

In his speech, Frost acknowledged there was a public good in contributions of money to charitable foundations. However, he noted pointedly that such gifts avoided succession duties and so the public was entitled to have the "fullest information" on their operations. He went on to speculate how the boards of such foundations might abuse their special status and not run the business in the best interests of the charity. "In other words, the charitable intent becomes secondary." No examples, however, were provided. Finally, he argued companies owned by foundations enjoyed a "tax advantage." Again, he did not elaborate and the words "*Toronto Star*" did not cross his lips. As he concluded his remarks, opposition MPP William Dennison, later mayor of Toronto, jumped to his feet, asking whom the bill was aimed at.

"Use your imagination," snapped MPP A.A. MacLeod.

"Why the *Toronto Star*, of course," quipped Liberal Harry Nixon.

Back at the *Star* offices, the news struck as a thunderbolt. The paper went into virtual "war" mode and copy boys remember running copy and fresh tear sheets from Hansard to 80 King. In one fell legislative swoop, all the carefully laid plans and the legal will of Joseph Atkinson had been destroyed. What next?

If there was any doubt as to the bill's true intent, it was put to rest the following morning by the banner headline in the opposition's *Globe and Mail*: "Bill May Force Sale of the *Star*." What struck Bee and other editors was the angle the *Globe* had chosen to describe the new bill. The *Globe*, along with the *Telegram*, was then owned by George McCullagh, a colourful, sharp-willed entrepreneur/journalist who rose to the position of financial editor at the *Globe* before leaving to earn a fortune in trading oil, mining, and gold stocks. McCullagh was a fervent supporter of the Conservatives and had once championed the creation of the Leadership League, an early lobby group pushing for smaller government and a one-party system directed by business. The *Star* had derisively dismissed the League as "fascist."

In the months before Frost took action, there had been occasional rumblings that the Conservative government was going to "fix" the *Star*, its great nemesis in the media. And McCullagh's name was usually linked to this conspiracy. Adding fuel to this fire had been McCullagh's abortive attempt to hire *Star* circulation manager Ralph Cowan to cross over and work for the *Telegram*, which McCullagh had just purchased. Cowan—who later became a renegade Liberal MP, forever known as the sole Liberal to vote against a new Canadian flag—had several conversations with McCullagh. In them, McCullagh predicted that the Atkinson will would soon be "torn to shreds."

Aside from the coverage in McCullagh's two papers, public reaction to the bill was swift and blistering. Across the province, the bill was linked to the *Star*'s criticism of the Conservative government and seen as the handiwork of both Drew and McCullagh. The *Star* labelled the legislation a "Shameful Retroactive Bill," a violation of the sacred right of a man to write his own will. It challenged the government to let the courts decide the validity of the will.

The bill was "destroying a newspaper," thundered the *Ottawa Citizen*, adding, "as a barefaced attempt to subvert a Canadian legislative body to personal and political vindictiveness, the proposed law has no precedent in the annals of this Dominion." The *Windsor Star*'s chief columnist described the act as "just a shady deal to tear down the *Toronto Star*." The *Fort William Times Journal* editorialized, "It is unthinkable that a government should be able to cancel out the wishes of a person who decides to leave his property to charity and rewrite the will to suit itself." The *Peterborough Examiner* wrote, "We are alarmed by a piece of legislation which looks so much like an attempt to silence criticism of the Ontario government." Even the staunchly Conservative *Ottawa Journal* analyzed Frost's rationale and concluded, "We think, in that [the act's] implications are dangerous and that should it become law, its consequences will be bad." Throughout it all, McCullagh denied he had conspired with the Conservatives but confided to friends, "I relish the blame."

Bee would always remember the arbitrary ruthlessness of this governmental intervention. The idea that a democratic government would deliberately subvert the legal will of an upstanding citizen for what appeared to be little more than a crass political purpose always stopped him short. In his retirement, Bee endlessly pored over documents and Hansard reports of the debates, as if trying to find a rationale hitherto unrevealed. He even sought out former Ontario premier Bill Davis, with whom he had a warm personal relationship. But although Davis had watched some of the debates from the public galleries as a student, he could add little. Bee would often talk to me about the bill, painstakingly bringing up every conceivable angle, but most discussions ended with little progress being made. He even wrote a booklet about the entire affair—an exhaustive study that provides the basis for this chapter. "We had no idea of what might happen," he would tell me. "All we knew was that the very future of the *Star* was at stake."

Subsequent events would certainly prove him right. Any thought the storm of public criticism might prompt the government to reconsider quickly dissipated. Five days after Frost first spoke, the Conservatives called for a second reading of the bill. This debate centred foursquare on Atkinson's will, with any pretense of another purpose now forgotten. Frost attacked both the Atkinson Foundation and the will, arguing the primary purpose of both was to operate a newspaper and perpetuate Atkinson's doctrines and beliefs. Charity was a secondary intent. "If the object is to perpetuate the business, then he should pay taxes and not ask the people to subsidize his business, which is competitive with other businesses," he said. It would fall to the newly elected CCF opposition leader and brilliant orator Ted Jolliffe to lead the fight. In a remarkable six-hour speech over two days, he met each of Frost's arguments, adding, "The government may not agree with Mr. Atkinson's intentions, but whether the government agrees or not, it was within the law at the time he wrote it and at the time of his death." He concluded by saying, "It is a vicious thing for any government to take unto itself the power of intimidation over any unit of the press, and it is going to be a black mark in the history of this country."

The debate was stormy and continued at intervals over the next five days, with the public galleries often full of protestors. At times, they even made it difficult for the Speaker to maintain order. Much of the debate was a head-to-head battle between Frost and Jolliffe, with the Speaker allowing Frost to intervene more than two hundred times as Jolliffe held the floor. The rump Liberals also joined in to protest, but the weight of votes was with the government. However, the joint opposition did result in Frost introducing several amendments.

First, the Foundation would have seven years, not three, to sell the *Star*. The Foundation would also be required to file with the public trustee annual balance sheets, statements of profit and loss, directors' fees, and all executive salaries over $8,000. Finally, the public trustee was given a veto over how much profit was to be paid to charities and a general power to perform any examination of the paper's finances he deemed advisable. Such an undefined oversight discretion set the stage for seven years of often acrimonious haggling between the paper's directors and Windsor lawyer Armand Racine, who had been appointed public trustee. Racine would become, in the words of one *Star* editor, the government's "relentless point man" in trying to force a sale of the paper.

The final amendment, however, would change the course of the *Star*'s future history. As a 100 per cent owner of the paper, the Atkinson Foundation would become, on passage of the law, an "illegal owner." And corporate practice would normally prevent foundation trustees from buying foundation assets, for it would be considered a fundamental conflict of interest. Yet the new provision specifically allowed for foundation trustees to buy foundation assets, subject to court approval. So an option that had been unimaginable for the *Star* when the bill was first introduced was now possible. In other words, those trustees running both the Atkinson Foundation and the *Star* might be able to work out a transaction. That slim sliver of hope would become the fulcrum on which a decade of intrigue would unfold at the *Star*, involving all senior players at the paper, including still-unsuspecting business editor Bee Honderich.

The new law was enacted on April 8, 1949, a mere two weeks after it had initially been introduced. Two weeks later, the Conservatives held a leadership convention and elected Frost as their new leader. He was opposed by A. Kelso Roberts, who at one point at the convention proposed a repeal of some of the most contentious sections of the law. He was abruptly told to sit down. And *Saturday Night* magazine later editorialized that support of the law was essential for Frost to be elected.

In reflecting back on it, Bee was determined this sorry chapter in Ontario legislative history would never be forgotten—hence his booklet. He wrote, "The act was an attack on a free press. Free speech and public discussion are cornerstones of our democratic society. They require the unimpeded flow of information, including criticism of the governments. The Conservatives, in trying to silence a liberal critic, were trampling on freedom of the press. Public opinion usually acts as a restraint on governments, but as the *Charitable Gifts Act* demonstrates, it is not foolproof. The act was conceived by the non-elected party leadership including Mr. Drew and Mr. McCullagh. They despised Mr. Atkinson and bridled at the thought he had found a legal way to perpetuate the *Star* in his tradition by giving it to a charitable foundation. Frost, as a leadership candidate, did not need much convincing. He needed their support to become premier."

What particularly irked Bee was that the new law deprived Ontario charities of millions of dollars, for Atkinson's will had specified that a varying percentage of profits would be paid to charities. Bee did the calculations back to the '50s and concluded that three times as much could have been paid out by the Atkinson Foundation. His conclusion was simple: "This law should be repealed."

It would not happen in Bee's lifetime, but sixty years after its passage, the *Charitable Gifts Act* was finally repealed by the Ontario government of Dalton McGuinty in late 2009. The repeal came without fanfare or even much notice, in sharp contrast to the tumult of its birth. Perhaps more telling is the fact that no other Canadian province ever followed Ontario's example. Critics often questioned the social purpose of banning charities from owning businesses. If such businesses were run properly and allowed charities to serve the public good, what was the harm? Charities had also argued that they should be allowed to own legitimate businesses that were closely related to their charitable activities.

These arguments, combined with the obscurity of much of the language in the law, led the Ontario Law Reform Commission to conclude in 1996 that it be scrapped. And so it was. Not surprisingly, there was nary a mention of the *Star* or the Atkinson will in this tranquil legislative debate. Yet the repeal, and the reasons for it, cannot be viewed as anything but a clear acknowledgement that the original act was one extraordinary and vindictive piece of legislation aimed squarely at the *Toronto Star* and at Atkinson himself.

For those back at the *Star* in 1950, however, there was only one question: Who would get to own the paper?

5

CORPORATE CHAOS AND
A NEW EDITOR-IN-CHIEF

During the eight years after the hated *Charitable Gifts Act* was proclaimed, ownership of the *Star* would be in full play, resulting in one of the most tumultuous periods in the paper's history. While Queen's Park inserted itself into almost every major decision, corporate suitors lined up, the Atkinson and Hindmarsh families feuded, and in an unexpected twist, Harry Hindmarsh (HCH) died. Ultimately, a half dozen corporate giants sought to grab the prize of Canada's largest newspaper. They included Argus Corp., one of Canada's most powerful conglomerates; Cyrus Eaton, a Canadian-America investment banker who rose to financial fame in the American Midwest; Jack Kent Cooke, the swashbuckling media and sports entrepreneur who created the NHL's Los Angeles Kings; Canada's venerable Southam newspaper chain; and even New York's Chemical Corn Bank.

Put together, their combined bids and counter-bids exemplified corporate battling at its most intense. All told, and counting principals and their advisers, the battle for control of the paper involved the best legal and financial talent in Toronto. Ultimately, it would take years of bluff, threat, counterthreat, and finally groundbreaking financial ingenuity for the *Star*'s fate to be determined. Throughout this period, speculation ran rampant outside 80 King Street. Yet inside, precious few really knew what was unfolding. That included Bee, who, since Atkinson's death, had gained experience as both a feature writer crisscrossing the globe and as editor in charge of the paper's financial section. His career seemed choreographed for his eventual appointment as editor-in-chief.

When writing as financial editor, Bee's articles, which read more as columns, were always sandwiched between the stock tables. His themes were sometimes straightforward news but more often commentaries. Not surprisingly, they fit squarely within the Atkinson tradition of concern for the common man. Yearly wage increases are one of the five "musts" for industrial peace, he wrote in '50. A week later, he argued that taxes on industrial profits hadn't crippled industrial growth during the war. Several times while on assignment in the U.S., he would highlight those pushing for a limit on corporate profits. An excess profit tax was essential in order to pay for defence, he wrote. On his next trip there, he pushed for the same tax, arguing it was required to curb inflation. He would also regularly highlight the fact that U.S. weekly wages were significantly higher than those in Canada. Back in Ontario, he repeatedly returned to the topic of "stockateers"—those taking advantage of the common investor by promoting dubious or fraudulent stocks. Indeed, he often called on the province to establish a royal commission to investigate the brokerage industry. And, as a change of pace in a column in '53, he wrote a letter to all federal political leaders arguing it was better to offer newlyweds a down payment on their first home than to provide subsidized housing.

Another major component of Bee's role as financial editor was to visit every region and province of Canada, often staying two to three weeks to study economic trends and industrial growth. Newfoundland and Saskatchewan appeared to be his favourites, with his close ties to their respective premiers, Joey Smallwood and Tommy Douglas, being no small reason. His fascination with the great social experiment in

Saskatchewan knew no limits. In one piece in '54, he crowed about how one decade before, Saskatchewan's debt level had been the highest in Canada but that at the time of his writing, it had become the second lowest. His appraisal of tax-averse Alberta was, unsurprisingly, not so positive. Over the years, however, no region was left uncovered.

It was the assignments to faraway destinations, though, that clearly excited Bee and allowed him not only to flourish but to flaunt his editorial prowess. It had been the tradition of both Atkinson and HCH to send reporters wherever there was a big story. There were no limits to this tradition. In '51, for example, Bee had been dispatched multiple times to Washington, D.C., to cover the slow and often tortuous legislative approval of the proposed St. Lawrence Seaway. This critical waterway was of vital economic import to Canada, but U.S. interest was decidedly tepid. Right in the middle of that fray, Argentinian dictator Juan Peron seized his country's great newspaper, *La Prensa*. Off to Buenos Aires went Bee, who wrote pointedly, "Here is a vivid example of what happens when a government, for spiteful reasons, interferes with the operation of a great newspaper." Then, for good measure, he flew to Montevideo, Uruguay, where he got an exclusive interview with the newspaper's editor who had been charged with "disrespect." It made for a spectacular page one splash.

In '52, Bee got the plum assignment to cover the sudden death of King George VI and the coronation of a young Queen Elizabeth. Later in life Bee would become an anti-monarchist, but on this solemn occasion he would write beautifully and reverentially, "A solitary figure in black, the young Queen walked through the yew trees in the early morning from Sandringham House to the little church of St. Mary Magdalene, 250 yards across. She stayed only a few minutes, alone with her grief, then walked back to take up the heavy affairs of state."

Later that year, Bee undertook perhaps the most life-changing assignment of his career, a forty-two-day around-the-world trip with then Prime Minister Louis St. Laurent. It was the first-ever circling of the globe by a Canadian prime minister. For the expelled

Mennonite from Baden, the poverty of India and the drama of the Khyber Pass to Afghanistan shook Bee to his spiritual core. "The fierce tribesmen, whose homemade rifles and swords are the law along the historic Khyber Pass, gave PM Louis St. Laurent the most colourful welcome so far on this world tour, where he motored through this centuries-old invasion route," read his page one dispatch. As a child, I will never forget my father later questioning how a loving God could possibly tolerate such abject and appalling deprivation. He became an agnostic thereafter. His subsequent assignments with St. Laurent in Canada were many, and his admiration fulsome. "He is by far the most effective politician on the hustings today," Bee wrote. "He has perfected his 'whistle blower' technique to a point that even staunch Tories cannot resist his charm."

The following year saw Bee off to Panmunjom, Korea, to cover the peace talks ending the devastating Korean War. His accounts of the "staggering" losses and destruction led him to conclude "the Koreans have little hope of rebuilding their nation themselves." He chronicled how the promised aid had not yet been forthcoming. On his way home, he stopped off in Japan to write an in-depth account of the then burgeoning Japanese economy.

And so it was for one more year. Two trips to Britain, several jaunts to the U.S., a solo excursion to Montreal, followed by several weeks in the Maritimes and another trip to Saskatchewan. Mixed in between was a small story on the death of John W. Honderich, Bee's father. He was described as a "printer by trade" who "also published a number of weekly newspapers." The words unquestionably came from his son, who was determined to provide a noble closure for a totally deaf parent who had struggled his entire life but to whom Bee had always remained ferociously loyal.

Unbeknownst to Bee, by the end of 1954, HCH had come to the conclusion the paper needed a new editor-in-chief. And by all reports, the eleven-year wartime replacement reporter turned financial editor turned worldwide correspondent was the natural and inevitable choice. Certainly, the announcement notice, which ran the day after New Year's 1955, read that way. The story emphasized Bee's "personal knowledge" of Atkinson's views along with his reputation for "penetrating comment." He was described as "an intense, industrious and incisive personality" whose personal beliefs were those of "a reflective reformer rather than a doctrinaire progressive." Finally, in his role as head of the editorial page—the soul of the paper—his aim would be "to champion social justice and social progress."

By any standard, it was as fulsome an appointment notice as one could ever expect. As an eight-year-old, I keenly felt the joy of the moment. Mother would shortly be pregnant with our younger brother David. Bee's travel would be less and we would be able to afford more. And professionally, Bee would now be at a level where he was made more aware of the corporate intrigue unfolding behind the scenes. Up to then, he had been away far too often. That was about to change dramatically.

Indeed, it was shortly after Bee's appointment that the corporate frenzy unfolded in earnest. In Joe Atkinson Jr.'s eyes, the *Star* was his birthright, and he had dedicated himself to finding a way for either him or the Atkinson/Hindmarsh families to buy the paper. "I'm not after the papers for myself," he once told his long-time counsel Allan Graydon, "but it's one way to keep it from the type of owners Dad didn't want." Sadly, this view was not shared by either his sister Ruth or her husband HCH. For years, they had stymied and openly blocked his ownership plans. Furthermore, in his general operation of the paper, the gruff and domineering HCH had done little to hide his disdain for Joe Jr. Their most infamous clash came some years before, over the location of new rotogravure presses. Not surprisingly, Joe Jr., as head of production, had felt his recommendation would hold sway. But the board, persuaded by HCH, simply decided otherwise. Joe Jr. appealed directly to Premier Frost but was rebuffed. By this time, the intra-family bitterness had become intense.

Despite this history of roadblocks, Joe Jr. decided once again to take a few tentative steps to buy the company; but his legal problems were twofold. As chair of the board that would ultimately weigh the offer, and as trustee of the foundation accepting it, he had two glaring conflicts of interest. He thus engaged counsel Graydon and his junior partner, Alex MacIntosh, to ferret out a possible solution. Just as this work began, however, Joe Jr. learned to his utter chagrin that Canadian corporate giant Argus Corp. was about to submit a $20 million pre-emptive bid for the *Star*.

Argus co-founder Bud McDougald yearned to get into the news-paper game and had been quietly but assiduously courting HCH. He proposed an Argus-owned operation in which HCH would stay on as president and son Harry Jr. would be appointed head of edito-rial. Ruth was a tougher nut to crack. At first, she was opposed because of Argus's controlling interest in the beer giant Canadian Breweries. Argus board chair E.P. Taylor, working in concert with McDougald, apparently read extensively on J.E. Atkinson's life and argued to his daughter Ruth that "beer is the beverage of the masses—of the little man." On that proletarian note, as the story goes, Ruth lined up behind Argus. To secure the third and deter-mining vote on the board, McDougald promised to double the salary of the flinty *Star* business manager, Fred Tate. At that time, the *Star* board had five members: Joe Jr., Harry and Ruth Hindmarsh, Fred Tate, and *Star* lawyer Alex Stark, whose obsession was living up to the Atkinson will.

With the Argus bid looming, the brilliant and creative Graydon strove to come up with a secret stratagem. He assigned two lawyers at his firm to check on every company Argus had acquired. "Find out how long their top managers survived" were his marching orders. After all, he understood that while Tate had been loyal to Joe Jr., the business manager's very comfortable lifestyle hinged on his *Star* salary. The answer of "six months" was relayed to Joe Jr. a few days before the crucial board vote on the bid. Though the Hindmarshes voted to sell,

McDougald was astonished when the three others, Tate included, voted against. The Graydon stratagem had worked.

A similar result unfolded one month later when noted American industrialist Cyrus Eaton submitted an offer to purchase. The board voted three-to-two against, with Joe Jr. and his allies prevailing once again. What amazed Joe Jr. throughout was the willingness of the Hindmarshes to sell out to right-wing industrialists. Both McDougald and Eaton were highly successful tycoons dedicated to establishing national or global conglomerates. Their records seemed irreconcilable with the dying wish of Atkinson that the *Star* be run by those "familiar with my doctrines and beliefs." It would be hard to imagine two less ideologically sympathetic candidates than these. However, HCH would counter that the constant meddling of the public trustee in the operations of the *Star* had become intolerable. This, he argued, was a far greater evil than a privately owned newspaper representing private, if not right-wing interests. That Joe Jr. was able to prevail should always be seen as a critical turning point in the *Star*'s history.

With two outside sales now blocked, Joe Jr. sought another legal opinion from the scholarly attorney John Arnup, who eventually ended up on the Ontario Court of Appeal. It was Arnup's advice that the company could be sold to its directors provided consent was secured from the Supreme Court of Ontario. Arnup's firm was asked for the legal plan, and the blue-chip firm of Clarkson Gordon was selected to devise a financial plan.

Just as their work began, the saga took yet another twist. In early '56, HCH was seriously hurt. According to the *Star* story, he arose at night, fell, and broke a hip. The real cause of his fall was a heart attack, but HCH insisted on keeping it secret. While later convalescing at Shorewood, the sprawling Hindmarsh estate on the shores of Lake Ontario, HCH received a surprise visit from Argus's Taylor and McDougald. Bearing flowers and a get-well card, they also brought the news that their original $20 million bid would be increased by several million dollars. At about the same time, queries came from other potential buyers, including the Southam chain of Canadian newspapers and Jack Kent Cooke. A New York newspaper broker also approached all five *Star* directors with a tentative offer of $22.5 million "on behalf of certain associates and myself." A copy of the offer letter mysteriously ended up on the desk of Premier Frost, with a cover note from Argus lawyer Wallace McCutcheon.

By now, the April deadline by which the paper was to have been sold under the law had passed. But the *Star* board opted several times not to vote on any of the offers. Instead, the directors met to consider the preliminary work done by Arnup and the financial advisers. At that meeting, the Hindmarshes repeated their desire to sell, arguing they were unalterably opposed to any "inside deal" involving current directors.

It was not until fall that Joe Jr. put the final touches on his plan to personally buy the paper for $25 million. This was the culmination of countless hours of study, consultation, and financial planning. At night, his teenage daughter Betsy often found him sitting up in bed, poring over law books. He would usually warn her that secrecy was critical, saying, "This is all sub rosa"—coincidentally a phrase I'd hear often from Bee. What the Hindmarshes never knew of or suspected was the closeness of Joe Jr.'s relationship with Premier Frost. At one seemingly happenstance meeting of the two men a year prior in Stoodleigh's, the restaurant in the basement of 80 King Street, Frost had casually brought up the *Charitable Gifts Act*. "You may not like that law, but it could prove to be the *Star*'s salvation," he mused. "Anyway, Joe, please keep me posted on your plans." Later, Frost let it be known he was not opposed to the concept of Joe Jr. taking over, marking a critical breakthrough.

Yet a few weeks later, at an informal meeting of the *Star* board, Joe Jr.'s hopes were dashed, with four of the five directors opposing his plan. Both *Star* officers, Stark and Tate, voted against, for each wanted a part of the sale, while the Hindmarshes were still strongly inclined to sell to Argus and opposed to any director buying the company. The deadlock continued. Director Stark then conferred quietly with Joe Jr. to see if there was any way to remove the Hindmarshes, adding it had been a mistake to have two of them on the board.

At a December board meeting, HCH formally requested to keep working past the company's fixed but often flexible retirement age of seventy. Stark decided to make his move. With support from Tate, he proposed deferral of any decision pending a medical assessment from a doctor. Stark reminded directors that HCH had not been forthcoming about his heart attack. He also went on to blast HCH for putting his son in charge of photo operations and for raising editorial salaries without board approval. HCH is said to have gone red with rage. Graydon later saw the episode as a golden opportunity. "There's your break, Joe," he said. "It's time to make a trip to Shorewood." Which is precisely what Joe Jr. did, an offering of a cut-glass ashtray in hand.

There at Shorewood, over soup and sandwiches, he and HCH decided not only to bury the hatchet but also to oust both Stark and Tate from the board. In their place would be advertising head Bill Campbell and production head Burnett Thall. The deed was done a few days later in the president's fourth-floor office, just off the newsroom. Despite his reputation as an accomplished hatchet-man, HCH was too stressed to swing the axe. So lawyers Graydon and MacIntosh gave the two directors a choice: either resign and receive generous pensions or simply be fired. Stark argued for a few minutes, then gave in. But Tate, a long-time staffer, began to weep, causing HCH to get teary as well. As MacIntosh later recalled, "The only dry eyes were the lawyers'." At a board meeting two days later, all changes were ratified and HCH's employment was extended for one year.

On December 20, the *Star* carried a straightforward news story on page one, matter-of-factly announcing the resignation of two directors and the election of two replacements. In the *Telegram*, however, it was bold headline news—"SHAKE-UP AT THE *STAR*." That same day, HCH's behaviour became very erratic. At one point, he called in reporter Mark Harrison to do "obits" on Tate and Stark. Then, swinging to a compassionate mood, he phoned Joe Jr. proposing a donation. Before hearing back, however, he went for lunch at his regular Stoodleigh's booth with Argus's McDougald, who was still pushing his $23 million bid. For whatever reasons, it seems HCH somehow felt he was in a superior position to conclude the deal. As he stood up to leave, he gave McDougald a strong handshake, declaring, "It looks like you boys have got yourself a newspaper." McDougald certainly thought that was the case.

But HCH went back up to his office and, under the weight of weeks of emotional stress, suffered a massive heart attack two hours later. He was pronounced dead at 6:15 p.m. in Toronto Western Hospital. And with him died forever the Argus bid. Naturally enough, the paper mounted huge coverage of the passing, centred on the obituary that HCH, with characteristic efficiency, had ordered written five years before. That very evening, the premier phoned Joe Jr. at home conveying his condolences, then adding, "By changing those other directors, Joe, you've probably saved the *Star*."

For Bee, with just two years under his belt as editor, this stunning turn of events dramatically and unexpectedly catapulted him into the limelight. A seat on the *Toronto Star* board was now a possibility, an eventuality not even imagined before HCH's death. But as was his wont, Bee strove hard for the appointment, including writing a seventeen-page memo to Campbell on the future of the *Star*. As editor, and given his extensive editorial background, Bee thought it not only logical but natural that he be chosen as HCH's board successor. Joe Jr. certainly agreed, as did the two new members, Campbell and Thall. Logic, however, isn't always the key motivator in decisions about corporate board succession in family-held companies. Thus, it didn't come as a surprise that Ruth was partial to her son Harry Jr., who, though widely acknowledged as a chip off the old block, was no journalistic heavyweight.

Within the newsroom, Harry Jr. had his backers, whom he quickly enlisted to buttress his case. Privately, both managing editor Jim Kingsbury and city editor Borden Spears—now reporting directly to Bee—advised against Bee's appointment, for reasons not known. Queen's Park reporter Roy Greenaway even went so far as to tout Harry Jr. to Premier Frost, urging him to intervene. The very next day, Ruth herself decided to visit Frost at his Queen's Park office, seeking his endorsement. The notion that the premier of the day could be the deciding voice on who should become a director only reinforced the prevailing sense that the *Star* had become the waif of the province.

To his credit, Frost refused to intervene. On January 25, 1956, Bee was voted onto the board by a three-to-one margin, with Ruth dissenting. At the next board meeting, she congratulated him, wishing him every success. With equal warmth, the following week she nominated brother Joe Jr. as president and publisher of the *Star*. Her bonhomie, however, lasted but a few days. With a daring and deftness that defied her genteel exterior, Ruth decided to toss a corporate grenade into the fray. After consulting noted lawyer Arthur Kelly, she sent identical letters to her four fellow directors urging the immediate sale of the *Star*. Then, she argued, the Atkinson Foundation could get on with the good works her father had intended. The board refused to buckle, but Bee had now witnessed first-hand the intensity of the intrigue.

The battle lines among the new players had now been set. Everyone knew a final decision had to be made very soon. What was different was the presence of a new combatant at the board table—a one-time high school dropout from Baden, whose resources and corporate experience were limited but whose tenacity and determination had already become apparent.

6

FROM BADEN
TO BAY STREET

As the newly minted director, Bee threw himself into the corporate fray without hesitation. Not surprisingly, he had a lot to learn about the prior wheeling and dealing. However, he did bring one advantage to the table. Over the past six years, he had developed a professional relationship with one of the principals of the drama, Premier Frost. It had evolved that whenever the *Star* sought approval from Frost for major expenditures, HCH would often send Bee. This became a habit. It seemed Bee's direct, no-nonsense approach fit well with the premier's disposition. And on more occasions than not, he returned with the approval HCH sought. What still astonishes is the fact of having to go to the very top of the political ladder for approval on such expenditures.

Long afterwards, Bee loved to regale others with the story of how he was dispatched in '54 to the Royal York, where Frost usually breakfasted, to seek permission for the *Star* to set up a special relief fund for the victims of Hurricane Hazel, a behemoth that ravaged Toronto and left eighty-one people dead. The promise of a page one photo of the premier promoting the fund the next day may have clinched the deal. Bee remembered the premier noting on another occasion that when it came to the reporting or editorializing on affairs at Queen's Park, he clearly knew a lot "and would certainly be open to consultation." Indeed, there were several occasions when Frost subtly tried to influence *Star* coverage of his government. That a premier had the audacity to do so always struck Bee as "absurd."

As a new board member, Bee also came to work more closely with his fellow director Bill Campbell, marking the beginning of a lifelong friendship and alliance based on mutual respect and admiration. Both were tough, highly principled, and totally dedicated to finding a solution that was consistent with the Atkinson will. And it would be better still if they, along with Joe Jr. and Thall, could somehow find a way to buy part of the paper themselves—a result unimaginable only a few months prior. Neither knew a whit about corporate finance, but they were about to get an extraordinary crash course.

In assuming the role of secretary-treasurer of the board, Campbell also took on the unenviable task of dealing with Ontario's public trustee. Like his predecessors, Campbell came to regard Armand Racine as a small-minded, officious bureaucrat who delighted in keeping the *Star* on a very short spending leash. A former lawyer for the city of Windsor, this dour, straightlaced official had ultimate veto power over how much of the *Star*'s profits went to the Atkinson Foundation and how much could go into company reserves. And his stated mission was to ensure that as much as possible of the *Star*'s profits went to charity. Ever since the law was passed, the *Star* had made it a policy to build goodwill by making well-advertised donations to worthy causes and to the Foundation.

Indeed, this had been the wise counsel HCH received from Prime Minister Louis St. Laurent in early 1950, when he went to Ottawa asking the PM to disallow the *Charitable Gifts Act*. St. Laurent turned down the request but gave him some excellent advice—build up a solid reputation of philanthropy and Frost won't dare take action against you. Shortly thereafter, the *Star* transferred $3 million to the Foundation, trumpeting the move with a page one story. This, in turn, resulted in forty-two donations to such worthy causes as the CNIB, Toronto Western Hospital, several universities, and the Art Gallery of Ontario. It was a practice that would be repeated every year, with celebratory stories in the *Star* to match.

Ever since the law was enacted, *Star* executives felt Premier Frost had been playing a good cop/bad cop game, using Racine as a foil. As Alex MacIntosh once remarked, "After all, he's not called the Silver Fox just for the colour of his hair." Undoubtedly the well-publicized history of charitable gifts deprived the premier of ammunition to attack the *Star*. Indeed, in '54 he publicly praised the paper's gifts, noting his objection was not to charity itself but to businesses owning charities.

But behind the scenes, the messages from Queen's Park were mixed, to say the least. In fact, it became a pattern. Frost would periodically pass a reassuring word to Joe Jr., and shortly thereafter, Racine would lower the boom, either demanding the paper be sold quickly or refusing to approve capital expenditures. Often when Racine demanded an immediate sale, good-cop Frost would step in and grant more time. Even when it came to the aforementioned purchasing of new rotogravure presses, Frost got involved. After Racine refused the request, Campbell and Bee appealed directly to the premier to reverse the decision. During that conversation, Frost spoke of the trustee's "quasi-judicial" status, remarking, "I'm here for a few years, but Mr. Racine expects to stay forever."

By August 1957, Racine all but ordered the directors to authorize a sale of the *Star*. Again, the board flatly refused. However, in order to placate him, they did promise to seek financial appraisals of the company. This would prove to be a necessary first step towards a final sale. Shortly thereafter, Armand Racine's "forever" came to an abrupt halt when he died suddenly and unexpectedly. He was "courteous and charming," a *Star* obituary allowed, with the merest trace of relief, "and had a way of smoothing over the ripples of discontent."

During this same period, Graydon and accountant Walter Gordon had been feverishly working on a daring and groundbreaking financial plan for the directors to buy the company. The major obstacle had always been coming up with the necessary capital. As the often sardonic MacIntosh once remarked, "The *Star* was worth about $25 million, and so far as I could see, Mr. Atkinson and the others were almost $25 million short."

In a two-page summary, Graydon reminded the five directors/ trustees that their primary two obligations were to ensure that the Atkinson Foundation received a fair price for the estate and that the doctrines and beliefs of Atkinson were maintained. The only way this could be concluded, he argued, would be to sell the company to themselves. He reminded them that such an unusual sale had become possible under the last-minute amendment to the *Charitable Gifts Act*. To succeed, however, the directors/trustees would require consent from both the premier *and* the Ontario courts. Graydon went on to propose that, before making any formal bid, the five families form a voting trust. It should be capitalized at approximately $1 million, with the shares divided in one of two ways—20 per cent for each of them, or one third each for Joe and Ruth, with the other three "outsiders" sharing the rest.

For Bee, Thall, and Campbell, the first option represented their wildest dreams come true, giving them 60 per cent and ultimate joint control. Just as naturally, Ruth would have nothing to do with it, insisting that she and Joe Jr. must control their father's estate. For his part, Joe Jr. was prepared to agree to any split that guaranteed ultimate peace. He was also mindful of Graydon's stern warning that total unity was essential for a successful bid.

The first step came shortly thereafter with Frost's affirmation that Queen's Park would not oppose a bid, provided it was unanimous. But there was an extraordinary condition. In return for this, as Joe Jr. noted in his diary, Frost required the *Star* to double its street price to ten cents a copy as soon as the *Globe* and the *Tely* did likewise. It seems Toronto's two other Tory-leaning papers were in great need of more revenue but couldn't risk being undercut by the larger and more successful *Star*. It was a steep price to pay, if not an exercise in blatant price fixing. But the *Star* announced the increase first, quickly losing sixty-seven thousand readers plus millions of dollars in circulation and advertising revenues. Those losses would take twelve years to recoup. But the prize was worth it—the premier was finally onside.

Then came another unexpected twist. Pursuing his quixotic dream of buying the *Star* himself, *Star* budget controller Al Griffis approached New York's Chemical Corn Bank, which became intrigued by his ambitious plan. Rather incredibly, with no security to offer but the *Star* itself, he secured a $22 million letter of credit from the bank. On December 3, he walked into the *Star* building and plunked down his bid. With the possible exception of Joe Jr., *Star* directors were stunned. "It didn't seem possible," Thall recalled later. "I felt he must be a front for someone else, maybe the Argus people again." For now, however, the board was not prepared to entertain any outside offer. They didn't even consider his bid.

Throughout this diversion, the five directors had still been unable to resolve their differences. On Christmas Eve, after the traditional Christmas handshake with *Star* employees, Ruth took Joe Jr. to Stoodleigh's for lunch. She argued again that the Atkinson/Hindmarsh families must control any new company, whereupon Joe Jr. offered to buy 32 per cent of the shares himself. Ruth would have 20 per cent—representing a voting majority for "the family"—with 16 per cent each for Bee, Campbell, and Thall. After a week, Ruth countered by paring her share to 19 per cent and the other three to 15 per cent, so that her son, Harry Jr., could buy 4 per cent. But—and it was a big but—all Atkinson/Hindmarsh shares would have to remain within the two families so they could control the *Star* forever.

Though her numbers were acceptable to the others, they all balked at the concept of lifelong family control. Bee felt strongly that such a limit would unnecessarily hamstring the company down the road. Joe Jr. hoped to broaden the ownership so that *Star* employees might share in the profits. "Personally," he wrote to Ruth in January '58, "I have no desire now or in the future to control the papers." Two days after that letter was sent, a round-table discussion of the situation brought the five directors, four lawyers, Walter Gordon, and Harry Jr. into the *Star*'s third-floor conference room. But consensus was impossible; Ruth was adamant on the issue of family control. It seemed clear she envisaged the day when her son would take control of the *Star* and she was not to be deterred. Watching her, MacIntosh couldn't help but admire her grit. "She never got rude or even raised her voice," he said. "Yet her determination was like steel. She was very much her father's daughter."

When the meeting ended in failure, the male trustees and their advisers gathered in Joe Jr.'s office to plan next steps. Since Frost was growing impatient, a breakthrough was deemed essential. As Ruth was clearly the stumbling block, Graydon proposed the seemingly unthinkable: if Ruth continued to refuse to budge, the board should vote to remove her—or at least threaten to do so. With no pleasure whatsoever, they set out to do precisely that.

The opportunity came one week later at an Atkinson Foundation meeting. Joe Jr. wore a "lucky" red necktie and kept his daughter's silver locket in a vest pocket. He led the discussion swiftly to his sister's insistence on family control. "In Dad's will," he reminded her, "he could easily have added a provision that control would go to his daughter, son-in-law, or son. But he didn't do that. Now you're trying to win control for your son, and we don't think that's what Dad wanted."

One by one, the others made their points. First, Campbell asked if Ruth was confusing control with a desire to wrap her son "in cotton batten." If she wanted security for Harry Jr., he said, the board would guarantee lifetime employment for him—and her sons-in-law as well. "And if I don't go along with you," she interrupted, "Harry and I expect he'll be kicked out." Before anyone could answer, she turned to Bee, saying, "It's your turn to speak. You see, I know all about your plans for this meeting."

It was pure bluff, but Bee was taken aback. He told her he greatly admired Harry Jr.'s ability to organize news coverage "even if his judgment in other matters is sometimes open to question." Thall then concluded the attack, accusing her of ignoring a clear command in her father's will that the decision of a majority of trustees should be binding. Frowning, she replied that she'd have to ask her lawyer about that.

Then Joe spoke again. With four trustees against, had Ruth given any thought to resigning? Ruth said she had considered it. As Joe Jr. noted in his personal files, the word "resignation" was the pre-arranged signal for action. A resolution moved by Campbell and seconded by Bee called for another meeting one week later "for the purpose of removing Ruth Hindmarsh as a director of the *Star* and trustee of the Atkinson Charitable Foundation." It carried four to one. Meeting adjourned. Yet nobody left.

Having given her fair warning and some time to think, the men didn't want to embarrass this doughty woman too crushingly, for they knew she would never truly disappear. As Bee remarked later, "We hated putting pressure on her. But Joe was making a sincere effort to save his father's paper and Mrs. Hindmarsh was getting in the way." For her part, Ruth continued to chat amiably, adding she still had a few tricks up her sleeve.

For four days, she talked with her family and lawyer. Then, largely at Harry Jr.'s urging, she finally relented. She called her brother and gave up her holdout "because that's what Father would have wanted." On January 27, 1958, she signed a six-page agreement to join with the other board members to buy the *Star*. There was no provision for family control. Harry Jr. would become a director with 4 per cent of the action. Like the husbands of his two sisters, he would also receive a ten-year employment contract. Unanimity—the elusive yet essential precondition for any deal—had finally been achieved.

Now, the money. By this point, the appraisers had priced the *Star*'s net assets at \$17.15 million to \$17.5 million. Accepting the larger figure, adding \$6 million for pensions and \$2 million for current liabilities, the final offer price became \$25.5 million. To present the offer, the directors formed the Hawthorn Publishing Company (its name derived from their initials) and they proposed to buy the company with a cash outlay of just \$1 million—less than 4 per cent of the total purchase price. "It was like we used to say in Nova Scotia," MacIntosh said later. "A dollar down and the rest when you catch me." In short, it was a leveraged buyout, but long before the term was even coined.

To begin with, only Joe Jr. and Ruth had much in the way of liquid assets—a block of *Star* stock they'd received from their parents. By selling it to the Foundation for \$1.2 million, they were able to pay \$320,000 and \$190,000 respectively for their portions. With a \$40,000 loan from his mother, Harry Jr. also acquired 4 per cent of the shares. But for the "outside three," the challenge was steep, and particularly so for Bee. His only real asset in life was his home on Haslemere Road, bought for \$21,000 in 1951. He had no significant savings and no wealthy family on whom to rely. To have thought six months earlier that he would even be in this situation would have seemed preposterous. There had been no goal to save towards. He did put a \$10,000 mortgage on the house in May. But where was the extra money going to come from?

Ten years old at the time, I can clearly recall the atmosphere at Haslemere as electric. First, there was the mayhem from our two-year-old brother, David. His arrival had been a joyous event for my sister and me, though my mother had suffered through a debilitating case of the mumps. Bee's constant trips and long workdays had not helped. Yet every night over dinner, he would recount, often in animated form, the latest twist and turn in the saga. I came to listen hard for the names and tales, but I couldn't fathom much of what was really going on. Alex MacIntosh was certainly around our house a lot. But the fact it was all very hush hush—or "sub rosa"—didn't mean much to me. One thing was clear, however. Money was a problem. While not strapped, our family all watched our pennies carefully and we were continually lectured on keeping within a budget. Our allowances were at the low end, although this was probably more my mother's doing. And the weekly ritual every Thursday at dinner would see Bee taking $100 from his wallet and passing it down the dinner table to our mother for the week's shopping. Anything extra would require an explanation. I don't recall ever hearing the figure of $150,000. It would have been unimaginable—as Bee later told me it was.

Enter lawyer Graydon who, along with Walter Gordon, took up the challenge of soliciting further funds from the Canadian Bank of Commerce, the *Star*'s long-time banker. He went directly to the top, meeting with the bank's chair, James Stewart. With the air of plausibility so vital to success, Graydon said the plan envisioned a cash payment of $17.5 million, with $8 million in debts to be met with future profits. Of that, $16.5 million would be sought from the public through the sale of bonds, debentures, and preference shares. Ever so casually, he added the six purchasers who would put up the final $1 million.

A parsimonious Scot, Stewart stared at Graydon as if the distinguished lawyer had lost his mind. "My God, Allan," he said, "there's hardly any equity at all." Indeed, in those days Bay Street usually called for an equity base of at least 50 per cent. "Look Jimmy, this is the largest newspaper in Canada," Graydon replied ever so softly. "Even though it hasn't been well managed, its net in the last seven years has been almost $9 million. Now that management's been united, it's bound to do at least that well. So you're not taking much risk at all!"

"Well, there's a grain of sense in that," Stewart replied. "So send those lads over." Thus Bee Honderich, Bill Campbell, and Burnett Thall walked the one block east along King Street to the bank's headquarters and each signed demand notes for $150,000 apiece.

Together they were now on the cusp of owning 45 per cent of the *Star*. They were excited, but also extremely leery of so much debt. This was certainly not how Bee had been raised in Baden. "Don't worry," said MacIntosh. "You're going to be wealthy men."

With full funding in place, Hawthorn formally tendered its offer on February 20 and applied to the Supreme Court of Ontario for the required approval. A date for the hearing was set for late March. But any hope the twists were over was soon dashed. The first came when, one week before the hearing, *Telegram* publisher John Bassett phoned Joe Jr. to say point blank he knew about the bid—and its exact size. Fearing a potentially negative leak, Joe Jr. agreed on the spot to let the *Tely* scoop the *Star* on its own story. The next day, the *Tely* lauded the deal because "control of this large and important daily newspaper (would) be retained in independent hands." The second shock came when, just the day before the hearing, Al Griffis raised his still secret offer to $26.8 million, more than $1 million above his bosses' bid. News of this wildly improbable bid broke in the *Globe*, stealing headlines just as the Supreme Court hearing began before Mr. Justice J.L. McLennan.

As counsel for Hawthorn, ex-jurist and distinguished lawyer Roy Kellock explained how the $25.5 million price had been determined—a price he said had been deemed "fair and reasonable" by the public trustee. Under Atkinson's will, Kellock argued the trustees weren't obliged to sell the estate to the highest bidder. Indeed, Atkinson had consciously stipulated that the paper was not to fall into private hands. This was why the trustees had rejected several outside offers and submitted their own. He also made the compelling argument that the directors of Hawthorn were committed to maintaining the doctrines and beliefs Atkinson had held so dear. Indeed, they promised to maintain them forever. Thus emerged formally the concept of the "Atkinson Principles" and the "promise to the court" to maintain and preserve them. This promise and its subsequent enshrinement in all corporate documents would make the

Star, and its subsequent parent Torstar, a unique body in Ontario's corporate firmament. Kellock concluded his argument by dismissing the larger bid by *Star* employee Griffis. He said Griffis had never been closely associated with Joe Jr. or Hindmarsh, as he had claimed. Rather, for $144 a week he was "keeping track of overtime."

Throughout the hearing, relay teams of *Star* staffers copied every word of the proceedings, then rushed to phone the paper to file for its afternoon editions. When the judge began delivering his ruling, senior reporter Buck Johnston listened a moment and then ducked out to call Bee. "Congratulations," he said. "You've won full approval, on one condition."

Bee shot back, "What condition?"

Suddenly Johnston felt like a cub reporter. "Oh, God. I didn't wait to find out."

It turned out to be a very minor matter. Before 5 p.m., the news was set in giant type: "Approve *Star* Sale." By then, the lawyers had returned to 80 King, where champagne was served. Joe Jr. even raised a champagne toast to his deceased father, whose posthumous wishes were now finally secure.

With all conditions met, *Star* shares, bonds, and debentures were put on the market by the establishment securities firm of A.E. Ames. While institutional investors stayed away, Atkinson's "little people" snapped up the *Star*'s first securities in short order. So did *Star* employees. They were offered 500,000 convertible preference shares, but the demand was so great, they bought more than 700,000. The deal was done and the $16.5 million required by the bank was raised.

For Bee, it turned out to be the bonanza of a lifetime. Over the next decade, the *Star* embarked on a period of great prosperity. So great, in fact, that he was able to reap enough dividends from his 15 per cent portion to erase his demand loan in just five years. The scheme had worked precisely as Graydon and Gordon had envisaged.

7

THE NEW EDITOR
TAKES CHARGE

It was to be a transformation the likes of which the *Toronto Star* had not seen since the early days of Joe Atkinson Sr. In the twelve years since he had first set foot in the newsroom, Bee had played by the editorial rules dictated by both Atkinson and HCH. Indeed, during much of the dramatic newspaper war of the '50s between the *Star* and the *Tely*, he was earning his stripes as financial editor and feature writer, away from day-to-day newsroom management. Yet upon his appointment in '55 as editor-in-chief at age thirty-eight, change took place immediately. The hurly-burly, let-'er-rip sensationalism that had characterized an HCH front page would become a thing of the past almost overnight. In its place surfaced a more restrained yet vital paper, clearly striving for editorial respectability rather than razzmatazz.

After Atkinson's death, HCH had been totally in charge of the paper's content and direction. His contempt, if not hatred, for Conservatives and their dastardly *Charitable Gifts Act* was so intense it often spilled over into the paper's coverage. The first change came when the paper, in an editorial, frankly declared itself to be Liberal, breaking with Atkinson's long-standing tradition of stated political neutrality. In the 1949 election campaign, the paper's coverage of

Conservative federal leader George Drew—whose provincial government had drawn up the *Charitable Gifts Act*—grew progressively
more hysterical. It reached a climax in the dying days of the campaign over Drew's designated Quebec lieutenant, former Montreal
mayor Camillien Houde. HCH had dispatched a crew of photographers to Montreal to dog Houde wherever he went, capturing him
in the most unflattering of shots. A portly man with a generous
paunch, he was the perfect target. But for HCH, that wasn't enough.
On the Saturday before the vote, the headline across the top of the
paper screamed:

KEEP CANADA BRITISH
DESTROY DREW'S HOUDE
GOD SAVE THE KING

It would become, perhaps, the most ridiculed and biased front page
in the paper's history. In succeeding years, HCH would also promote
a tradition of sensationalism that resulted in razzle-dazzle scoops
but established a much-criticized reputation for a tabloid mentality
under which allowed editorial standards were often trampled in pursuit of the story. While Bee had thrived in that era, he had secretly
chafed at what he had seen. As soon as he took over, he took dramatic steps to change it.

The first step was to recruit a raft of new writers, contributors, and
columnists under the rubric of "the best money can buy." In those
days there were no consultants or strategic surveys. Bee would tell me
later, "These were some of my proudest moments." Certainly, the list
of recruits read as a who's who of Canadian journalism at the time:
writers Pierre Berton, Peter C. Newman, Jeannine Locke, Lotta
Dempsey, Nathan Cohen, and Ron Haggart; editors Ralph Allen
and Martin Goodman; managing editor Charles Templeton; photographer Boris Spremo; and cartoonist Duncan Macpherson. Each
contributor on this impressive list achieved fame either at the *Star* or

afterwards. Nor did the list or range end there. Also hired were Sovietologist Mark Gayn, who read *Pravda* every day and knew Mao Tse Tung; Canadian literary giant Robertson Davies, who wrote a weekly column; author Robert Fulford, who wrote a daily book column; and future CBC icon Barbara Frum, who wrote a weekly radio column. As Fulford said at the time, Bee's goal was to create a new *Star* for the new middle-class Toronto. "He seems to have had in mind a combination of populism and sophistication, a paper that could be read by large masses of people but could also impress the most knowledgeable readers," said veteran reporter Val Sears, who felt that the genius in the new approach was "finding readers in the young middle class who were striving to move up." *Time* magazine had a different spin: "The *Toronto Star* turned grey one day last week."

Undoubtedly, Bee's acquisition of Pierre Berton from his *Maclean's* magazine perch was nothing short of a triumph. For four years, Berton wrote a daily column that instantly became Canada's best-read newspaper feature. He was fearless, dogged, and penetrating, letting loose wherever he felt injustice, con games, or criminal activity might be in play. For him, there was no such thing as a sacred cow. And his range of topics knew no limits: "I tried to keep people wondering, 'What's next?'" he'd say. In '59 he was awarded the Leacock Memorial Medal for Humour for a collection of satirical columns.

Berton prided himself, along with his indominable wife Janet, on reading every note he received. One of his many famous columns, on the public beating of gambler Max Bluestein, was initiated by a phone call. That column led to three men being imprisoned and an eventual royal commission on organized crime. Another tip led Berton and his researchers to scrutinize real estate records in York Township. Berton wrote a critical column that then reeve Chris Tonks dismissed as "old hat." A further column revealed the reeve's own house was on a choice lot he'd bought for forty-one cents per square foot, a purchase hidden by a dummy corporation because it was illegal. That, in turn, led to Tonks being unseated and ordered to hand over the property.

His range was truly vast. For example, there were several columns on dishonest sewing machine repairmen. There was another on a Greek travel agent who demanded money from immigrants for visas. In a profile of Berton at the time, writer Sidney Katz quoted him as saying, "I believe that nostalgia, not sex, is the most powerful of human emotions." He then listed subjects Berton had waxed on—everything from old radio programs, old movies, and old magazines to the Boy Scouts, one-cent candy, old comics books, and player pianos. One of my all-time favourites was his hilarious series of columns on a houseboat trip he, his wife, and their six children and two Siamese cats took on Ontario's Trent-Severn waterway. No one could tell a story better.

It was Berton who pressed Bee to hire his old pal Duncan Macpherson, who would later prove to be one of Canada's greatest cartoonists. The jowls and furrowed brows of former prime minister John Diefenbaker proved to be a cartoonist's delight. Perhaps Dunc's most famous cartoon was his portrayal of Dief on the announcement of the cancellation of Canada's Avro Arrow fighter program. The public outrage over the loss of fourteen thousand jobs was palpable. How to capture the moment? In a stroke of brilliance, Macpherson turned to the offhand remark of France's last queen, Marie Antoinette, on hearing the news her country had no bread: "Let them eat cake!" What emerged was a dazzling drawing of a jowled Diefenbaker in the plumes, jewels, and feathers of a French queen of the eighteenth century. This level of brilliance was repeated again and again.

From the *Globe*, Bee lured away veteran municipal columnist Ron Haggart, whose fearless pen was the scourge of many a municipal politician. One famous series of columns involved a request from the Toronto Dominion Bank to the city to donate a $245,000 piece of public land for the new TD Centre. Since TD's spokesman was former Metro Toronto chair Fred Gardiner, a seamless deal seemed a foregone conclusion. But Haggart attacked the bank's arrogance, calling the transaction "a sad comment on Bay St.'s attitude toward the plaything called government." He also went after Gardiner for "rattling the tin cup for big business." When a further column went after TD president Allen Lambert, the bank immediately caved and paid for the land. "He got things done. He got laws changed. He was a spokesman for those who could not speak for themselves," said Berton of his raucous colleague.

Perhaps the most flamboyant of Bee's recruits was theatre critic Nathan Cohen. Lured from the *Tely* in '59, he was by his own admission the country's best dramatic critic. His sartorial splendour only added to the lustre as he made sure he was one of the last to take his seat on opening night. A flowing black cape and gold-tipped cane were usually the order of the evening. Cohen was famous for writing generous reviews of small productions while savaging the big shows. He once called Richard Burton's *Hamlet* "an unmitigated disaster." On seeing it again, he pronounced it even worse.

During this period, Bee also hired two young, hungry reporters who each would play a huge role at the paper for decades to come. The first was Martin (Marty) Wise Goodman, a strapping, super-energetic graduate from McGill who joined in '58. It took the new hiree only a few weeks to make his mark. Noticing a brief news item from Alabama that said a Black man named Jimmy Wilson was soon to be executed for stealing $1.95 from a white woman, he told city editor Borden Spears, "The *Star* should get moving on this." Once he got approval, he immediately headed to prison in Montgomery to interview Wilson. The fifty-five-year-old handyman swore he had asked the woman for a little drinking money. He insisted she'd given it to him voluntarily for he had once done work for her. When she told a policeman she'd been grabbed, Wilson was immediately handcuffed and confessed.

In his page one story, Goodman set out that robbery with violence was a capital crime punishable by execution in Alabama. He also interviewed local jurists who couldn't recall such punishment being handed down for a Black man merely touching a white woman. More than three thousand *Star* readers ultimately sent letters of protest to Alabama governor Jim Folsom, who thereafter commuted Wilson's death sentence to life imprisonment. Marty had made his mark.

For Ray Timson, a tough, wiry reporter from Toronto's east end, the breakthrough came in '59 during the bitter loggers' strike near Grand Falls, Newfoundland. Premier Joey Smallwood had stripped the loggers' union of all bargaining rights, and Timson happened to be the only reporter present when a cadre of sixty-six RCMP and provincial police, brandishing long steel billyclubs, bore down on the strikers. He reported witnessing about a dozen loggers being beaten unconscious while another was pounded to the ground after taunting the police with chants of "You sure have guts." In his page one piece, Timson wrote, "It was a dark day for Canada's finest and the beginning of violence that could set all central Newfoundland aflame." Ultimately nine loggers were jailed and one Mountie lay dead, hit squarely on the head with a piece of wood.

The following day, Timson's report was read in the House of Commons. The RCMP commissioner resigned, accusing the *Star* of "distortions." But PM Diefenbaker would have none of it, saying, "I was not prepared to sacrifice the reputation of the RCMP to save either Mr. Smallwood or the reactionary corporations which owned the Newfoundland forest industry." Meanwhile, Timson was hiding out at a U.S. naval base near Argentia because he had heard Smallwood had issued an arrest warrant for him "for disseminating false information." Avoiding the police by staying away from the civilian airport, Timson, who was married to a U.S. citizen, managed to convince the base commander to give him a flight to New York.

While assembling this star-studded stable of quality journalists was an auspicious start, Bee's more daunting task was dragging the paper kicking and screaming towards a new editorial vision. In his tell-all autobiography, *An Anecdotal Memoir*, Charles Templeton—the one-time evangelist, TV and radio star, and political leader who ran the *Star* newsroom for several years—put the transformation in blunt terms. "The *Star*, for all its merits and crusades for the underprivileged, was a biased, dishonest and unprincipled newspaper," he wrote. "Almost single-handedly, he [Bee] turned it around and made the *Star* the antithesis of what it had been."

Banished almost immediately was much of the sensationalism of the past. Edicts from the top, or "Honderich rules," became the new order for the newsroom. Photos of naked bodies and grisly crime scenes, heretofore a staple of page one, were banned. Crime reporters were forbidden to name suspects until they had been formally charged. The main headline on page one (the "black line") was to be no larger than the main story demanded. And the black line was never to be used for crime stories. Pictures were bigger, headlines smaller, the writing brighter, and risky stories were vetted by company lawyers.

Furthermore, page one had to be "balanced," presenting world news, Ottawa news, other Canadian news, and local news. But to offset the serious tone, a change of pace or offbeat story was to be covered. And every story had to include, close to the top, a background paragraph to provide context to readers perhaps unaware of a subject. At the same time, Bee continued the practice of dispatching staffers across the globe to report on everything from a devastating earthquake in Morocco to life in Fidel Castro's Cuba, to the election of Pope John XXIII, to Tommy Douglas's CCF government in Saskatchewan.

In addition to the edicts, Bee also involved himself on a daily basis in the news file, a level of engagement not seen elsewhere in North America, as noted in *Marketing Magazine*. His day began at 6 a.m. with reading the *Globe* and then listening to CBC and CFRB on his twenty-minute drive down to the office. Upon arriving, usually before 7 a.m., he would quickly scan the overnight news files. To the despair of some, he'd say, "There's something wrong with that story.

Fifth paragraph down—second line—doesn't sound good, doesn't ring true." And the explanations from editors had better be good. As Bee told *Marketing*, "Even on its best days, a newspaper is a very imperfect institution. The newspaper offers virtually unlimited opportunities for human misjudgment and errors."

Changes of this magnitude upset some in the newsroom, particularly old-timers who saw them as a rebuke to the good old days of HCH. Not surprisingly, this led eventually to clashes with HCH's son Harry Jr. Bee went out of his way to avoid any showdown, but when Harry Jr. openly defied one decision, he was called in for a private meeting. "If we get into a fight," said Bee, "you can't possibly win. So, you'd better decide what you're going to do." A realist, Harry backed off for good. A few others sniped from the background, including one who penned a few lines of anonymous doggerel:

> Bless this crap, O lord we pray,
> Keep it dull in every way,
> Keep it free of sense and verve,
> Keep us free of guts and nerve,
> Bless the banal, bless the trite,
> And Bee will love us every nite.

This kind of creative resistance to orders from the top is endemic to every newsroom. For example, one of Bee's orders mandated that before a new editing pencil be provided, the stub of the old one must be turned in. So editors artfully responded by turning in their stubs and receiving new pencils that they then quickly cut into five pieces, which in turn were quickly redeemed for five more pencils—not the economy drive Bee had envisaged. Sometimes the vilification became more personal. One of the more common snipes was "Bee's not in today. He's over at the foundry getting a heart transplant." Or, after the *Star* moved from King Street to its Queen's Quay location: "Honderich moved the plant to the waterfront to be closer to his U-boat."

What no one doubted, however, was who was in charge. Bee was nothing short of relentless in his pursuit of journalistic excellence. How one defined that "excellence," though, was another matter. "In enforcing his view of what the *Star* should be, he was often arbitrary and unreasonable," wrote Templeton. "He seldom praised and was inflexible in disciplining carelessness or slovenliness." There is no doubt he was exceedingly difficult to work for. Again and again, the message to those at all levels was that their efforts weren't quite good enough. And his close eye stretched to all sections of the paper. He always had a reason for the change, often valid. Yet to many, it seemed like change for change's sake.

The concept that as boss you might tolerate a different approach to promote creativity or encourage a promising editor was inconceivable to him. Plaudits came very rarely. This would be his modus operandi for his entire career. In some respects, this rule-from-the-top approach was what he had learned from both Atkinson and HCH. The constant stream of managing editors and city editors did not appear to faze him. Under Bee, eighteen persons, generally alone but also in pairs and troikas, would hold the title of managing editor. Timson would hold the job three times. Legendary police reporter Gwyn "Jocko" Thomas used to say his best remedy for insomnia was to remember in order the forty or so city editors he served under during his half-century career. When asked later to explain this rapid turnover, Bee would say, "Mr. Atkinson had his Harry Hindmarsh. And I was probably looking for mine."

In retrospect and given my own experiences with him, I came to view Bee's management style as carefully crafted and deliberate. Never let anyone get complacent or settled. Keep them on their toes. Always keep them guessing. Never let them feel they were safe or immune from criticism. And if they defied ordered changes, make it clear termination was the logical outcome. For those in senior roles who lasted for years, such as Goodman and Timson, this was the reality they came to accept. I will never forget an obviously shaken Bee recounting his last face-to-face conversation with Goodman from his hospital bed before he succumbed to pancreatic cancer. Of all his senior executives, no one had been more faithful or dogged in trying to do exactly what Bee had wanted. "My greatest regret," Goodman had confessed, "is that I was never able to fully please you."

If Bee was serious and controlling, his counterpart at the *Tely*, John Bassett, was the direct antithesis of these qualities. The son of a newspaper publisher, Bassett revelled in his role and became a celebrity in Toronto's elite circles. He was an extrovert who didn't shy away from the unconventional and who sought out the limelight whenever possible. Bee, on the other hand, was much more the introvert—intensely private and averse to any publicity. In some sense, the two editors' differences were reflected in the type of paper each put out. While Bee led the editorial transformation at the *Star*, the *Tely* stuck to its raucous, guns-a-blazing style, with punchy headlines and a heavy tilt towards crime.

Life has a strange way of bringing adversaries together, and so it was with Bee and Bassett. The link was divorce, something both men were seeking. As Bassett told Val Sears in his entertaining memoir *Hello Sweetheart . . . Get Me Rewrite*, "Honderich was practically unknown as far as the general public was concerned. He was a very shy man. I called him and said: 'Bee, I want to make a deal with you. If you guarantee there'll be nothing in the *Star* about my divorce, I'll give you the same guarantee.'" Bee quickly agreed and Templeton later confirmed he had to kill a *Star* story being done on the Bassett divorce. Needless to say, I confronted my father much later about this fabled story, for it represented the kind of editorial compromise he always abhorred. He never denied it.

But none of this got in the way of both papers waging one of the great newspaper wars in Canada. It began in the early '50s, when Bassett took control, and continued unabated through Bee's term as editor. "The Old Lady of Melinda Street"—as the *Tely* building at the corner of Melinda and Bay Streets was affectionately called—was situated only a few blocks away from the *Star* but had only half the circulation. Bassett's mission was to beat the *Star* at every opportunity. Perhaps the most fabled *Tely*-related story centred on the day Bassett apparently read both papers only to find a report that was in the *Star* but not in his beloved pink-coloured paper. He reputedly summoned all his editors and delivered a scathing tirade on their incompetence. The story goes that as he paused to take a breath, a senior editor blurted out, "The reason it wasn't in today's paper is that we had it yesterday!" To which Bassett reportedly shot back, "Gentlemen, happiness is a day when you find the publisher is full of shit!"

Most of the infamous battles between the two papers involved crime. There was the chase in Simcoe County after a bank robber killed two people and fled. The *Tely* sent nineteen reporters, four more than the *Star*. After a three-day chase, the two *Globe* reporters unexpectedly decided to share their info with the *Star*, providing a great scoop. Then there was *Star* police reporter Jocko Thomas, who convinced editors to send him to San Quentin penitentiary in California to interview a felon named Stan Burkowski. Toronto police suspected Burkowski of committing murders in Canada but had had no success in interviewing him. Thomas got in to see him and managed to sweet-talk and cajole out of him a confession to three shootings in Toronto. That death row confession won Thomas his first of three National Newspaper Awards and sold more than 450,000 papers—a record.

Star scoops also came from travels around the globe. Bill Stevenson covered the Korean War and secured a world-beating interview with Vietnam's Ho Chi Minh. Intrepid reporter James Nichols once took a dog-team ride to cover Arctic radar stations, and for the coronation of Queen Elizabeth II, the *Star* dispatched no less than seven staffers. The nadir of such adventures came in '55 when reporter Alf Tate and photographer Doug Crook, on assignment, flew deliberately into the eye of a hurricane, never to be seen again.

Perhaps the wildest of *Star–Tely* capers came in '54 when, against all odds, sixteen-year-old Marilyn Bell became the first person to swim across Lake Ontario. As a promotional gimmick, the *Star* sponsored both Bell and Winnie Leuszler, twenty-eight, who had once conquered the English Channel. As Bell came to be the only one left in the cold, eel-infested waters, she was closely followed by reporters, among them the *Star*'s George Bryant in the twenty-two-foot *Mipepa*. At one point, when a *Tely* launch came too close, Bell's father pelted it with empty glass bottles. As an exhausted Bell approached the Toronto shore after twenty-one hours in the water, more than 150,000 people were lining the shore. On arrival, Bell and her coach, Gus Ryder, were whisked into the *Mipepa* and taken to the harbour police dock, where an ambulance was waiting. However, the *Star* team spotted a *Tely* reporter dressed as a nurse. So good old Jocko Thomas, sensing sabotage, took out the distributor cap from the secret *Tely* ambulance so it couldn't move. And the *Star* had Bell to themselves. But the *Tely* was still not be outdone. It ran a first-person account labelled "Marilyn's Story" on page one, with her signature across the top—which had been stealthily lifted from her high school yearbook.

The aftermath of the assassination of President John F. Kennedy provided another epic moment in the *Star–Tely* rivalry, one that pitted *Star* veteran Rae Corelli against the *Tely*'s legendary Peter Worthington. Corelli was assigned to cover the transfer of accused assassin Lee Harvey Oswald from the police station to the county jail. The first press release gave a time of 5 p.m. for the transfer, but a later press release upped that time to 11 a.m. Sadly for Corelli, he was at dinner with Peter Jennings of *CTV News* and so missed the scheduling change. Thus, when Oswald was led handcuffed into the jail and was suddenly shot by Jack Ruby, there in full TV view was Worthington. Later in the day Worthington ran into Corelli, saying, "Jesus, I'm sorry. I know how you must feel." Corelli replied, "No, you can't possibly know."

This era also marked the emergence of one of Canada's most famous investigative reporters, Bob Reguly. The story that catapulted him into fame involved Hal Banks, the brutal boss of the Seafarers' International Union (SIU). Banks ran the SIU from Montreal for fifteen years before being jailed for five years for ordering the near-fatal beating of a rival. Released on bail in '64, he vanished, with both the RCMP and the FBI saying they couldn't find him. Managing editor Ralph Allen picked Reguly to find Banks, later saying the young reporter was a natural investigator with common-sense instincts. Asked where he thought Banks might be hiding, Reguly replied New York or San Francisco, where the SIU had offices. "That's where he'd find protection. In trouble, you run home to mama."

So off to New York Reguly flew, heading immediately on arrival to the offices of the National Maritime Union, the bitter rival of the SIU. Explaining his mission, he requested and received a list of SIU properties in New York, along with an unmarked union car and bodyguard to boot. When they eventually drove power boats to a Brooklyn dock area, Reguly spotted a white convertible with Quebec licence plates. Lounging nearby was an older man, smoking a cigarette. "Hal Banks?" Reguly asked. "Ya, whaddya want?" the man snorted. "I'm from the *Toronto Star*. I want an interview." To which Banks growled, "Get lost!" Reguly left the scene quickly to purchase a Kodak Brownie to snap a photo. When he returned to get his shot, he was attacked by four thugs, suffering blows to his head. Managing to escape with the help of his bodyguard, he quickly phoned Allen with his scoop. That same day, federal justice minister Guy Favreau did a TV interview insisting Banks could not be found. But half an hour later the *Star* emerged with its banner headline "*Star* Man Finds Hal Banks."

Reguly grew to even greater fame in '66 with his discovery of Gerda Munsinger, a woman infamously linked to two federal cabinet ministers. The issue first arose publicly in the House of Commons when then Prime Minister Diefenbaker was dared to explain the "Monseignor case." The Ottawa bureau chief, Marty Goodman, told *Star* editors the name referred to "a hushed-up sex and security scandal." The woman involved was reportedly a Montreal call-girl named Olga, who was rumoured to have left Canada in '61 and to have since died of leukemia.

Allen turned once again to Reguly, assigning him the task of finding Olga. Reguly's first trip was to Montreal, where, after visiting several German clubs, he concluded Olga's surname was probably Munsinger. Searching through old telephone books, he came up with a Munsinger listing. From there, Quebec bureau chief Bob McKenzie found a janitor and his German wife who knew her well and who had an old address for her in Austria. The next morning a German-speaking picture editor at the paper, Jack Granek, phoned the address and was told that Gerda Munsinger (not Olga) was alive and living in Munich. Granek phoned the place where Gerda worked and, for $100, got her home address.

In Munich the next day, Reguly went to the address and waited until 6 p.m. when a woman arrived at Apt. 5. Reguly knocked and asked, "Gerda Munsinger?" "Yes," she replied, to which Reguly responded, "Well, your name has come up in Parliament." Her first reaction was, "Perhaps it's about Sévigny," referring to cabinet minister Pierre Sévigny. She then talked about her life in Canada, her three-year affair with Sévigny, and casual lunches she'd had with another cabinet minister, George Hees. After drawing up a contract and paying $980 for her story, Reguly had the scoop of a lifetime.

The next day, Allen let the paper's huge second edition go out with a headline saying a judge would be probing the case. After two thousand copies were printed, including the usual batch for the *Tely* newsroom, the presses were stopped and replated with a secret, new blockbuster front page: "*Star* Man Finds Gerda Munsinger." "I found her in a chintzy flat in an affluent district of Munich, wearing a gold September birthstone ring that was the gift of a former Cabinet minister," wrote Reguly. After this version's release, plans were immediately hatched over at the *Tely* to try to catch up. Editor Doug MacFarlane had already sent a reporter to Europe looking for Gerda's grave. He then dispatched six more, with one sliding a note under Gerda's door promising $10,000 for a five-minute interview. Ray Timson, who the *Star* also sent over to watch guard for Gerda, intercepted the note. He also negotiated a deal with a German news agency, which paid Gerda $50,000 for her story.

All in all, it will go down as one of the greatest eras in Canadian newspapering. The Gerda story, in particular, brought the *Star* huge acclaim, embarrassing a government and cementing Reguly's reputation forever. The accumulation of scoops and investigations also had a profound impact on the business. By the end of Bee's decade-long term as editor, the results were in. *Star* circulation had risen by 75,000 to a new high of 395,000 while the *Tely* had gained less than 12,000 for a total of 235,000. The *Star* ranked fourth in advertising linage and first in classified ads among all afternoon dailies in North America. The editorial transformation had brought a raft of awards, leading American publishers in '61 to rank the *Star* among the world's very best "foreign" papers, behind only Manchester's *Guardian*, London's *Times*, and Argentina's *La Prensa*.

As it turned out, this was no time for Bee to rest on his laurels. The ever fluid Toronto newspaper market was about to be shaken to its core.

8

A NEW PUBLISHER AND
THE DEATH OF THE *TELY*

I t was never going to happen easily or without rancour. As Joe
Atkinson Jr. began to ponder his succession, the prospect of yet
another intra-family imbroglio seemed inevitable, if not preor-
dained. For almost seven decades, an Atkinson or Hindmarsh had
run the *Star*, leading to the entrenched myth of a family dynasty.
Enter Harry Hindmarsh Jr., son of the now deceased HCH and
nephew to Atkinson. Having been passed over by Bee eight years
earlier in his appointment of a new editor, Harry Jr. had never given
up hopes of taking over if not the whole company, at least editorial.
Indeed, Atkinson had penned a memo to himself much earlier,
writing that Harry was his "natural successor." But he had quickly
added that a lot could happen.

Indeed, by 1966 Atkinson had changed his mind, to the point of
becoming almost obsessive in his insistence that production boss
Burnett Thall succeed him as CEO. Theirs had always been a close
working relationship, with Atkinson acting as a benevolent, admiring mentor. The problem for Thall, however, was a complete lack of
support from other directors. Simply put, none of them felt he was
up to the task. But this wall of opposition was not stopping Atkinson
in his drive to promote Thall. Finally, there was Bee, the new editor,

replete with a record of editorial accomplishment and an ambition that seemingly knew few limits. While still a relative newcomer to the board, Bee was not going to let inexperience or fate impede his will to prevail. Once again, the ingredients for a Machiavellian, internecine battle were all in play.

After months of backroom negotiation, principally between Atkinson and his sister Ruth, the battle broke wide open. Harry Jr., having failed to convince his uncle to back him, suddenly turned the tables on him, informing the other directors of Atkinson's secret plan to unilaterally install Thall as boss. Harry Jr., Bee, and advertising head Bill Campbell immediately confronted Atkinson in his office, accusing him of improperly bypassing the board of directors. They also reminded him that under the voting structure of the voting trust, Atkinson and Thall together could muster only 47 per cent of the votes, while Bee, along with the Hindmarshes and Campbell, controlled 53 per cent. So long as they held together, they would prevail. Furthermore, for Atkinson to act without board approval and in defiance of the majority would be a sham, they declared. Atkinson admitted discussing several "possibilities" but insisted that no final deal had been made. To which his nephew roared back, "You're a liar!" On that rancorous note, the meeting ended.

At a special board meeting the following week, Atkinson faced the ire of his nephew, the suspicions of other directors, and the veiled hostility of his sister, with all not sure what he was up to. Atkinson had long tried to bring his sister Ruth onside, but her loyalty had always been to her son, Harry Jr. On the issue of Thall, her brother's pleadings fell on deaf ears. Looking around the table that afternoon, Atkinson promptly rattled them all by proposing to resign and sell all his shares. He then firmly but quietly told them to leave.

Almost immediately, Atkinson confided to company lawyer Alex MacIntosh that he felt he had made a big mistake. MacIntosh was astounded by the turn of events, reminding Atkinson that he didn't have the votes at the board to win. "If you force the issue, you'll lose," he told him, adding, "You've got to correct the situation as soon as possible." Meeting later with all of the directors, MacIntosh warned that they were at risk of losing control of the *Star*. All knew the voting trust rules would oblige Atkinson to offer his shares first to the other directors, but MacIntosh reminded them that the value of the *Star* had grown from $320,000 to over $15 million in eight years. Atkinson's share was one third of that, and few banks would lend such a large sum to directors of a company that was in obvious turmoil, he said. A compromise had to be found.

Behind the scenes, Bee had been taking his own steps to make a point about his erstwhile competitor. Realizing he was an outsider and relatively new to the board, he was intent on not leaving anything to chance. He enlisted his new managing editor, Charles Templeton, to build a file listing every foul-up or delay in the composing room, which was under Thall's control. In his memoir, *Inside the "Toronto Star,"* Templeton recalls, "There was little trouble in fattening Honderich's file: almost every morning there were delays or problems to document." At a showdown meeting a few weeks later, Templeton witnessed Bee in full fury as he chastised Thall for the delays, threatening to take the issue to Atkinson and the board unless there were improvements. Templeton speculated this might be the opening salvo in a showdown fight for power, adding Bee was "tougher, more ambitious and better equipped as a journalist to be publisher than was Thall." There seems little doubt Bee made this material known to all of the directors. Indeed, it has become a key element in the company mythology of Bee's ultimate success.

Given the need for resolution, MacIntosh intervened, stressing the importance of compromise. With the backing of both the Campbells and Hindmarshes, and having made his point about production issues, Bee knew he was in a stronger position. He acceded to Thall's being his second-in-command but ruled out completely any thought of Harry Jr. heading up editorial. In May, without any leak regarding the power struggle, Bee was named assistant publisher. Six months later—and in accord with the compromise—he took over as president and publisher, capping what the *Star* called "a rags to prominence story." On his first day, he penned a two-page letter to all two thousand employees, setting out his general vision. "When the *Star* was founded 75 years ago," he wrote, "it succeeded where others failed because of two things: the leadership and sense of purpose provided by J.E. Atkinson and the co-operation and loyal support of the staff." He continued, "As president I will try to provide the leadership the company requires. . . . I can only succeed, however, if I have the active support of the people who really constitute the *Star*."

I remember feeling great pride when the announcement was made, but not much surprise. While I had been entrusted with very few details of the battle—with Bee now living alone in a spacious, well-appointed apartment looking out at a forest glen off Yonge Street—he looked, appeared, and acted very much like the man in charge. His experience of running editorial, particularly of engaging aggressively with political leaders at all levels, had left its mark. He had earned their respect—if not in some cases, their fear. Jim Coutts, principal secretary to former prime minister Lester Pearson, would tell me later how the *Star*—"and by that I mean your father"—played a "huge role" in the medicare and pension debates. "Your father knows how to wield power," he added. Bee's iron-fisted control of the news department had also revealed an executive not afraid to utilize the levers of power. In most respects, he had become the face and essence of the paper. His accession to the publishership was, thus, a reaffirmation of that reality.

The battle did produce, however, a schism and bad blood between the Honderichs and Thalls that never disappeared. In the frenzied events leading to the creation of the voting trust, Bee and Thall had collaborated well, enjoying a common purpose. I can remember friendly visits to the Thall cottage on Lake Simcoe. But that bonhomie dissipated into a deep sense of mistrust and resentment that would rear its head periodically over the next six decades. Whether the subject was the Thall family's right to have a director on the board, the chairship of the voting trust, or special working privileges for family employees, the two families would repeatedly come head to head. Within the voting trust, the Thalls would often take a dissenting view, much to the chagrin of the others. By the end, they even refused to pay their share of legal expenses. And the Atkinson–Thall alliance, with their combined 47 per cent of the votes, became a new dynamic for Bee to handle. Indeed, he would tell me that keeping the 53 per cent onside was something he never forgot about or ignored.

Within a year of his stepping back, Atkinson, a widower, married Elaine Barrett, a twenty-two-year-old *Star* secretary and a friend of his daughter Betsy. Four months later, he was rushed to hospital, where a giant brain tumour was discovered. Too ill to resume working, he died within nine months. Doctors and *Star* lawyer MacIntosh wondered if that tumour affected Atkinson's behaviour adversely near the end of his run. "Joe was a born peace-maker," MacIntosh observed. "Turning so confrontational was completely out of character for him." In its obituary, the *Globe and Mail* said, "Mr. Atkinson stood by the social principles which his father had inculcated in the *Star*. But he changed the paper's tone and approach; he helped it to grow and mature." At his daughter's request, he was buried in his favourite red tie.

About this time, my father decided to marry Agnes King, the widow of a former IBM executive killed in a Trans-Canada Air Lines crash north of Montreal in 1963. We had known the Kings for years as they spent holidays, as we did, at Chateau Woodland Lodge in Haliburton. It had been a relatively low-key courtship and Bee opted for a small ceremony at Toronto's Cricket Club. He asked me to stand beside him, an honour that caught me totally by surprise.

In the newsroom, the ongoing rotation of managing editors continued, but in the '60s, two figures stood out. The first was Charles Templeton, who caught Bee's eye while conducting three simultaneous interviews on a CBC program. Bee invited him to edit what was then the *Star*'s op-ed page—newspaper-speak for the page opposite the editorial page. Templeton's friend, Pierre Berton, advised him against taking the job, citing the past record of short tenures in this position. But Templeton decided otherwise and showed great talent as he climbed the ladder. As then editorial page editor Bob Nielsen commented, "Charles proved that a vigorous, intelligent man with little or no background in newspaper work could master just about any job at the *Star*." Eighteen months after joining the paper, Templeton was running the newsroom.

He would hold that job for more than three years before he left to run, unsuccessfully, for the leadership of the provincial Liberal Party. Throughout his tenure, Templeton had figured out his own distinct way of working successfully with Bee. Indeed, Bee tried his damnedest to dissuade Templeton from leaving, arguing he could do more for society at the *Star* than in politics. The two seasoned newsmen didn't always agree, but a mutual respect persisted between them. Templeton admired Bee, but not blindly. As he said on his departure, "Bee was a notoriously difficult man to work for. But the fact remains he took a lousy newspaper and turned it around, by being stubborn as a mule in what he wanted, even ruthless in dealing with people who got in the way."

The next newsroom leader would be legendary sports columnist, war correspondent, novelist, ex-editor of *Maclean's* magazine, and mentor to a generation of gifted journalists Ralph Allen. Bee was so determined to land this legend he offered him a salary $1,500 above his own. More important to Allen was the agreement struck between them. Their joint goal was to produce the best paper they could, but Allen insisted he be left alone to do it. Given Bee's notorious "hands-on" modus operandi, most newsroom observers felt clashes were inevitable. Yet that simply didn't happen, at least publicly. A famous anecdote tells the tale. Unaware Bee was standing behind him, Allen asked an editor about a Jimmy Breslin column from the *New York News*. Before the editor could speak, Bee interrupted, "I don't always like his stuff." In response, a surprised Allen told the editor, "Put that in the paper—right away!" Bee departed, a wry smile on his face.

As newsroom leader, Allen brought a deep knowledge of the country, a zest for new ideas, and a reverence for good writing that was contagious. Veteran sports columnist Trent Frayne once said of his friend, "Ralph wanted nothing more than your best, and he'd accept not a damn bit less. Under him, Bob Reguly became Canada's most famous investigative reporter. Tragically, slightly more than two years after joining the *Star*, Allen died at age fifty-three, after surgery to remove a tumour from his throat. Within hours, the *Star* ran an editorial about its loss, as well as tributes to one of the country's greatest journalists. Years later, Bee would sum up his feelings by saying, "Ralph Allen was simply the best."

Unquestionably Allen's most celebrated act on the personnel side was his hiring of Peter C. Newman, then the most feared columnist in Ottawa, having just written his devastating critique of the Diefenbaker years, *Renegade in Power*. A native of Austria, Newman started his career in the Royal Canadian Navy before he entered the world of journalism. Allen had worked with him at *Maclean's* magazine and knew only too well the reporting panache of this writer/journalist who would ultimately become one of Canada's most celebrated chroniclers of politics and business. At the *Star*, Newman continued breaking story after story while covering the Liberal government of Lester Pearson. Indeed, Pearson became so incensed with the leaks from his cabinet that he threatened to fire any minister caught spilling secrets. Walter Gordon, then a cabinet minister, recalled the PM saying, "We must not discuss this matter in any detail because Peter Newman is listening. He's lying under the table right now." As Gordon related, "Three cabinet ministers were so dumbfounded that they actually peeked under the table." The next day, that was in Newman's column too.

Within the newsroom, the news editor is charged with the daily task of pulling together all the disparate stories and features that will comprise the next day's paper. Legendary in his time, the brittle and crusty Tommy Lytle held that role throughout this era, working tirelessly for more than forty years. He was the epitome of a hard-bitten, hard-driving manager, and it would be his judgment that ultimately shaped the paper's front page. Lytle was famous for his dictum "News is what I say it is." Profanity was his stock in trade, as were accuracy, dedication, and an intense desire to be first. Bee totally respected him, and was even occasionally the willing object of his acerbic wit. Once during a newsroom discussion, Bee gave Lytle's arm a gentle squeeze. When he did it again, Lytle frowned, "Bee, what do you want me to do? Squeak?"

Throughout the '60s, Bee never lost sight of the competitive position of the *Telegram*. Indeed, he became, quite appropriately, fixated on it. Perhaps his biggest personal defeat by his afternoon rival came in '60, when the Diefenbaker government decided to award private TV licences in major cities. In a bid for the Toronto franchise, *Tely* publisher John Bassett led a consortium that included the retail Eaton family and broadcaster Joel Aldred. A staunch supporter of Diefenbaker, Bassett let it be known he had the inside track. Despite this, eight other bids were submitted, including one by the *Star*. Every bid contained promises of superb programming, rich in Canadian content. But the *Star*'s proposal was truly unique in that it promised to run the station as a public utility, taking only 7 per cent of the profits and giving the rest to charity.

I remember Bee's particular pride in his bid, as well as his total disbelief that the fix was in. Rival bidders, on the other hand, took a dim view of Bee's initiative, seeing it as a ploy to undermine them. In preparation for his oral presentation before the Board of Broadcast Governors, Bee spent hours and hours at home practising, often recruiting me to act as audience. I was totally caught up in the drama, while feeling great pride in the *Star*'s attention-grabbing proposal. At my insistence, Bee allowed me to attend the actual hearing, which, unsurprisingly, received massive play in the *Star*. It all turned out to be for naught, however, as Bassett was awarded the licence. Bee was totally crushed, a state I had very rarely witnessed.

In the head-to-head news competition throughout the '60s, the razzle-dazzle of the past became far from the norm. But from time to time there were exceptions. One was in '60, when seven-year-old Roger Woodward was swept over Niagara's Horseshoe Falls but lived to tell the tale. *Star* reporter/photographer Ed Roworth was dispatched to get the requested exclusive. By the time he arrived at the hospital, the *Star* had already presold the boy's story to a British tab for $4,500. *Tely* reporters were also there, wrangling to get their exclusive. Having heard Woodward's father was a construction worker, Roworth, noticing a man at the admitting desk in muddy work boots, smoking nervously, headed straight over. Sure enough he was right, and on the spot, he offered the father to pay all his son's medical bills plus $100 in cash. The deal was done and the *Star* had its exclusive. In drafting the boy's account—"How I Rode over Niagara"—Roworth also slipped in a small fiction to protect the *Star*'s copyright. "The boat started to jump around and buck just like my old rocking horse," he wrote. In fact, the boy never owned such a toy, and when that exact detail appeared in the matching *Tely* account, *Star* lawyers quickly moved to get the story killed.

The following year there was a Canadian National Exhibition promotion that saw marathon walker Dr. Barbara Moore walk from Montreal to Toronto. A *Tely* reporter accompanied the doctor for three days before quitting with sore feet. The *Star* countered with reporter Dottie O'Neil and her friend Roslyn Robb, turning the trek into a race along Highway 2. After eleven days, pipers welcomed the women to Toronto's city hall, cheered by a crowd estimated at ten thousand by the *Star*, four hundred by the *Tely*, and "about a thousand" by an impartial police officer. Dr. Moore complained the *Star* team had been driven most of the way, inspiring two headlines the next day: "I walked every painful step—Dottie" and "Not on those short fat legs—Dr. B."

Much more the norm became in-depth features and serious investigative reporting. In '65 the *Star–Tely* competition turned on the mighty Eaton family's plans to develop a prime downtown area of twenty acres into a $250 million shopping and office complex. The project included the demolition of the city's iconic Old City Hall to build a forty-four-storey highrise, prompting a public outcry to preserve this Romanesque structure. As 70 per cent owners of the *Tely*, the Eatons received full editorial support from that paper. The *Star* at first balked at the demolition but gradually tilted more towards the plan. When the Eatons suddenly cancelled their entire proposal the next year, the *Tely* blamed "small-minded, petty politicians." But in an exclusive break, *Star* columnist Ron Haggart revealed that the return on investment for the project had become less than expected. Some politicians warned that the Eatons would take their plans elsewhere in Canada. But Haggart insisted in multiple columns that this was simply a power play. Just as he predicted, the company later built the much larger Eaton Centre for $265 million, with Old City Hall thankfully left intact.

As the *Star* and *Tely* continued their editorial battles, a far more profound battle for survival was bubbling underneath. In the eighteen years since publisher John Bassett had purchased the *Telegram*, its circulation had inched up to a daily average of 235,000. Meanwhile, the *Star*'s circulation had jumped to more than 400,000 a day. In 1971, as labour bargaining for all Toronto papers was set to begin, the *Telegram* registered a loss of more than $2 million, whereas that same year the *Star* turned a profit of just under $6 million. Production costs for both papers were about the same, but the difference in advertising and circulation revenues was substantial—and growing. Thus, as bargaining began with the Toronto Newspaper Guild, the *Star* could well afford to offer reporters a hefty hike in salaries. Bassett, on the other hand, swore such an increase would force him out of business and took the unprecedented step of allowing labour reps to inspect his books.

As a swashbuckling, old-style publisher who relished the lime-light, "Big John" had always boasted he would never sell his beloved paper. Indeed, two years before, he had openly declared, "This paper is not for sale—not in my lifetime, not in my sons' lifetime and hopefully not in my grandsons' lifetime." In the background, how-ever, the story was entirely different. Through brokers, Bassett had already offered the *Tely* to several Canadian and English publishers, without success. He even sought out two ex-*Star* giants, Pierre Berton and Charles Templeton, to see if they might be interested in entering the fray. The two considered the proposal for several days, with Berton later recalling, "At one point Chuck said, what the hell, if we bought the paper and it didn't pan out right, we could always sell its circulation to the *Star*."

Little did they know that back at the *Star*, Bee was crafting a strikingly similar strategy as he watched his cross-town rival sink deeper into debt. Bee knew only too well how Atkinson Sr. had coveted the *Tely* right up to his death. But when the paper suddenly went on the market six months later, Atkinson's trustees shied away from making an offer. Sensing the time was right to pounce, Bee first dispatched his circulation manager on a fact-finding mission to several U.S. cities where one of two afternoon dailies had folded. In one case, the survivor's advertising and circulation revenues had increased only moderately. But in the second, where the survivor bought its rival's circulation list, the gains were significant. As Bee recalled later, "We concluded that we should go after the *Tely* lists— and before the *Globe* did."

After considering various options, Bee called his designated "fixer," Walter Gordon, to act as consultant and go-between. In August 1971, Gordon contacted Bassett directly, saying he had a question to relay from Bee: If Bassett could no longer operate the *Tely*, would he sell its subscription list to the *Star*? Five days later, Bassett replied that he had approached the *Globe* about buying the *Tely*'s spanking new Front Street printing plant, but while insisting other interests were in play, he acknowledged the *Star* was the "logical" purchaser of its circulation lists, given that both were afternoon papers. As negotiations unfolded quickly, Bassett proposed that he alone would shoulder responsibility for discontinuing the paper. The *Star* would purchase the circulation list but nothing else. Bassett would assume all *Tely* liabilities, including $5 million in severance pay for his employees, and would later sell its property and plant to the *Globe*.

Both sides haggled over the value of the list, eventually agreeing on a $10 million price tag. Meanwhile, lawyer MacIntosh went to Ottawa to secure an advance tax ruling that concluded such an expenditure was tax deductible, citing the "failing company doctrine" as the principal reason why the *Star* should not be accused of stifling competition. In the newsroom, an elite group of senior editors drew up a list of nineteen journalists they would like to hire. And one features editor quietly urged the purchase of *Steve Roper*, *Mary Worth*, *Peanuts*, and other popular comic strips. The list of senior executives made aware of the deal was kept as tight as possible. Indeed, Bee would later tell of how one of the *Star*'s corporate directors sent him a memo saying Bassett was on the verge of selling the *Tely* to Lord Thomson of Fleet.

With an eye on the future, Bee also kickstarted another hush-hush project. Led by Marty Goodman, the *Star* began laying the plans for the launch of a down-market morning tabloid on the first day of 1972, to compete against the more upscale *Globe*. Bee turned to his old buddy Milt Dunnell to be publisher of the new daily, dubbed "The Alternate *Star*" in internal memos. Planning for this new upstart had reached a fever pitch by late fall. In one memo, Goodman set out plans for an "all *Tely*" editorial staff—"Andy MacFarlane or Mel Morris in charge, Peter Worthington and Bob Pennington as writers. Sandy Ross as columnist, of course." Another memo from Bee set out a timetable for the announcement of the new paper—"several days prior to the suspension of the *Telegram*." Timson later recalled being asked to cancel an upcoming jaunt to

Cyprus in order to work on the project. Timson's reaction was immediate: "We've bought the *Tely*!" Goodman reportedly winced, adding, "On second thought, you'd better go to Cyprus. But keep your mouth shut!"

In the second week of September, Bassett convened a meeting of the ten directors of the Telegram Corp. in the library of John David Eaton's elegant mansion—the Eatons holding a majority of company shares. Bassett outlined the terms of the deal, emphasizing that with the proceeds from the *Star*, there would be enough to cover the paper's debt and meet all severance requirements. Bassett's son, known by all as Johnny F., was the only dissenter. The following day Bee convened a meeting of the *Star* board, which unanimously approved the deal. The only variation from Bassett's initial proposal involved the *Star* leasing the *Tely*'s plant for two years for $2 million, to handle the increased circulation until the *Star* could install additional presses. At meeting's end, Bee took Goodman and several others to the National Club for a celebratory lunch, allowing himself two of his favourite Manhattans.

That very same afternoon, Bassett met with *Tely* union officials, rejecting out of hand their offer to accept IOUs instead of cash raises. Strategically unmentioned was any word of the *Star* deal. So that evening the unions proceeded with their pre-arranged employees' meeting, seeking strike authorization. When that was approved, a *Star* reporter phoned Bassett at Mr. Tony's restaurant, where he was dining with senior *Tely* executives, including political editor Fraser Kelly. Told of the strike vote, Bassett repeated his earlier warnings of financial doom, but amazingly added he was prepared to meet with union leaders again "and bargain in good faith." In her Bassett biography, Maggie Siggins relates how dinner guest Kelly decided to take Bassett head on. He said, "First, people say you don't give a shit about the paper anymore. Second, they say you've already sold it. Finally, they're saying the *Telegram* is dead. Is that true?" In response, Bassett supposedly looked Kelly straight in the eye, declaring, "Right on every count."

Believe it or not, it would be another two days before Bassett, just before midnight, finally marched into the *Tely* newsroom to write his newspaper's obituary. In a personal statement, he announced the ninety-five-year-old paper's closing, saying, "This decision is the saddest that I have ever had to make in my life, in war or in peace." At the *Star*, four reporters worked through the night producing eight articles on the history of the paper's legendary competitor. All stories were held, however, for the second edition, allowing the *Tely* a scoop on its own demise, in accord with fine competitive tradition. Even Bee was quoted, saying, "The *Telegram* has made a valuable contribution to the life of the community and the nation."

It is hard to overestimate the dramatic impact of the *Tely*'s demise. A Toronto institution was going down. Senior newspaper executives labelled the failure inevitable, but labour leaders decried it as a "tragedy." Lord Thomson of Fleet decided to take a swipe at Bee, who only a few months before had told a royal commission how important competition was in the newspaper business. "It amused me to see Honderich come off his high horse about unlimited competition," Thomson said. "When the crunch came, he wasn't ashamed to make a deal that was very much in his own interest."

On radio station CFRB, veteran host Jack Dennett implied that Bassett had been bribed into giving the *Star* an afternoon monopoly. His charge was prompted by *Tely* union complaints that the $10 million for the subscription list was a "payoff." Since the *Star* was picking up the *Tely*'s newsboys, the argument ran, *Star* reps could have easily traced *Tely* subscribers. Those lists weren't worth the paper they were printed on, let alone $10 million, they complained. In an internal memo, Bee countered that securing the lists was essential to stop them from being sold to the *Globe*. However, when *Globe* executives publicly disavowed any such interest, Bee found himself in a tough public relations position. In a dramatic turn, he declared in a page one story in the *Star*, "We are still of the opinion the *Telegram* is no longer a viable economic operation. But even at this late date, if anyone is prepared to come forward to try to arrange purchase of the newspaper and operate it as a going concern, our directors would be willing to withdraw from our agreement provided, of course, that Mr. Bassett would release us."

Mining tycoon Stephen Roman would offer $12 million for the paper, but with so many conditions, Bassett wasn't interested. Indeed, the *Star* had already made the first of two $5 million payments for the lists of 164,263 *Tely* subscribers. And, in a private letter, Bee said his offer to cancel the deal would stand until the *Tely*'s final day—now set for October 30—provided any buyer would also cover the *Star*'s expenses. In an interview with Ken Lefolii in *Toronto Life* the following year, Bee seemingly acknowledged the relative worth of those circulation lists. With the *Tely* no longer in business, the *Star* could sell an additional one hundred thousand papers, but it had no way to print them, said Bee. "We made the deal for the list to get access to the *Telegram*'s plant," he added. "The subscription list alone was worth nothing." I have always believed that this description was far closer to the truth.

As the shutdown day approached, key *Tely* advertising and circulation employees were recruited to cross over to the *Star*. More than twenty editorial staffers were also offered jobs, including film critic Clyde Gilmour, veteran Queen's Park columnist Ron Haggart, and young city hall reporter Ian Urquhart, who would later rise to be the paper's managing editor. Goodman would subsequently rescind the offer to Haggart, citing his offence of writing favourably for an NDP election pamphlet. "One cannot assume a partisan political stance of this kind and still achieve the elements of a Queen's Park column that the *Star* policy demands," Goodman wrote. More than sixty reporters appealed this decision to Bee, but he stood firmly behind Goodman. "News reporting must not only be fair, it must appear to be fair," he wrote.

For most of the *Tely* editorial staff, however, a very different outcome was in store. Many of them were enlisted to work on a feisty new morning tabloid that would ultimately be dubbed the *Toronto Sun*. Conceived in amazingly short order by the trio of *Tely* executive Doug Creighton, veteran newshound Peter Worthington, and syndicate manager Don Hunt, the new paper received a financial boost from long-time *Tely* lawyer Eddie Goodman, who raised a quarter of a million dollars. The team rented an old building on King Street and wasted no time broadcasting the newspaper's future. Two weeks before the *Tely* officially died, Creighton put out a press release proclaiming that the new *Sun* would be "an outspoken, independent voice in Toronto." Moreover, the new paper would be printed by Bassett's Inland Press as soon as the *Tely* shut down.

With this dramatic and rapid-fire birth, Bee's idea for a morning tabloid hit the dustbin. In retrospect, it seems clear the *Star*'s secret plans were not secret as they might have wished. The *Sun*'s creators got off to a faster start, and worse still, MacIntosh warned that federal competition officials would not look kindly on the *Star* fighting a new paper. It has always been assumed that each side knew of the other's plans. Ultimately, the *Sun* became a fierce competitor, changing forever the strategic outline of Toronto's crowded newspaper market. Had the *Star* been able to enter the tabloid market, the story of this market would, undoubtedly, have been much different. For veterans of that era, it has remained one of the great "what ifs."

On the second last day of October 1971, the *Tely* proclaimed its own death with the headline "THIS IS IT: Our last day." Beside it was a montage of old front pages with a big red "30" superimposed on top—30 being journalists' traditional symbol for the end of a story. This was truly the end of an era.

But for Bee and the *Star*, a new one was about to begin.

PART II

9

GROWING UP WITH BEE

The setting was the magnificent Jasper Park Lodge, with its heritage cottages and giant stone fireplace, on the shores of Lac Beauvert. Against the backdrop of the rugged Rockies, the publishers and editors of Canada's major newspapers gathered in '64 for the annual meeting of Canada's national news agency, the Canadian Press. All the great names I had heard of were there: J. Patrick O'Callaghan of the *Edmonton Journal*, Frank Swanson of the *Calgary Herald*, St. Clair Balfour III of Southam, Stuart Keate of the *Vancouver Sun*, and Howard Webster of the *Globe and Mail*. The only one missing, to my saucer-wide eyes, was the *Tely*'s John Bassett. What made this CP meeting different was the planned presence of some of the progeny of these newspaper giants. So there I was. Bee's eldest son.

There was no doubt this was a true busman's holiday, with the meeting meticulously planned around a daily round of golf on the spectacular championship course. I vividly remember bear tracks in the early-morning dew on some greens, with a few pins unceremoniously yanked out. I also recollect Bee sitting at the board table, quite forcefully arguing some point that had others riled up. That didn't surprise me in the slightest. I was very used to his argumentative approach and felt a son's pride as he pressed his point. It was also clear that as editor of Canada's largest newspaper, his voice came with clout. He might have been brand new to the table at that time, but that didn't deter him one iota. Those were the moments I enjoyed the most.

Then there were the multiple social gatherings, meals, and drinks that are a staple of such get-togethers. There I encountered the various sons—the thought of bringing a daughter being inconceivable in that era. I'm not sure I had imagined what to expect. For certain, I didn't expect any special treatment, nor did I feel I deserved such. I was Bee's son, after all, and coddling his children was, I'm sure, unthinkable to him. But as an eighteen-year-old, I remember being sharply taken aback by the deference broaching on sycophancy that I witnessed in these sons. It was as if they felt they deserved to be part of this group. It was their birthright. This was the world as it should be, and they acted accordingly.

Not so for me. The very notion struck me even then as false. For whatever deep psychological reasons, it seems I was already feeling intensely that I did not want to be identified primarily as the editor's son. Aside from taking a *Star* paper route and a brief summer job in the photoengraving department, I had deliberately avoided doing anything remotely linked to the paper. Indeed, I never worked on a student newspaper or a yearbook, or even thought of writing a letter to the editor. My early ruminations on career, linked in no small way to the wildly popular *Perry Mason* show, had me practising criminal law. Indeed, that would be my sole career aspiration, give an occasional variation here and there, until I actually completed law school. While I may not have been entirely familiar with the concept of nepotism, it seems I knew what it felt like. And I was intent on doing my own thing, being my own person. It was a deeply ingrained feeling that has never left me and that, given my eventual career path, has produced great internal turmoil. It also presaged some major battles that lay ahead with Bee.

Paradoxically enough, it would be that Jasper experience that was uppermost in my mind as I wrote to Bee eight years later. In that letter, meticulously saved by Bee to his "John" file, containing my lifetime correspondence with him, I described why I had decided to change careers. "For the past 26 years, I have studiously avoided any involvement in anything that might faintly be regarded as linking me to you," I wrote. "All this in spite of the fact I have been keenly interested in communications, journalism and the *Star* . . . so it is time to stop cutting off my nose to spite my face and realize what I want. Although the image of the fawning, obsequious sons crowding and yessing their fathers at Jasper is still vivid, I am now determined to try to enter the communications field."

Bee would tell me decades later he found this letter "cruel" and "unfeeling." It seems he felt the victim, interpreting some of my deepest desires for independence as a personal attack on him. Looking at my words now, I can see how he might have felt I wanted nothing to do with him or what he did. Yet I remember clearly my intent was exactly the opposite. In making this momentous decision, I knew the person in the world I most wanted to have understand was Bee. I spent several days on a rock promontory in Lighthouse Park in West Vancouver writing and rewriting this letter. The dramatic view of the sparkling ocean seemed appropriate. I chose my words carefully and remember thinking he would be most happy for me. While being frank, I thought he would respect my desire to go my own way. Certainly, throughout my life, he never once told me what to do. Not once. He would always say, "It is up to you. It is your decision." And I very much respected that—and often told him so.

One decision, however, was non-negotiable. "I wouldn't start of course in Toronto," I wrote, "but as to where I go and what I do, I would like to talk to you later." First, I had no experience in journalism. Second, to be fair, Bee had always said any aspiring journalist should earn his chops at a smaller paper before coming to the big city, just as he had done. And third, I was even more determined than ever to prove my independence. On that point I wrote, "My preference presently is to go to Vancouver and there, 3,000 miles away, find out if I am even any good." When we spoke a few days later, Bee didn't reveal any of his hurt feelings. That wouldn't have been my father. But we did have a good conversation and it was then that the idea of me working in Ottawa first surfaced.

What had always been self-evident were the special life and experiences I had enjoyed growing up with Bee. And I said so unequivocally in the letter. "I have lived with you long enough to see the day-to-day routine, the pressures, the experiences, the people you worked with, the environment in which you were stimulated, the people you met and the lifestyle you had. To put it bluntly, I have constantly been fascinated and envious of it all." Who else would have been able to attend, for the allotted half hour, the "drinks parties" Bee held in our house basement after his appointment as editor-in-chief? There, to mingle with Pierre Berton, Lotta Dempsey, and Milt Dunnell or to watch Nathan Cohen swish down the stairs in his black cape were unforgettable moments. So unforgettable, in fact, I recalled them as one of the eulogists at Berton's funeral. The image of a very inebriated Duncan Macpherson also persists. Then there were the dinners with the Newfoundland contingent. Bee had met Premier Joey Smallwood in his reporting travels and the premier dropped by from time to time. A more regular visitor was Alfred Valdmanis, the wily Latvian immigrant who spearheaded Smallwood's scheme to industrialize Newfoundland. With his connections in Germany and the Baltic countries, Valdmanis had hoped to entice European companies to set up shop on the Rock. In '54, all of that came to an end when he was charged with defrauding the government. Bee, however, would always defend him, and their tennis game up the street usually preceded a lively dinner.

Then there were the three giants, as I remember them, who all played pivotal roles in Bee's life as well as my own. The first was Alex J. MacIntosh, the wily, wise, and totally dedicated lawyer from the *Star*'s legal firm, Blake Cassels (Blakes). A proud Scot from Nova Scotia, Mr. MacIntosh, as I always called him, was a superb counsel in the truest sense of the word. He first met Bee during the formation of the voting trust and was without doubt his closest confidant until he succumbed to cancer thirty-five years later. No major decision was taken without "Alex's" advice. A shrewd, tough negotiator, he was also a ferocious advocate for top-quality journalism. He cared deeply about what appeared in the paper and had a well-formulated position on virtually every political issue, which, in many cases, he felt compelled to share with either Bee or, laterally, me. My "A.J." file is full of such letters, each one of which always necessitated a detailed response. However, once his point was made, that would be it. MacIntosh also provided libel advice in the newsroom, weighing in on contentious investigative stories and starting a tradition with Blakes that has lasted ever since. Periodic visits to his cottage in the Kawarthas, replete with a mandatory sailboat ride, were always a treat.

The second giant was the patrician ex–finance minister Walter Gordon, who, along with Bee, championed the cause of economic nationalism in Canada. Mr. Gordon was the epitome of Toronto's financial establishment, with his fine three-piece suits and elegant white hair. A senior partner in the accounting firm Clarkson Gordon, he chaired the Royal Commission on Canada's Economic Prospects. In the commission's two reports in '56 and '57, Gordon sounded the alarm about the growing foreign ownership of the Canadian economy. Bee took up this cause with a ferocity after hearing Gordon declare in '60 that Canada must choose between independence and satellite status vis-à-vis the United States. Every speech from Gordon received page one coverage, Bee spoke often on the subject, and the *Star*'s editorial page rang out regularly on the perils of foreign ownership. While Peter Newman once called Gordon's writing "as interesting as a manual on bee keeping," that did not curtail its prominence in the paper. This was a crusade of the highest order and it had an impact across Canada. By the end of the decade, a majority of Canadians felt foreign ownership was a matter of great concern. Over the occasional dinner at our home, Mr. Gordon never failed to impress.

The third giant played an entirely different role with Bee, as fishing buddy, fellow thoroughbred horse enthusiast, and regular betting partner. For Bee, Milt Dunnell, the *Star*'s legendary sports editor, was as close to a good old pal as anyone. After all, it was Milt who first proposed the idea of Bee moving to the *Star*. The loyalty and bond between them were unique. They would forever be placing bets on anything sportif, with Milt the usual winner. During the newspaper war, when *Telegram* publisher John Bassett tried to lure Milt away with a much higher salary, Bee quickly flew to New York where Milt was on a story, to fend off the defection. It became an annual ritual for our two families to go to the Queen's Plate, an occasion preceded by a lavish luncheon. Fishing jaunts while in Haliburton were also a mainstay, and those would be the only times I saw Bee drink to excess. An exuberance and mocking sense of humour would also emerge, traits I rarely saw in him otherwise. Milt would also become a great confidant to me later, always loyal to the paper and constantly concerned about Bee's welfare.

In addition to my fondness for the three giants, my other great memories are of periodic visits to "the office." I just loved going to 80 King Street West. The foyer was so grand, with its brass elevators, carved floral motifs, magnificent chandeliers, and chiselled stonework. The elevator attendants, always clad in impeccable white gloves, usually gushed over my younger sister Mary and me. We were somewhat known locally, for Bee had regularly "volunteered" us for family photo shots in the paper—seeing Bee off at the airport, opening Christmas presents, working on train sets or doing kid stuff. I never thought of this as unusual. But I do remember that whenever the paper needed kid "props," Mary and I were always made available.

At the office, Bee would usually let us amuse ourselves while he was off doing his work, although we never went too far astray. The smell of lead that permeated the building from the cylinder plates is forever etched in my memory. Going down to see the presses rolling, watching the typesetters tap away furiously, or seeing editors stuff marked-up paper copy into pneumatic tubes soon to go down the chute became familiar sights. Our treat would be either getting a candy bar from the first vending machine I ever saw or going for lunch at Stoodleigh's in the basement. We never tired of the routine or the visits.

The other moment of consequence that fuelled my independence came as I began a brief summer job in August of '64, during one of the most bitter strikes in *Star* history. It involved the Toronto branch of the International Typographical Union (ITU), which was fighting the introduction of a new technology that allowed the typesetting of data and stories by tape rather than humans. The three Toronto papers joined forces to fight the ITU. Several contracts were agreed upon by the local Toronto branches but were summarily rejected by ITU headquarters in Colorado Springs. This automation, if accepted, would undoubtedly cost union jobs everywhere and ITU central decided to put a stake in the ground in Toronto.

Management of the three Toronto papers was equally adamant that this new technology had to be allowed. In their arguments, they relied heavily on the fact that the local units had wanted to settle but the "ugly" American international headquarters hadn't let them. With the *Star* composing room empty, all hands were called on deck to put out the paper. And Bee, even as editor, did precisely that, working every night to lock up pages. In the process, he badly mangled one finger, earning much respect for his dogged contribution. As I had just completed grade thirteen, I was in desperate need of a summer job before I started university. We had amicably worked out a deal that persisted throughout my nine-year-long academic career. Bee would pay for my tuition and I would be responsible for all other costs. So Bee suggested a brief stint in the photoengraving department, which was not affected by the strike, so I could earn pocket money.

Going to this job obviously necessitated crossing a picket line, an impediment I overcame. I do clearly recall Bee's argument that the local units had wanted to settle, and his insistence that newspapers had to constantly keep up with new technologies. This latter rationale would ultimately confront me four times more in my career as I endured various strikes. My belief in unions and the rights of workers paralleled Bee's in many respects. After all, he had been the first president of the Toronto Newspaper Guild when it was formed in the late '40s. Indeed, he played a major role with the union in negotiating the first newsroom contract at the *Star*. I would later become a union steward at the *Star* before joining management. I can even recall once voting to reject a contract settlement that was overwhelmingly approved by my colleagues. Heading to work my first day that late summer, I was also aware that the photoengravers, like the members of all other *Star* unions, had voted to cross the ITU picket line daily to keep the paper running.

My greeting, however, was totally unexpected. Clearly the engravers had not been told the name of their new summer intern. And when they were informed, they all gathered around, genuflecting and proclaiming in near-unison "Swami!" I remember feeling acutely mortified, with very little to mutter in reply. My only remedy was to work extra hard, carrying every heavy lead cylinder and finishing every piece of paperwork as quickly as possible. My strategy was swiftly diagnosed by the engaging and always entertaining Charles Stockey, a veteran photoengraver who played the role of philosopher king for his mates. Stockey regaled me daily with his tales of conquest, be they motorcycling, amorous, or financial. Obviously, his investment prowess was acute, for his $1.7 million endowment led to the construction of the stunning performing arts centre in Parry Sound that bears his name and hosts the annual Festival of the Sound.

The summer of '64 also marked my return from a transformational year in Europe, where I had completed grade thirteen at Neuchâtel Junior College in Switzerland. The idea to go abroad had first been raised by my mother, but I subsequently embraced it enthusiastically. I felt very comfortable, perhaps too comfortable, in my North Toronto surroundings. The idea of breaking loose, learning French, living in a local *pension*, and seeing Europe all had tremendous appeal. The only problem was that my formal acceptance to the college, the year before, had arrived just a few weeks after my parents had separated.

Throughout my high school years, marital unhappiness had enveloped our household. It was a constant emotional drain for my sister and me. My brother, nine years younger than me, felt the pain differently—indeed more severely. While Bee was away a lot, the tension that surrounded nightly family dinners was palpable. Arguments would break out regularly, often over the most trivial of matters. A consistent guarantor of friction was money, not its need but rather how much was spent. My mother was proud of her Presbyterian frugality, which led, for example, to the family returning from trips to Florida with half our spending money unspent. This would enrage Bee. The differences in their family background and upbringing also played a huge role in my parents' discord. My mother was raised by her great uncle and aunt after her mother died in childbirth with her second child. Discipline, conformity, and regular church service, all within a relatively comfortable setting, determined my mother's course. Bee's poverty-racked childhood and his obsession with breaking boundaries stand in sharp contrast to this sense of calm and ease.

In his five-page type-written apologia to Mary and me a few days after he left our home, Bee outlined with brutal honesty why the marriage hadn't worked. First, he described it as "unfortunate" that he had been away travelling so much. "Young married couples need most to get to know each other," he wrote. "They should not be separated for long periods as we were." He could have said the same about his children, as my earliest memories are of a father constantly travelling. He seemed always gone, and a perusal of his dispatches from across Canada and abroad underlines the point. I simply never expected him to show up for my hockey games, choir recitals, or symphony concerts in high school. And indeed, he did not. Nor would he express much, if any interest, in how my life was going. Report cards, however, were always an important point of reckoning, although my record on that score was usually decent. But I was constantly reminded that I could do better.

Second, he wrote, "I have been too interested in my work for my own personal good." He admitted to a "compulsion" to work, adding, ". . . everything I have anything to do with must be done perfectly. No doubt these characteristics have contributed to my success in the newspaper business, but they have also cost me the things I value most in life." On this point, Bee was stating the obvious. Throughout my living with him, it was an accepted truth that business always came first. Whether the demand was a telephone call, a meeting, or a trip, the *Star* was paramount. On our annual two-week summer stay at Chateau Woodland Lodge in Haliburton, calls from the office came regularly, almost always at dinner. In *Star* lore, much is made of the tale that on his honeymoon trip to Hawaii, Bee called "the office" from the airport to check on things. This didn't surprise me one iota. Of course Bee would call. He had extra time on his hands, and this is what publishers do—at least publishers like Bee. "This compulsion to work makes me difficult to live with," he wrote. "I tend to think of my work to the exclusion of other things. If I have a business problem on my mind, I cannot go out socially for an evening, I feel I must solve the business problem first."

His third and final point was directed specifically at me. "Finally, John, I am a non-conformist." While arguing this trait made for a good newspaperman, he conceded that "it does, however, make it difficult for people around me for it seems my ideas are constantly changing." Later he acknowledged, "I may not appear to be an affectionate father and at times I may seem stern and indifferent." And then he professed great love for us in a way we might not appreciate "until you look into the face of your own children."

It was a stirring and emotive cri de coeur. Never before had I heard my father write or emote this way. I remember being almost dumbstruck by its honesty and critical self-analysis. Expressions of love for his children were simply not something I had ever experienced. Hugs were unknown. Indeed, the only time he reached out for a hug was the last time he picked me up at the Vancouver airport, a few months before his death. Taken aback, I wasn't quite sure what to do. Yet, ultimately, it was how he chose to separate from us that struck deepest, something he was completely oblivious to. On that dark January evening, I had taken my brother David to the annual track meet at Maple Leaf Gardens. It always ended very late, so we were late getting home and Bee chose to speak only to my sister. In his letter, he began by apologizing for not telling me directly, arguing it would not have been "fair at that hour of night, to subject you to such a serious and disturbing conversation."

I had felt exactly the opposite. As eldest son, I felt entitled to hear directly from him. To be told by my mother the following morning seemed deeply unfeeling on his part, particularly when I learned Mary had been foretold. This breach also underscored my deep-seated conviction that Mary had always been my father's favourite. Not only that, I had deeply resented Bee's constant attacks on my mother, feeling she had become the innocent victim of a marriage gone sour. She never stopped trying to make it work, whereas I felt he had given up. Mary and I would talk endlessly about the poisonous atmosphere at home, and both of us felt a palpable sense of relief when the separation occurred. There is no question my loyalty lay completely with my mother. I was often described as my mother's son. I was her favourite and I knew it. I also identified more closely with her gentility and sense of fairness. Mary, on the other hand, had much more empathy for my father. It was a dynamic that never changed.

The meting out of discipline also left its mark on us. As younger children, it seemed any transgression could be met with "the strap," which Bee had brought back from Argentina. Depending on the seriousness of the mischief, we would be forced to extend hands for a few well-aimed swats. My mother also adopted the practice, although with somewhat less vigour. Both my parents were unapologetic products of a strict upbringing, with little thought of the rod being spared. They both firmly believed this was how children should come "to learn a lesson," the justification I heard most often. Seemingly innocent requests could also be met with cruel rebukes. My most poignant memory centres on my appeal to have the family buy a few fireworks for May 24th. In one of his periodic foul moods, Bee thrust a five-dollar bill in my face, suggesting I take it outside, light it, and then watch it burn.

Politics, both national and provincial, were paramount in Bee's life. Dinnertime conversation often revolved around issues of the day. I will never forget being challenged to take one side of an argument, with Bee stubbornly taking the other. It became a mealtime ritual, one I often chafed at. However, the mutual insights on political leaders of the day and the passion we expressed on certain issues, particularly U.S. domination of the Canadian economy, made up for it.

Ultimately, the solo trips I made with him to Washington and Ottawa would remain strongest in my memory, while cementing forever my interest in politics. The trip to America's capital came in the early '60s, when I was in my late teens and Marty Goodman was in residence as Washington bureau chief. We toured Washington's stunning national monuments and were entertained that evening at a fancy dinner hosted by Marty's redoubtable wife Janice.

My memories of the trip to Ottawa are by far the strongest, centring on a lunch in the storied Parliamentary Restaurant on the top floor of Parliament Hill's Centre Block. It is the place to which MPs and senators regularly go for lunch when Parliament is in session and has stunning views of the Ottawa River and the Gatineau Hills beyond. The buffet tables then were resplendent with sumptuous offerings of fine salads and desserts. We were seated in the middle of the restaurant when veteran Liberal MP and leadership hopeful Paul Martin Sr. came to visit. The Windsor native could not have been more solicitous of my interests and life—in obvious deference to the editor of the *Star*. I will always remember him telling me, "My door is always open." But it was the next visitor who literally took my breath away. Lester B. Pearson, leader of the opposition and recent winner of the Nobel Peace Prize, dropped by. Wearing his trademark bow tie and a V-neck pullover, he pulled out a chair, placed a foot on the seat, and rested his elbow on his knee. Compared to Martin, he was more casual, if not relaxed, in his questions; however, he had a definite point to make with Bee. His manner was certainly not as deferential as Martin's either. Quite simply, it felt such a great honour to meet him.

After that encounter, Ottawa always occupied a special place in my mind, as did federal politics. So perhaps it was no surprise it ended up being the place I would start my fledgling journalism career. The thought of working on "the Hill" was enticing, but that would obviously come later, if at all. First, it was time to learn the basics and find out—did I have any aptitude for this?

10

OFF TO OTTAWA

It would be, paradoxically enough, on the eve of April Fool's Day 1973 that I began my journalism career in Ottawa. At the pre-arranged time, dressed far too nattily, I strode up to the Queen Street entrance of the old *Ottawa Citizen* building. Landing a job had been a long, tortuous process, and as I arrived that night, I still didn't know exactly what to expect. But one thing had been clear. I didn't want any help from Bee. I had been determined to do this on my own—and so I did.

After initial thoughts about Vancouver, Ottawa had become my ultimate preference, that love of federal politics probably showing through. So I applied to both the *Ottawa Citizen* and the *Ottawa Journal*. From the latter, there was politesse but no offer. From the former, the paper's kindly and jovial editor, Bill MacPherson, waffled for several months and then finally told me to show up. A job would be waiting, curiously undefined. At the time, it seemed far too presumptuous to ask for any details about the position, let alone the pay. I had a job in journalism! Here I was an honours graduate in political science and economics, and one of Her Majesty's most recently minted lawyers. But my journalism experience was nil—not so much as a freelance piece, essay, or even letter to the editor to boast of. That is how determined I had been to avoid any whiff of involvement in journalism.

Certainly, I was under no illusions as to how I would be regarded. Nothing I said or did, particularly at the beginning, would make a difference in what people thought. I was a Honderich, plain and simple—Bee's son. The assumption would be that I came from a plush, privileged family that had undoubtedly pulled strings to arrange for this job, particularly given my lack of journalism credentials. The fact that I had two university degrees would undoubtedly be lost in the newsroom shuffle. Right from the get-go, my strategy was to do any job, take any assignment, and try hard not to react to any jibe or insult. I would let the results—in this case, stories— speak for themselves. I knew I would never escape a perception of favouritism, a sense that I had been accorded special advantages. But nothing shuts down assumptions better than proven performance. I may always be seen as the son of privilege, but my goal throughout my career was to be known as the son who did the job—and then some! It was a career-spanning credo I never forgot. And it would be tested my very first day.

As I entered the dark, smoky *Citizen* newsroom, I became aware of the abrupt end to the clatter. It was as if every pencil dropped and every eye fastened on the new recruit. Not just any new recruit, as I was told later. They all knew what I'd be doing—and the pay rate. Managing editor Lyndsay Chrysler, one of the jovial grand ole patriarchs of Canadian journalism, suddenly emerged and introduced himself. "Let's take a tour," he began. It all seemed a blur as I met several reporters, all seemingly dressed in jeans and variations of black. In my beige, checkered sports coat and matching slacks, I was hopelessly overdressed—and embarrassedly self-conscious. We then approached copy editor Paul Cavell, his sometime state of inebriation still at an early stage. "So, the big cheese has finally arrived," he growled. "My guess is the first week you'll figure out how we run, the second, you'll take us over, and the third, you'll buy us out." Welcome to your new life, I thought, unable to muster any appropriate retort.

Sensing my unease, Chrysler quickly ushered me to the notice board, where my new life was about to become clearer. "I imagine Bill told you about the job," he began. "No," I replied, hesitantly. "Well, well," he muttered, clearly caught off guard. "You'll start at the bottom as a copy boy. I can't really oversell the position, but it's a good place to learn the business." Then he pointed to the schedule showing a start time of 7. Stunned by the news, I quickly mumbled, "Okay, I'll see you tomorrow morning." To which he quickly replied, "Oh no, John. That's 7 p.m. You start tomorrow evening and work 'til 3." The thought of working nights had not even crossed my mind, let alone that I would be "copy boy." I had just assumed I'd be working days.

In retrospect, I've often wondered what I had expected. But certainly not this. I managed to ask about the pay and was told it would be $73 a week, with a few extra dollars for "night differential." What had I done? Was I crazy? I felt completely shell-shocked. I quickly bid Lyndsay goodnight and headed to the bar of the Château Laurier Hotel, at that time the only watering hole in town I knew. Then, for the next several hours I drank double scotches, drowning my depression the sole purpose. Any comparison to Bee's slightly more auspicious yet decidedly less dramatic debut in Kitchener thirty-six years earlier would only come later.

The following evening, I summoned every ounce of fortitude and headed for work. My boss, the night editor, would be Russ Mills, a high school teacher turned journalist who would later rise to be the *Citizen*'s long-serving publisher. He was ultimately sacked in 2002, in an extraordinarily public spectacle, when Canwest mogul Leonard Asper showed him the door for editorializing that Prime Minister Jean Chrétien should resign. Indeed, Asper was so vicious in his comments that I would later be moved to write a strong column in Mills's defence, which began: "Russ Mills was my first boss."

On my first night, almost three decades earlier, Mills was ever so much the gentleman, explaining in straightforward, workmanlike terms what was required. The essentials of the job were not difficult to fathom: clear the teletype machines of wire service stories and place them in three distinct piles: local, national, and world. Do odd jobs, get the midnight food and drink orders for reporters and editors, and write the occasional story—if there's time. It took about fifteen minutes to outline, at most. Then I remember sitting down and staring intently at the clock. I kept on staring til 7:40 p.m., when I had a stern conversation with myself: *You made this choice; you know why you're here; so get on with it.*

Even in those early days, the paper seemed an ideal place to start. Established as the *Bytown Packet* in 1845 by local businessman William Harris, it was renamed the *Ottawa Citizen* six years later with the motto "Fair Play and Daylight." It went through a succession of owners until 1879, when the Southam family purchased it in the process of creating a cross-country newspaper group. For nearly a century, the Southam chain boasted a tradition of quality journalism and a commitment to the craft that resulted in vibrant newspapers in such cities as Vancouver, Calgary, Edmonton, Montreal, and Windsor. Editorial policy was left to local management, and each paper had a mandate to reflect and tell the stories of its respective community. In sharp contrast to other chains, there were no overarching political policies or orders from on high as to how each paper should be run. The elegant, silver-haired Bob Southam was publisher of the *Citizen* when I began. In every respect, this quiet yet towering figure represented all the values his family stood for in newspapering.

Editorially, the paper was progressive, aligning itself often with the Liberals and styling itself as the smart, urbane alternative. Unlike its competitor, the *Journal*, it also strove to cover and reflect the burgeoning capital in those heady days of Pierre Trudeau, rather than the more stolid, conservative traditions of the Ottawa Valley. It was a winning formula that eventually led to the *Journal* closing up shop in 1980. In accord with its aspirations, the *Citizen's* newsroom was also replete with a cadre of young, ambitious, and exceptionally talented journalists who would later make their mark across the country, some at the *Star*: Carol Goar, Colin MacKenzie, Murray Campbell, Charles Gordon, Rick Mackie, Orland French, Sarah Murdoch, Bruce Ward, and Richard Labonté.

For me, the immediate task was making friends with, if not earning a little respect from, these curious if skeptical colleagues. From the outset, it was obvious no one had the foggiest idea what to make of me, which was a reaction I came to expect throughout my career. It wasn't every day a fully fledged lawyer accepted a job as a copy boy. Nor was it every day the son of a big city publisher worked nights for minimum wage. The opportunity I was seeking came in week two. It was a test—and I knew it. Reporter Phil Carter approached me asking for a favour. He needed background info on a story he was doing and the *Citizen* clippings file had "gone missing." Since I was new in town and wouldn't be recognized, could I go over to the opposition *Journal* library and nab some of their clippings? "Sure," I said. And off I went, returning shortly with their entire file. "Here," I declared triumphantly.

Over the next few weeks, I scrutinized the paper every day trying to figure out how to write a news story. I knew the five Ws of journalism (who, what, when, where, why) and the need for copy to be tight. But not much else. So it was a process of writing, rewriting, and rewriting even more, often on the simplest of news breaks or press releases. I was clearly at the bottom of the pecking order and so got stories to do only when everyone else was busy—which suited me just fine. I silently rejoiced at the smallest of assignments that appeared. Six weeks in, I got my first front-page story involving the sentencing of a local thug. Not yet a story above the fold—the aspiration of every journalist—but I was so excited I sent Bee the carbon copy of my original draft, which found its way into his "John" file. Not surprisingly, Bee was keen to hear how I was doing, what kind of stories I was working on, and what it was like "starting from the bottom." He always thought that was the best way, just as he had done. But he didn't interfere or offer advice on my writing or approach. That was for me to figure out, which I found most appropriate.

My first byline came with a fortuitous last-minute assignment to cover then Finance Minister John Turner's defence of wage and price controls to his local Ottawa constituents. Turner, ever the gentleman, took more than the usual time to speak to me. The story marked a turning point for me in getting more assignments out of the office. But the process of writing, rewriting, and honing my reporting skills was non-stop.

By summer, the grind of working nights plus filling the midnight food orders of every reporter and editor—some of which I can still recite—began to wear. Was there any chance of a move? I inquired. While the televised Senate Watergate hearings in the U.S. had kept me mesmerized during the days, I felt I had paid my dues. Sure enough, an opening arose in the *Citizen*'s consumer column called Action Line. With my legal background, it seemed a perfect fit, and so I happily began my new job—thankfully in daylight—doing research and writing up stories on my findings.

Much like Bee, however, I would need a big break to really jump-start my career. Six weeks into this new assignment, I had settled into a comfortable routine. One sleepy Friday afternoon in August, I was handed a letter from a woman who had lost her deposit on a new housing lot in Marlborough Township. Initially it didn't strike me as too suspicious, but I decided to call her lawyer. Much to my surprise, I got through. He mumbled something about "a Section 29 Planning Act problem," adding dismissively, "You probably wouldn't know anything about that." Turns out I did, as a law student who had serendipitously revelled in the intricacies of real estate law. So, the following Monday I camped out in his reception lounge all day until he finally relented and agreed to meet with me. In return for a promise to never reveal his name, he took me through the details of the "checkerboarding" scheme. Instantly, I realized I was onto something big.

For a week I furiously researched the scheme, which involved the reeve of the township along with several developers, including the uncle of legendary Ottawa crooner Paul Anka. When I presented my work to my boss, Roger Appleton, he told me it would run, following his usual rewrite, in the big Saturday edition. While it was standard procedure for Action Line stories to run on page two, without byline, I considered it a pretty big scoop that deserved the front page or, at the very least, a pointer from the front. Instead, it ran in the usual spot with the surprisingly innocuous headline "Action Line special report." It was also clear Roger had told no one about the story, nor had anyone editing the column thought it worthy of special display. I remember waking early and rushing to read the paper, only to be crushed by both the story's tepid treatment and the absence of any acknowledgement of my contribution. Complaining, however, was out of the question. New boys don't do that, especially one with my last name.

So, I said nothing, not even to Roger. But a journalistic storm erupted immediately in the newsroom over the fact we had badly underplayed the story. There was also a sense that Roger had unfairly taken all the credit. That was remedied the following Saturday when regional reporter Bert Hill, unbeknownst to me, included in his page one story that the scandal had emerged through "the investigative work of staff member John Honderich." Justice was done, and one month later I was promoted to reporter. Parenthetically, the provincial government rushed in to take over the administration of Marlborough Township and the minister involved gave me the scoop, resulting in my first headline story. Bee was very impressed by this and reminisced about his big break with the barn fires in Baden.

After a brief stint in the newsroom as a general reporter, most often covering police, I was moved to the courts beat. For someone who had once aspired to practise criminal law, this was a dream job. The cases, the defence lawyers, the Crown attorneys, and the judges all fascinated me. The courthouse was downtown, and I was even able to skate to work on the Rideau Canal during winter. The big murder trials—of which the Ottawa Valley seemed to have more than its fair share—along with the usual stream of juicy cases provided an endless stream of stories. And in what I will always see as an act of contrition, my old Action Line boss gave me a tip on another checkerboarding scheme, which led to more front-page exposés. A few months later, there would be a third checkerboarding case in Silver Lake, and this time I was served with my first libel suit. It would be the first of six I received, none of which ever went anywhere.

By now, my reputation, writing skills, and bona fides seemed accepted by all. A big hurdle had been cleared, and just seventeen months after first starting, I got a big promotion to be the paper's investigative reporter. It was a glorious assignment allowing me to combine my legal background and inquisitive reporting to produce a stream of exclusive stories. In short, I was beginning to make a name for myself while always honing my writing and reporting.

I would be only a few months into this job when another career-changing jolt occurred. In the co-op where I lived with two others in Ottawa's Centretown, it was a tradition to celebrate birthdays with a grand feast. That January night in 1975, I was cooking dinner when my housemate Marilyn Sleeth sashayed into the kitchen to tell me we had a "surprise guest." That guest turned out to be one Barry Forsythe, who had that very day shot his way out of Kingston Penitentiary and found his way to Ottawa. Armed robbery was his trade and he was supposedly en route to a tree outside Pembroke, where he had secretly stashed the proceeds from one of his earlier heists.

Could he stay for dinner? asked Marilyn, a Kingston native who had met Forsythe a few years earlier during her weekly visits as a Pen volunteer. Not only was the news all over the radio but my other housemate, Chas Pearson, was an articling student with the Justice Department. Nor could I ignore that I was a lawyer and reporter. The prospect that police might find out we were harbouring an armed escapee did not sit well with us. Career and reputations might be at risk. Just then, Forsythe showed up, the outline of a small gun quite obvious in his rear pocket. Following a brief and surprisingly courteous chat, he agreed to leave. "Don't worry," he told me. "I understand why you are doing this. Happy times." However, he did not get out of town but opted instead to hide out in a nearby theatre. In a subsequent gun battle with police, he shot three officers, seriously wounding one. It was huge news, but thankfully we had contacted the police, who showed up twenty minutes after he left.

We were shell-shocked. Would the cop die? Would we be hauled in? Were we somehow responsible? Then it hit me. This was one helluva story—and I was a reporter. I should write it. After consulting with my housemates, I headed to the office, not sure what I was emotionally able to produce. I will be forever grateful to my hard-driving and no-nonsense city editor, Scott Honeyman, who sat me down and did his best to calm me. He said, "Just write it straight. Not fancy, just straight." Which I did, and the story not only topped page one in the next day's *Citizen* but ran across the country, along with a photo of a moustached, rather shaggy-looking reporter. The reaction everywhere was overwhelmingly positive. I had done it— and coincidentally, it too landed in my father's "John" file, along with the photo. I wouldn't realize until the following year how game-changing that story would be.

Over the next eighteen months, the investigations continued, many of them involving crooked or questionable real estate and developer deals. But my targets also included everything from the Church of Scientology to medical issues at Pembroke's general hospital, to vice rings, to a troubling cover-up by the Sûreté du Québec over a tragic car crash involving one of its officers on Ghost Hill. This last investigation was done in conjunction with Sheila Copps, the *Citizen*'s West Quebec reporter, who later turned in her reporter's badge for a hugely successful career in federal politics. Had she stayed a journalist, I have no doubt her nose for a great story and extraordinary ability to connect with people would have made her equally unstoppable.

I had just turned thirty and it was about this time my craving to cover politics became all consuming. It crescendoed in the winter of '76 as the Progressive Conservatives were holding their leadership convention, most fortuitously in Ottawa. That allowed the *Citizen* to open the journalistic floodgates and send ten reporters to the convention site a few kilometres down the road. The meeting to decide who would cover which of the nine candidates started with all the senior political and feature reporters picking off the supposed front-runners—Brian Mulroney, Claude Wagner, Jack Horner, Sinclair Stevens, and, of course, Flora MacDonald. I was seventh in line due to my relative inexperience, and was left to choose the little-known thirty-six-year-old MP from Alberta named Joe Clark. For the next three days, I followed Clark like a hawk, being one of the very few reporters of any paper to do so. And when he defied all expectations, climbing to the victory podium, I was assigned to write how he had achieved this miraculous, come-from-behind victory. Several front-page stories followed, and I realized then that political reporting was my passion.

Weeks later, I headed in to see managing editor Nelson Skuce, whose love of local Ottawa stories knew no bounds. Would I have a chance to cover Ottawa City Hall or Queen's Park or even Parliament? His answer was immediate and ultimately decisive. The system at the *Citizen* was established: all political reporters could stay in their posts until they decided otherwise. Though I was aware of the "system," I had somehow hoped my investigative work and three years' experience might prompt a promotion. Unbeknownst to me, publisher Bob Southam had penned an assessment of my work to his superiors, noting, "In a relatively short period of time, he has developed into a first-class writer and will obviously move ahead very quickly." I was never aware of this appraisal or that a copy of it had found its way to my father. Certainly, Bee never spoke of it.

But Skuce's answer altered my career. I was not prepared to wait. Had something developed, my storyline might have been entirely different. I loved the *Citizen* and was very happy in Ottawa. But I wanted a job covering politics, preferably federal. And I felt I was ready to do it—anywhere except the *Toronto Star*. As I started my search, that option was completely out of the question. Nor did I even let Bee know I was planning a move.

I started with the *Globe and Mail*, who informed me ever so politely they had no interest in training me only to see me walk cross the street to work at the *Star*. The *Financial Post* was next. Editor Neville Nankivell asked me to write a piece on the Supreme Court, which later was published. However, he went on an extended holiday and weeks went by without any word. During that period, I was at my desk when the *Star*'s then managing editor, Ray Timson, was suddenly at the other end of the line. "So, John, we hear you're looking for a change," he began in that unmistakable gravelly tone. "Why haven't you let us know?" My reply was instant: "You know why, Ray." Ever the consummate arguer, he shot back, "Well, nothing hurts in you at least having a conversation. You can always say no."

I didn't have an answer for that. So after some reflection I decided to fly to Toronto—needless to say, without a word about it to Bee. When I entered Timson's office, there on his coffee table lay my first-person, guess-who's-coming-to-dinner story on the escapee from Kingston Pen. "You've clearly made your mark, John. You've shown everyone you can do it." After a lengthy chat, he tabled the offer—reporter in the Ottawa bureau covering primarily the finance minister. It was as close as could be to the dream job I was seeking and here it was before me. Was Bee aware of this? I asked. Timson sidestepped the question, confirming what I should have known. Of course he was. However, Timson insisted the decision was his alone. Indeed, Bee was later asked by Doug Fetherling of *Saturday Night* magazine about my prospects at the *Star* and he replied, "I'd never make a decision as a father or as a publisher to affect him."

It took me several weeks to come to terms with it all. Virtually everyone said I should accept, but I hesitated. Was I caving in? How could I ever prove myself there? Would I not be ever tagged as gaining the job through nepotism? On the other hand, the job was perfect and I was desperate to move on. Ultimately, I came down on the side of giving it a try. There is always a three-month probation period for new employees. In this case, I asked Timson for the same three months from my side to see if I felt I could work for the *Star*. Probation in reverse, I called it. When I finally informed my city editor, Charlie Gordon, that I was leaving, the die was cast. Two weeks later, the *Financial Post* offered me its job in Ottawa. Too late. The deed was done.

11

TWO CAPITALS

It was with trepidation, certainly not awe, that I crossed the *Star's* threshold in September '76 for my first early-morning editing shift. A few weeks working in the main newsroom was standard fare for any new Ottawa reporter. Of course, I had been in the "new" office at One Yonge Street, but not often. Certainly, I remembered well the groundbreaking ceremony five years prior where then Ontario premier John Robarts joined the Reichmann brothers of Olympia & York Developments. This was the Reichmanns' first commercial tower, built on lakeside land Joseph Atkinson had bought dirt cheap half a century before as a hedge against possible printers' strikes. Atkinson, ever the business realist, wanted to ensure ready access to Lake Ontario, where boats could unload newsprint in the case of a nasty labour dispute.

A twenty-five-storey edifice built in a nondescript international style, One Yonge lacked any of the architectural aspirations of its King Street predecessor. At that time the sole building south of Toronto's railway tracks, its greatest asset was its iconic address— number "one" on the world's longest street, Yonge Street. And in an ironic twist thirty years later, when the paper asked its readers to name the ugliest building in town, some 20 per cent nominated One Yonge. Certainly, that early September, the place felt cold and brutish as I strode in as the boss's son to start my shift. I stayed at my mother's but had dinner with Bee the night before.

To say he was in fine form would be an understatement. I can honestly attest that never once did he ever express a desire for me to work at the paper. He was clear that any reporter coming to the *Star* should work first in a provincial daily. I had done that. But to suggest this might have been the first step in a succession plan is not to know Bee. First, in '76 Marty Goodman was running editorial on all cylinders and was widely viewed as Bee's likely successor. More importantly, Bee never thought or acted in terms of family succession. In fact, his earlier brushes with both the Atkinson and Hindmarsh families had soured him completely on any such arrangement. His advice to me was always "Go prove yourself." And that advice fit perfectly with my own career strategy.

Yet I did wonder much later if my coming to the *Star* validated him in some unspoken way. The sparkplug for that thought came with his reaction to the letter I had written him five years before, laying out my reasons for entering journalism. He took it as a personal attack, as if I wanted nothing to do with him. And yet here I was, joining the fold. He had certainly heard all my declarations of independence and I had always assumed he understood the reasons why. If he felt a lingering sense of grievance, it was never expressed. But my decision to join him in common purpose at the *Star* certainly resonated with some force. He seemed a very happy father.

While I felt I had legitimately earned my reporting spurs, the stark reality of being a Honderich at the *Star* suddenly hit home as I strode in that first day. What was I doing? Didn't I know this could never work? Why had I ever agreed to take Timson's call? I will never forget my shortness of breath as I entered that expansive newsroom, unsure of what indignity to expect. My fears, as it turned out, were completely unfounded. This was all in my mind and seemingly not in others'. No pencils down, no strange looks—or not that I saw—no rude comments. Just sit down, learn how things work, and meet your colleagues, including Lou Clancy and Geoff Chapman, who would both later work for me as senior editors. I had never worked on a desk before as a copy editor, and that inexperience certainly manifested itself quickly. Nor had I ever seen the likes of Jim Rennie, an explosive force of impatience and invective who ruled over the early-morning newsroom as a volcano. His temper was legendary but his news sense impeccable. No one wanted to be at the other end of his stare. This was the big time as I had expected it to be.

The next hurdle came a few weeks later when I showed up at the *Star*'s Ottawa bureau, on the ninth floor of the National Press Building. This time I did not feel hesitant or ambivalent. I strode in cheerily and my mates for the next four years were as welcoming as could be. "It's not as if we didn't know who he was," the often sardonic Peter Lloyd would say later, "but we knew what [he'd] done at the *Citizen*." However, they were all somewhat taken aback when I told them later over drinks at the National Press Club that I was starting with a "reverse probation." Not only was I under probation, but so was the *Star*. "Would that we all could get that," Lloyd shot back.

My speciality was economics, and so my focus instantly became the then finance minister, the amiable and patrician Donald Macdonald. The fact that my civically engaged Aunt Ruth had been a loyal stalwart in his local Rosedale campaigns helped open the door. A minister in the cabinet of Pierre Trudeau since 1968, Macdonald was made of the finest public service timber. He was direct, totally on top of his file, and unfailingly professional. "Big Mac," as he was affectionately labelled, would later declare he lacked the "royal jelly" to run for the top job, which was undoubtedly Canada's loss. Macdonald's preoccupation then was the Anti-Inflation Board, a body set up by the Trudeau government to combat inflationary pressures. As subjects of huge public interest, both Macdonald and the future of the board provided ongoing fodder for my daily stories, most often given prominent play.

When Macdonald resigned in '77, the finance job went to the first French Canadian ever to hold the portfolio—the inimitable Jean Chrétien. We hit it off immediately, and I probed and poked regularly. Along with his trusty sidekick, Stormont MP Ed Lumley—who was a treasure trove of great exclusives—we spent much time together. So much so that, one day, out of the blue, Chrétien offered me the job of executive assistant. Temperamentally, we had a great connection and a mutual respect that has never waned. We got along. I did consider his offer, but journalism, not party politics, was my passion.

As the economics reporter, one of the monthly rituals was going in early—shortly after 7 a.m.—to report on the unemployment and inflation figures. In the '70s, the *Star* still had a five-star edition whose deadline was before noon. Since both inflation and unemployment were anything but dull subjects, these stories would usually become the headline or "blackline" stories. So much so that I clearly remember the always sardonic Val Sears coming to the Ottawa bureau one day and chortling out, "So, mister blackline! You're all over the paper. But when are you going to learn to write?" A celebrated wordsmith whose political dispatches were legendary on Parliament Hill, Sears cut right to the quick with this comment. Indeed, I had been quietly impressed by all my blackline stories. *Better think more about your writing*, I told myself. It was a lesson I never forgot.

My first trip outside the capital brought me into close contact with one of the greatest wits and firebrands Newfoundland has ever produced, John Crosbie. It would be his by-election entry into the House of Commons in the riding of St. John's West that I was dispatched to cover. I was the only reporter in attendance as he spoke in the tiny fishing hamlet of Trepassey on the Avalon Peninsula. Needless to say, he wasn't going to let this fact go unannounced to his followers, proclaiming the "mighty *Toronto Star*" had deemed to show up "despite its Liberal cravings." Crosbie never forgot that meeting; nor did I. As he was the Tory finance critic of the time, I would regularly seek out his comments, which he provided unfailingly and always with gusto. It would be Crosbie's ill-fated budget, of course, that led to the collapse of the Joe Clark government, a budget he infamously memorialized as "long enough to conceive but not deliver."

Ironically, it would be that collapse that led to my career unexpectedly catapulting upwards. Trudeau having just retired, no one had expected the Liberals to regroup and bring down the Tory government. But at the Christmas parties the night before the non-confidence vote, unmistakable election drums were beating. The following morning, incredulous senior *Star* editors were calling the Ottawa bureau demanding to know what was happening. I took those calls, with other bureau members insisting I do so. Our bureau chief, the implacable and somewhat taciturn Terry Wills, had failed to show up, a bender being his affliction. He never did appear, and so I was called upon to arrange complete coverage for this momentous upheaval.

For the 1979 general election, I had been paired with my garrulous and endearing colleague Steve Handelman. Taking turns on the campaign plane, we chronicled the Joe Clark campaign in daily small columns designed to provide a different "take" on events. Surprisingly, Bee enjoyed this non-traditional approach, mailing me several columns with compliments. He also enjoyed our regular phone chats as I regaled him with tales of campaign lore. All this experience meant my links and connections with the Clark government were many. I always admired Clark, with whom I had a no-nonsense professional relationship dating back to the leadership convention, along with his closest policy adviser and former MP Jim Gillies, also the source of many exclusives. All these connections meant I felt ready and able to choreograph *Star* coverage as the fateful non-confidence vote loomed.

As expected, the government did fall, and *Star* pages were filled to the brim with coverage, garnering the bureau great praise. The following day, a chagrined and contrite Wills was relieved of his position and I was named the new bureau chief, which thankfully went over well with my colleagues. I had my first corner office. Handelman and I did propose writing a book on Clark's Tories, but our proposal never took off. I can remember thinking of the question I posed to Clark at the press conference following his win. How would he govern given that he was a few seats short of a majority? He replied that he would govern "as if he had a majority"—the story that ran as our blackline and garnered considerable attention. Ultimately, Clark was true to his word, but he paid the price for doing so.

In the election that followed, I opted to stick with the tradition of the bureau chief covering the PM. The fact I had experience, not to mention ties with the Tories, dating back to the prior election, reinforced my choice. The paper opted to stick with our format of writing small columns each day as we travelled with a party leader. The hugely unpopular Crosbie budget, with its eighteen-cents-a-gallon gas tax, rendered the outcome almost inevitable. A rejuvenated Pierre Trudeau romped to victory, making those long campaign bus trips and plane rides with Clark much more desultory. Once again, Bee made a point of congratulating me on certain columns.

One incidental outcome of my reporting principally on finance ministers, followed by two campaigns covering Clark, meant I spent very little time with Trudeau. The one major exception was his dramatic speech at Montreal's Paul Sauvé Arena near the end of the 1980 Quebec referendum campaign. The country's future was in play. The federalists were ahead, but not comfortably so. Standing near where pucks would normally be dropped, and enveloped by a frenzy of supporters, I witnessed what I still consider one of the greatest political speeches in Canada's history. Days before, Trudeau had been mocked for not being a true Québécois because his middle name was the English "Elliott." He recounted how his mother's family had come two hundred years earlier to Quebec, "where you can still see their names in the cemetery." In response to deafening roars of "Elliott, Elliott," he declared, "Mon nom est Québécois." Seconds later, he added, "But my name is a Canadian name also."

Now called the "Elliott speech," it was as powerful and emotional an assertion of being both a proud Quebecer and a proud Canadian as one could imagine. The federalists went on to win by a wide margin. As a reporter, I still consider this the most momentous event I ever covered.

That evening also produced an infamous moment that has gone down in *Star* lore. As I was standing in that cold arena, an editor was anxious to hear what was going on. The whole event was delayed, and of course cellphones didn't exist, so I had not checked in as was the usual routine. "Get Honderich!" the editor barked to a subaltern. Moments later, he was told his call was ready, and he seized the phone. "You son-of-a-bitch, why haven't you called? We've waited for hours." There was a silence on the line, followed by that familiar flat voice that had so often terrorized the newsroom. "I think you must have the wrong Honderich," Bee replied.

About that same time, word filtered down from One Yonge that the Washington bureau would be opening up just in time for the epic showdown between Jimmy Carter and Ronald Reagan. With five years under my belt at the bureau, I was ready to make a move and thus applied. I never heard who else might have been in the running, but I learned quickly the job was mine. A new chapter was about to begin for me professionally. But this was true in my personal life as well. The day after Clark's victorious press conference following his '79 election win, I was in Edmonton en route back to Ottawa. Sitting in a hotel bar, I picked up a local paper and came across a bubbly account of an Alberta writer done well, Katherine Govier. I had met Katherine several times—once when we were maid of honour and best man in a wedding—and when I hadn't asked her out, I thought to myself, "There's a lost opportunity." With her living in Toronto, our paths had understandably not crossed. My itinerary back from Edmonton took me through Toronto, so I decided to call her from the airport. To my delight and surprise, she answered and responded she would be tickled to get together. That was all the spark required for an intense year-long relationship to develop, involving countless back and forth trips between Ottawa and Toronto. Katherine was a celebrated short story writer and *Toronto Life* columnist, which meant she and I had friends in common and a mutual interest in fine writing. We both also had careers and an interest in starting a family. This we committed to do as equals, so it seemed only natural that we move together to Washington, where we would both be able to write in our respective fields. Unmarried upon arrival, we eloped two months later, the ceremony conducted at city hall by the chief marriage clerk of Washington, D.C.

Unfortunately, my new commitment was not exactly what Bee had in mind. A more traditional partner, able to bake apple pie— parenthetically one of my own culinary specialities—was more to his way of thinking. Not someone who chose to retain her last name or who was so openly career driven. Indeed, his feelings on the matter reflected exactly the kind of spouse he had chosen. I understood that, as well as his insistence that unmarried partners not share the same bedroom in his house, regardless of their age.

What was intolerable to me was that he openly revealed his views right in front of Katherine. It happened at a dinner table in Florida when, in a voice loud enough to be easily overheard, he told my sister he didn't think Katherine "was the right one." Of course, she heard his comment, and it was not something easily forgotten. Nor was his constant written referral to her as "Mrs. John Honderich." When he later sent a dozen roses to her under that name at the Washington hospital where our first son Robin was born, it took hospital staff a full day to track them down.

On the other side of the ledger, I had a simply amazing relationship with my father-in-law, George Govier, "Mr. Oil of Alberta," that lasted until his death. The architect and first chair of Alberta's Energy Resources Conservation Board, Govier was the former dean of engineering at the University of Alberta and a former deputy minister to Alberta premier Peter Lougheed. On our many family visits to Calgary, George—as he always insisted on being called—and I would talk both business and politics for hours. Our politics weren't the same, but that never stood in the way of our having lively and respectful debates. He would always inquire about the newspaper business and how I was faring. Quite simply, we clicked. He also reached out several times to establish some connection with Bee. Those efforts were never reciprocated. This sharp contrast in our relationships with the two fathers often made for many uneasy discussions with Katherine.

Indeed, it was George who was my inspiration to wear only bow ties as a statement to start the '80s. Until then, far from being formal in appearance, I had sported an unruly moustache. But I had always been impressed as an imperial George held sway at his board meetings or cut a swath on the dance floor of Calgary's Petroleum Club—invariably in a lively bow tie. So, as the New Year was about to begin, I stood with him facing the hall mirror in his Calgary home, learning the intricacies of the tie-up. From then on, I was—and still remain—a bow tie man.

My first foray into U.S. politics came in the two months leading up to the 1980 election. I was dispatched to cover the campaign, along with the current Washington correspondent, the ever-reliable Joe Hall. To me, the impact of leaving Ottawa, where my calls and requests were handled with dispatch, for Washington, where I was relatively unknown, was immediate. I used to say that in the U.S. Canadian journalists ranked "somewhere between the Swedes and the Greeks." Whenever you asked for access to a campaign plane or bus, it was virtually a given that you were placed on standby. Most often the question would be, "And how many voters read you?" As for access to a candidate, that simply was never offered. Of course, this was all understandable, but it was still a radical change from what I had been experiencing up to that point. Right away, this new dynamic forced me to carefully reconsider how I would approach my new assignment. Everyone loved covering the big story, but that story was readily accessible through news wires. How to be different and relevant?

One way, I discovered, was to specialize in Canada–U.S. relations. This was a subject not covered—or even mentioned—by American media. With the Trudeau government's introduction of the new National Energy Plan and its negative impact on the U.S. oil and gas industry, tensions between Ottawa and Washington had heightened. The huge bilateral trade through the longest unprotected border on the planet could also be a treasure trove for stories. But it would be the nascent beginnings of undoubtedly the greatest change to our economic relationship in the twentieth century that first caught my eye. With three weeks to go before election day, Reagan delivered a major TV address on foreign policy, eager to allay fears he was a warmonger. Under the rubric of developing a "more realistic hemispheric policy," he proposed what he called a new "North American Accord." No details were given. But it would be my mania, joined by the CBC's insightful Susan Reisler, to press Reagan's special foreign policy adviser Richard Allen for more details. They never came, for they didn't exist. But Allen used to spot the two of us approaching at campaign stops so often he would usually beat us to the punch: "Here come the Canadians. No, I have no more details." My first story on the Accord was nine paragraphs long and ran on page seventeen, in retrospect certainly not the play it deserved. But no one then had any idea of what would ultimately be in store—NAFTA, a free trade agreement among Canada, the U.S., and Mexico.

While my experience covering two Canadian federal campaigns was useful, the scale and grandeur of a U.S. campaign was something else. First, the world's press was there, particularly for the last two weeks. Second, where else would you see Nancy Reagan rolling an orange down the plane aisle on every takeoff, accompanied by Willie Nelson's "On the Road Again"? Or where could you see Ronald Reagan deliver his iconic "shining city upon a hill" speech?

The phrase, borrowed from an early Pilgrim settler, referred to those first settlements in Massachusetts as being a beacon for liberty to the world. I heard that speech several times on the campaign trail—each time, Reagan's delivery was impeccable. Indeed, I still regard him as the most effective political communicator I've witnessed.

One of my most emotional experiences after the inauguration was going to West Point, New York, to cover the return of the fifty-two U.S. embassy hostages from Iran. To watch them kiss the ground as they disembarked, surrounded by a supportive throng of tens of thousands, was nothing short of spectacular. And the following week, my fellow Washington correspondent from *La Presse*, Jean Pelletier, broke the story of Canadian ambassador Ken Taylor's heroic efforts to hide six Americans, also from the embassy, in his residence. The story of their exit from Tehran, disguised as a film crew, was later memorialized in the box-office hit film *Argo*. It was an amazing time to be a Canadian in Washington, with effusive thanks proffered every time an American learned of my nationality.

The shooting of President Reagan a few weeks later evoked a *Star* response reminiscent of the good old days of the '60s. I was dispatched immediately to George Washington Hospital—a fifteen-minute walk from the National Press Building—where literally dozens of reporters waited outside for any tidbit. Back in Toronto, the super-charged foreign editor, Mike Pieri, ordered up a charter Falcon jet to whisk my predecessor, Joe Hall, veteran scribe Christie Blatchford, and chief photographer Fred Ross to the American capital. Talented wordsmith Bruce Ward caught the late plane to Denver, with a mission to track down the family of the shooter, John Hinckley. Meanwhile, Ross had hustled directly to the ABC network offices, seeking out the shooting video, from which he selected and shot the best images. Once done, he raced back to the airport, boarded the jet, and delivered several rolls of film to the main *Star* newsroom in time for the next day's editions. As was custom for such a major event, a power-packed, special eight-page section also rolled off the presses. This was *Star* go-big journalism at its finest.

The days after the shooting, however, were filled with an ongoing debate among us three writers as to how far we could "push" the story. Both Blatchford and Hall were more in line with the "don't-believe-'em" school, intent on proving Reagan was in much worse shape than publicly stated—which turned out later to be the case. I realized I was seen by them as more trusting, leery of pushing the envelope too far. They were the rough and tumble, I was the doubting traditionalist. Our debate reached a climax when the renowned Blatchford declared the only really good reporters were those who had to fight to get their job, who never stopped fighting, and who didn't come from a background of privilege. A native of Rouyn-Noranda, she was the epitome of such. I was certainly not. I said nothing, but the sting was there. It was an attitude I knew I would face again.

A year later, when an Air Florida Boeing 737 slammed into Washington's 14th Street Bridge over the Potomac River, I bolted out of my office to the crash scene down 14th Street. Seven vehicles were struck on the bridge before the jet tumbled into the freezing river. Four motorists and seventy-three passengers died. In the raging snowstorm, I was among the first reporters to arrive and I witnessed first-hand the stunning bravery of bystander Lenny Skutnik. As one of the few survivors escaping from the fuselage lost grip of a lifeline, Skutnik dove into the water from the riverbank and rescued her. It made for a stunning front-page story with details not mentioned in any wire stories. I remember foreign editor Mike Pieri phoning to ask if I was sure about my facts. "You're damn right I am," I shouted. No holding back that day. And a note of praise arrived the following day.

One of my finest joys as a foreign correspondent was being able to travel and ferret out engaging stories anywhere. Why not travel to Plains, Georgia, and see what a defeated Jimmy Carter was up to? Or cross the country chronicling the new conservative think-tanks fuelling the Reagan revolution? Or trek to the Chicago suburb of

Morton Grove where possession of a handgun was just banned? Or travel to the United Nations for a special plenary on world peace? Or crash an invite-only press conference for British PM Margaret Thatcher, simply to ask her if she was prepared to let PM Trudeau repatriate the Canadian constitution? (She was not amused by the question.)

Most of my time, however, was spent in Washington, where I made it my speciality to chronicle the slings and arrows of the Canada–U.S. relationship. There was a whole series of hot-button economic issues, many of which prompted testy hearings in Congress. Periodically, I was able to interview the Michigan head of the House Energy and Commerce Committee, John Dingell, a crusty pol whose dislike of Canada's National Energy Plan was intense. Acid rain was also a growing concern, sparked by the first-ever Canadian lobby group to go to Washington full time to make its case—the Canadian Acid Rain Coalition. Their ultimate success in getting congressional action became a textbook example of how to lobby in the capital. Cocktail parties at the Canadian embassy, then at its social pinnacle under the tutelage of ambassador Allan Gotlieb and his wife, Sondra, were also a hit. I was able to strike up quite a regular conversation with Katharine Graham, the legendary owner and publisher of the *Washington Post*. She was as impressive and engaging as legend has it.

As my two-year anniversary at the *Star* was approaching, calls from Toronto to return to the newsroom intensified. Coming right from the top, they included a plea from newly minted executive managing editor Gary Lautens. "John, you've had a great run in Ottawa and Washington," he said. "Time to learn how to be an editor." At first, I resisted. Our new son Robin had just turned one and was well ensconced in local baby groups. Indeed, Katherine and I had discovered the joys of raising young children in Georgetown's lush parks and ravines. Much to our surprise, we also learned Katherine was pregnant, with our daughter Emily expected in a few months. As usual, Bee stayed neutral, saying it was my decision. I loved working in Washington. But I remember waiting one late night outside the Canadian embassy, once again, for then Environment Minister John Roberts to provide a comment on the acid rain issue. It was a long wait and I thought, perhaps, I might like something different. Ultimately, I agreed.

12

PROSPERITY AND
A CONGLOMERATE

E ver since Atkinson's death, the *Star* had dedicated itself, without hesitation or reserve, to its mandate to "observe and promote" the Atkinson Principles. The words of that precise directive
did not come by chance. Rather, they were plucked directly from
Atkinson's last will and testament, in which he specifically insisted
that the *Star* be run "in accord with my doctrines and beliefs." While
the spirit of his wish was clear, the specificity of his beliefs was anything but. It would be in the '70s that Bee, in conjunction with
editorial page editor Bob Nielsen, would give written meaning to
"The Principles." It was far from an easy task. Much later, Bee would
do his own review of every editorial of the Atkinson era, discovering
that consistency on some major issues was not self-evident. Capital
punishment was a particular case in point. But when it came to any
aspect of support for working people—be it medicare, pensions,
unemployment insurance, or family allowances—the calls were
clarion and unrestrained. Ultimately, six concepts were codified as
"the Principles": "A sturdy and self-reliant Canadianism, public
ownership of public utilities, equal rights and full civil liberties for
minorities, town planning, the right for labour to organize, and
freedom of the individual from fear, want and injustice."

It has been common in some newspaper circles to describe the *Star* as a "Liberal rag," tethered to the Liberal Party and whatever dog-eared candidate or howling party platform it might adopt. Indeed, those were the words *Globe* publisher George McCullagh used in the late '40s when pressuring Ontario to move against Atkinson's will. "I'm going to knock that pedagogic rag right off its pedestal," he told *Maclean's* magazine. That the *Star* is probably the most progressive of Canada's mainstream dailies is beyond debate. Indisputably, the paper has usually supported the Liberals. Certainly, throughout the terms of Prime Ministers Mackenzie King, Louis St. Laurent, and Lester Pearson, dating all the way back to 1917, that editorial support was unwavering. But in the '70s, Bee forever ditched the "must always" aspect of the tradition, codified a few years prior by HCH. In Pierre Trudeau's first re-election campaign in 1972, Bee personally wrote the editorial backing Robert Stanfield's Progressive Conservative Party, citing the Liberals' refusal to adopt a wage and price controls policy. In '74, the *Star* reaffirmed its support for Stanfield on the same issue, but in '79 it opted to support the NDP's Ed Broadbent. (The paper would also support the NDP's Jack Layton in his 2011 campaign. Provincially, Bee supported William Davis's Progressive Conservatives in several campaigns, and in 2018, the paper supported the NDP.) Thus, while *Star*'s earlier support for the Liberal Party generally continued, it was no longer a given under Bee—a tradition I was most anxious to maintain.

Whoever occupied the office where editors of the editorial page toiled always knew Bee was never far away. In fact, it was for him just a short walk down the hall. No matter how small a matter, Bee usually had an opinion—and more often than not, a strong one. Over the years, the paper had fulminated against rum-running censorship, capital punishment (latterly), nuclear stockpiles, second-hand smoke, and Sunday sports. On the other side of the ledger, it had crusaded for Sunday shopping, voting for women, higher taxes on the rich, affirmative action, creation of the St. Lawrence Seaway, and expanded French in Ontario schools.

For Bee, a passion bordering on obsession was born of the warning from Walter Gordon that Canada was headed towards becoming a mere satellite of the United States because of the huge amount of U.S. investment in the country. Year by year in the'70s, the paper ran hundreds of stories and editorials arguing that so much investment was costing Canadian jobs and exporting profits. Gordon, for a time Canada's finance minister, made many speeches proclaiming that Canada's very independence was in danger after years of heavy U.S. investment. Stories on most of those speeches invariably found themselves on page one. The federal government eventually created the Foreign Investment Review Agency, a version of which still exists. After his departure from politics to join the *Star*'s board of directors, Gordon became one of Bee's principal trouble shooters.

By this time, Peter Newman had left his roost in Ottawa to become editor-in-chief at the *Star*. It would be in October 1970 that Newman made his own unwanted headlines, a story that began with trade commissioner James Cross's abduction in Montreal by four members of the separatist movement Front de libération du Québec (FLQ). A week later, another FLQ group kidnapped Quebec labour minister Pierre Laporte. Quebec premier Robert Bourassa went into hiding and called the deeply respected editor of *Le Devoir*, Claude Ryan, asking for advice. Ryan, in turn, urged him to add prominent outsiders to his cabinet as a sign of Quebec unity. Rumours started circulating in elite circles that Quebec was setting up a provisional government.

Shortly thereafter, Prime Minister Trudeau famously invoked the *War Measures Act*, enabling police to round up more than four hundred Quebecers because of the "apprehended insurrection." The very next night, Laporte was found dead, strangled by the chain of the religious medal he wore around his neck. Newman and his then wife Christina McCall were in Ottawa and spent an hour, with guards outside, conferring with one of Trudeau's closest advisers, Marc Lalonde. Newman asked about the wild rumour that Ottawa had resorted to the *War Measures Act* because of the whispered plot to replace Bourassa with a provisional government. Far from denying it, Lalonde acknowledged the rumour had caused grave concern in the Trudeau cabinet. And then, to Newman's amazement, he set up a telephone interview to have his claim confirmed—by Trudeau himself.

Back in Toronto, Newman wrote a very carefully worded story headed "Plan to supplant Quebec government caused Ottawa to act." Bee also got involved and phoned Ryan in Montreal, reading him the story. Ryan hotly denied his involvement in any plot and angrily demanded his name be removed. Bee told him the story would run, knowing its ultimate source was the prime minister himself. In Parliament, Trudeau claimed to have "solid information" on the plans for a provisional government, but insisted it was not a factor in his invoking of the *War Measures Act*. Ultimately, no evidence was found of any shadowy provisional government, leaving both Bee and Newman to feel—very legitimately—they had been cravenly used.

On the news side, however, the *Star* scored two scoops thanks to an RCMP informant. The first came after a *Star* reporter discovered Montreal police had raided a woman's apartment and found one of Laporte's killers in the closet. Days later, reporter Tom Hazlitt broke the story that the other three killers were only inches away, hiding behind a false wall. When twenty-two hours later the police guards left to get some food, the killers escaped, slipping away to a farm where they were eventually caught. Hazlitt won a National Newspaper Award for breaking the story.

In '73, Newman left to be editor of *Maclean's* magazine, replaced by long-time *Globe* columnist George Bain. For years, Bain's column occupied one of the most prestigious pieces of newspaper real estate— the bottom left-hand corner of the *Globe*'s editorial page. Known as a contrarian, principled writer of the highest integrity, Bain agonized long and hard before taking the posting, knowing only too well the history of Bee's demands. He worked out a deal with Marty Goodman, stating that if the job didn't work out, Bain would be given a foreign assignment. Later he would admit he was struck by Bee's artful ability to act, or seem, a bit slow: "'I don't follow you, George,' he'd claim. 'Why do you say that?' And he'd keep on not following me until he'd extracted all the best arguments I could muster."

The breaking point for Bain came during the '74 federal election. After writing an editorial only to have Bee reject it, he wrote another, but then discovered Bee had gone to someone else. He resigned at once and left to be the paper's London correspondent. Upon departing, he left his successor a tongue-in-cheek job description: "Writing editorials is like wetting your pants while wearing a blue serge suit. Nobody notices, and it leaves you with a warm feeling."

On the news side of the paper, the budget for editorial almost doubled to $18 million in the '70s, the decade following the *Tely*'s demise. But the formula for emphasizing the local angle was, if anything, reinforced. On every story, reporters and editors were told to play up "the Metro angle." In story meetings, new ideas would usually be put through the prism of "what does it mean to Metro?" Bee had commissioned a series of readership surveys from marketing guru Martin Goldfarb, all of which reinforced the hunger for local news. So, while others might poke fun at the obsession with the "Metro" angle, it worked. And when a local story broke, there was no such thing as too much coverage. No city editor would ever be upbraided for sending too many reporters. Quite the opposite. Never was that more evident than in the paper's response to the '79 Mississauga train derailment, when a 106-car freight train carrying chemicals and explosives derailed in a fiery blast twenty-five kilometres from downtown Toronto. More than two hundred thousand people were told to leave their homes, making it, at that time, the largest peacetime evacuation ever in North America. Three dozen reporters were dispatched, filling page after page. The page one headline read "KEEP OUT—Mississauga Is Closed Until Further Notice."

Going the extra mile also paid dividends during the first Russia–Canada hockey series in 1972. For hockey-mad fans of both nations, this eight-game series between the Soviet national team and Canadian stars from the National Hockey League would be an exciting first. The final four games were in the Soviet Union, but the *Star* decided, as was the custom, to send its own photographer to capture the magic or grab a unique shot. That moment arrived when Paul Henderson scored the dramatic winning goal with just thirty-four seconds left in the final game, giving Canada the series win in a moment no Canadian will ever forget. *Star* photographer Frank Lennon had positioned himself perfectly—with the split-second foresight of the world's best photographers—to capture the miracle of a possible last-minute victory. His prescience resulted in a close-up capturing of that split-second joy of Henderson, his arms raised in exultant triumph, embraced by teammate Yvan Cournoyer, with Russian goalie Vladislav Tretiak sprawled in defeat. This iconic photo has been reproduced countless times in books and posters, while also being used as an image for a Canadian coin and a Canadian postage stamp.

The following year, legendary photographer Boris Spremo was in Vietnam, sending home evocative images of the jungle war. Spremo was truly one of a kind, capturing a bevy of iconic images, be they former Canadian prime minister Pierre Trudeau either winging a paper clip or making a clown face to reporters, former prime minister John Diefenbaker lounging on a beach, Muhammad Ali fighting, or the Beatles holding a press conference.

The *Star*'s tradition of sending correspondents and photogs to war zones started with Atkinson during South Africa's Boer War at the turn of the twentieth century. Curiously, Atkinson also acquired then the rights to dispatches from British correspondents, including a young Winston Churchill. Perhaps the paper's most celebrated correspondent was Ernest Hemingway, who spent much of his four years at the *Star* in Paris, chronicling contemporary postwar Europe. During World War II, Fred Griffin, Matthew Halton, and columnist Greg Clark—who'd won the Military Cross for his service at Vimy Ridge—reported from the battlefields of Europe, North Africa, and Asia. While danger lurked for all of them, it would not be until much later, in Afghanistan in 2002, that a *Star* reporter was seriously injured on the job. Reporter Kathleen Kenna and her husband were travelling along a deserted road in the back seat of a van, along with photographer Bernard Weil in the front, when a grenade was tossed into the van. It landed under Kenna's seat, resulting in her suffering serious injuries requiring emergency operations and airlifts. Thankfully, she survived, and Weil escaped largely unscathed.

During the '70s, the paper's fine tradition of evocative foreign reporting carried on. Gifted wordsmith Frank Jones won acclaim for his vivid reporting of Israel's "Yom Kippur" War with Egypt and Syria. After one savage battle, he found a bleak plateau strewn with burned, twisted hulks of Israeli and Syrian tanks. "In a eucalyptus grove beside the Sea of Galilee," wrote Jones, "Israeli war hero Col. Isaka—the famous warrior with only one name—jabbed at a map with a snake-embossed walking stick and described for the first time how Israeli tank units, outnumbered 12–1, absorbed terrible losses as they held on desperately to the lip of the heights that command much of northern Israel." This was war writing at its finest.

The same could be said of veteran correspondent Jack Cahill, who spent five years reporting mostly from Vietnam. In April '75, when two hundred thousand Viet Cong troops encircled Saigon, a desperate Cahill nabbed a ride on a U.S. helicopter, ending up on the cargo ship *Sgt. Andrew Miller*, which was crammed with 7,000 Vietnamese refugees. For six days, the ship trekked east across the South China Sea towards the Philippines. "The holds smelled of urine and sweat," wrote Cahill. "Families were crowded so tight in them they could hardly move. It was so hot down there you could see the air. Hot, stinking air is yellow or purple. . . ."

Perhaps the most notorious of *Star* foreign correspondents was the irascible and continuously talking Gerald Utting. On hearing reports in June '77 that Ugandan dictator Idi Amin might have been ambushed, he took off within hours from Toronto for neighbouring Kenya, since foreign correspondents were barred from Uganda. Utting then sent Amin a fawning telex begging him to do an interview on Commonwealth affairs. After eleven days with no reply, a visa-less Utting decided to fly to Uganda's Entebbe airport, where he was quickly clapped into prison. After eighteen days, with Canadian diplomats desperately searching to locate him, he was suddenly whisked to a resort where Amin was waiting, a pistol in his belt. There, the self-styled "Big Daddy of Uganda" spoke about his four wives, South African apartheid, English rugby, his fondness for the Queen, the upcoming Commonwealth Games in Edmonton, and Canada's need to fight against U.S. domination of its economy. After a brief return to jail, and a personal farewell from Amin, Utting flew out to Britain on a cargo plane full of cows. For his extraordinary exploits, Utting received two National Newspaper Awards.

Despite all the awards—and the *Star* won by far the most in Canada and more than all its Toronto rivals combined—the '70s proved a challenging time in the newsroom. Following the *Tely*'s death, morale in the *Star* newsroom sank very low. It seemed many reporters missed the spark of head-to-head competition. Long-time reporter and rewrite pro Jim Emmerson recalled, "It felt for a long while as if I was working in a vacuum, with no opposition to test ourself." And, in order to keep his troops on edge, Bee became an even stronger presence in the newsroom. As Robert Perry wrote in the *Financial Post*, Bee's "demanding perfectionism and peculiar management style have driven subordinates to rage, despair and strong drink." In '73, a consultant's report discovered "wall to wall unhappiness." Thus, it was not surprising the paper lost a dozen notable journalists, including investigative ace Bob Reguly, reporter

Walter Stewart, books editor Kildare Dobbs, and Insight editor Shirley Sharzer, the paper's most senior woman.

There is little doubt Bee's ultra-strict management style and his inability to adapt to changing times were a large factor in the departures and low morale. All his life experiences—his early days in Mennonite Baden, his learning the ropes in Kitchener, and his early days at Atkinson's *Star*—took place in an environment where discipline and a no-questions-asked obedience to orders were taken as given. This was what he was used to. It was a style he understood and that he felt provided the best results, both financial and editorial, and it was an approach he never abandoned. While he would often speak of his "duty" to uphold the Atkinson Principles, my sense was that this was sometimes a false rationale used to justify his actions. Whenever the need for a dismissal arose—and there were many—I never sensed much remorse. Rather, in his mind, the situation demanded action and this was a necessary consequence.

For my part, I was never accepting of or comfortable with this approach. Indeed, in my early days at the *Star*, I sensed the frustration and heard the complaints first-hand. While at the *Citizen*, I had experienced a much more collaborative environment, where regular reporters' meetings were held, where ideas from below were heard, and where there was a real concern for newsroom morale. This struck me then as the more sensible, sensitive approach. Nor did I accept that quality or performance would be adversely affected by allowing more flexibility. Rather, I felt the opposite was true. In Bee's days, the reputation of the *Star* as a top-down, strict, editor's paper sometimes became a negative factor in attracting prospective reporters. It seemed Bee accepted this difficulty as a given part of the ebb and flow of any newsroom. That would never be my view.

Amid the '70s departures, there were still occasional capers that one could only imagine happening at the *Star*, harkening back to the shenanigans of the '50s. The most notorious of these, which became known as "*Star* Trek," came one evening in '77 when city editor Bruce

Garvey, business editor Al Dow, and senior editor Jim Rennie lingered long after others had left the seafood restaurant where they'd gone after putting the paper's afternoon edition to bed. Their nourishment was mostly liquid, consisting of screwdrivers. Then, according to various sources, ensued a debate about where to get the best glass of orange juice in London, England. Now well soused, the trio decided to catch the very next plane to London to find out. Upon arrival, without passports or plans, the trio told immigration officials they were "big shots" at the *Star*. When those officials called the *Star* early the next morning, then managing editor Timson was heard saying, "Send them back immediately. Those men are terrorists."

The '70s also marked the era when Marty Goodman took ultimate control of editorial, having been elevated to the position of editor-in-chief by Bee. While fully immersed in daily news coverage, Goodman also held greater and greater authority within the company. Near the end of the decade, Bee promoted him to the role of president of the newspaper division, clearly signalling he was in line to succeed Bee as *Star* publisher. At this time, Goodman had just shepherded the paper through the strategically important decision to launch a Sunday paper, fighting back the ever-growing circulation and influence of the *Sun*. Almost as a badge of honour, Goodman had made it his business to find a way to work with Bee, always deflecting any criticism from him.

Certainly, the inevitability of Goodman as Bee's successor was accepted by one and all, myself included. We got along very well, and I was most impressed with his energy, passion, and commitment to the traditions of the *Star*. When I had first signalled an interest in journalism before going to Ottawa, Goodman had offered me a job at the paper. I never was sure how serious the offer was, but I had turned it down immediately, citing both my lack of experience and the fear of nepotism charges. I totally admired his ability to work with Bee, however frustrating that might be. Tales abounded of Goodman ordering one approach to a news story only to have Bee switch it unceremoniously a few hours later. Yet he developed a practice of carrying on as if this was the ordinary course. Goodman would often describe his approach to Bee's aversion to new ideas as akin to baseball, his favourite sport. In baseball you get three strikes, he'd say, and you should use them all before you give up. While Goodman might not have had the creative flair of a Ralph Allen, his news instincts, knowledge of national affairs—particularly national unity, which was his passion—and dedication to the job knew no equal. Not only that, Bee had told me Goodman had all the skills to succeed him.

With the death of the *Tely*, one of the biggest issues facing the *Star* was a lack of printing capacity due to additional circulation. The presses at 80 King Street had been in place for half a century and the space was necessarily limited. The interim solution was to rent the *Tely*'s relatively new plant for two years. However, a more permanent solution was essential and this is where the Reichmann brothers of Olympia & York would play a large role. Orthodox Jews from central Europe, the Reichmanns had lived through the Second World War in Tangier, Morocco, before emigrating to Canada. Their original business centred on household tiles, but eventually, led by younger son Paul, they entered the property development world.

When Paul Reichmann went directly to Bee with his proposal, it would mark O&Y's first venture into a commercial development designed for business use. The Reichmanns had a vision to build a dazzling new world headquarters for the Bank of Montreal on the northwest corner of Bay and King Streets. The *Star* building directly adjoined the existing bank property and the Reichmanns wanted 80 King to allow for a grander design. So they proposed O&Y buy that *Star* property and build a new five-storey production plant and twenty-five-storey office tower for the paper at the foot of Yonge Street, a site where the paper had run an ink factory.

It would be the first high-rise development on the city's waterfront, south of the Gardiner Expressway. For the *Star*, the proposal was enticing given that the company already owned the land for the new headquarters. When Reichmann arrived at Bee's office, he found the *Star* boss surrounded by a phalanx of lawyers and accountants. Upon hearing Bee's price, Reichmann surprised them all by accepting the proposal—no questions asked. The process of signing the lease, on the other hand, would take almost a decade to finally complete.

The selection of new presses for One Yonge would be a decision Bee always regretted. The choice came down to price and reliability. The paper's traditional supplier, Hoe, had far more experience dealing with North American dailies. A British press upstart, Crabtree Vickers, was desperate to break into the North American market and thus offered new untested presses at a lower price. Right from the outset, the presses were not able to produce at the promised volumes, leaving subscribers fuming over delivery delays. As any publisher will attest, the greatest risk to any paper's future is the ill will of unhappy subscribers. The decision would cost dearly in overtime, leading to the *Star* buying an extra press and using those at the *Tely* plant longer than expected before stability was maintained. Meanwhile, the *Star* sued Crabtree Vickers over the performance issues.

A valuable lesson was learned, to be drawn on two decades later when presses were bought for the paper's newly built $400 million state-of-the-art printing facility in Vaughan, north of Toronto. This time, the final winner was a German producer, MAN Roland, whose offset presses were already installed and in operation elsewhere, allowing *Star* crews to inspect the equipment for themselves. The German firm was looking to gain a foothold in the North American market, which resulted in very competitive pricing. But when the *Star* team went to the board for final approval, Bee had a surprise in hand. The proposal was for five lines of presses, based on ambitious volume-printing projections. Recalling how he had been burned by similar projections before, Bee declared, with a certain emphasis, "You need a sixth." There was no debate.

Following the *Tely*'s demise and other headline-grabbing developments in the Canadian newspaper market, the federal government
set up two commissions to study the concentration of newspaper
ownership. The first, the '69–'70 Senate Special Committee on Mass
Media under the chairship of Senator Keith Davey, recommended
Ottawa establish a press ownership review board. The second, the
Royal Commission on Newspapers, chaired by Tom Kent, was
created after the simultaneous closure in '80 of the *Ottawa Journal*
(owned by the Thomson chain) and the *Winnipeg Tribune* (owned
by Southam). These highly controversial closures resulted in each
chain gaining a monopoly in one of those two markets. The Kent
Commission recommended newspaper owners not be allowed to
hold both radio and TV broadcasting licences in the same market.

For Bee, the prospect of government regulation of any sort was not
one to be relished. Since the *Star* was not part of any chain, its position
vis-à-vis concentration of ownership was relatively unique. But ever
since 1960, when the paper had lost a bid for a TV licence in Toronto,
Bee had sought other investments in a bid to diversify the company's
assets. The first was the acquisition of national magazine publisher
Comac Communications Ltd. The prize of that company was
Homemakers magazine, a widely distributed money maker, along with
City Woman and *Western Living*, the latter aimed at western Canada.
The second initiative, developed by the company's new investment
team of Roy Megarry (later to be publisher of the *Globe and Mail*) and
David Black (later to head up the western community group Black
Press) was to buy a stake in Western Broadcasting. In addition to
maintaining a strong broadcasting presence in Vancouver and Victoria,
Western owned a Hamilton TV station and another station broadcast-
ing into Toronto. The third and ultimately most lucrative initiative was
the purchase of the romance publishing giant Harlequin.

The prospect that any of these investments might not be allowed or
that they would be subject to government regulation was anathema
to Bee. Yet he was also very responsive to arguments that big-time

newspaper proprietors had a responsibility to be sensitive to readers and their grievances. While such proprietors in Canada were unanimous in their opposition to any government regulation, they were badly split on the need for a press council to adjudicate reader complaints. It was here that Bee decided to step in, playing a leading and decisive role.

The premise of the press council is that newspapers must have a secure, unfettered right to freedom of expression. But that freedom only has a legitimacy, the argument goes, if it is exercised with a sense of responsibility. When norms are broken or reputations smeared, a way must exist to check and control it. Thus, the idea evolved that readers' complaints should be adjudicated by peers of the newspaper industry, along with discerning laymen, in a body called a press council. The first such council was established in Sweden in 1916, and Bee became the idea's most prominent Canadian advocate.

In 1972, pursuing his relentless and driving obsession, and overcoming much peer opposition, Bee created the Ontario Press Council, much to the delight of federal officials. Representatives from all newspapers eventually joined, along with interested members of the pubic. Each complaint is heard by a panel in which the public members always constitute the majority. No lawyers are allowed, so costs are minimal. Complainants usually appear on their own behalf, and the proceedings are far less structured and formal than court hearings. The Council has had a tradition of strong leadership, beginning with former CBC head Davidson Dunton and ending with former Ontario cabinet minister Robert Elgie.

(When the Ontario Council folded in 2015, I took the initiative—following in fine family tradition—to create a national press council representing all of Canada, save Quebec, called the National NewsMedia Council. Former *Globe* and *Star* columnist John Fraser took over from social advocate [and later senator] Frances Lankin as head of this new body. Most importantly, there has not been any talk of government regulation for a very long time.)

The *Star*'s investment in Western Broadcasting turned out to be the critical missing link in another major move by Bee, one that would have a profound impact on the company's prosperity for the next half century. This one involved community newspapers and flyers—eventually flyers by the billions. As part of Bee's aim to establish a broadcasting arm, Western had been the principal vehicle to gain entry. Closer to home, however, another opportunity arose in '71 that suddenly took priority. Inland Publishing, a community newspaper group owned by the Bassett and Eaton families, indicated an interest in selling. The Bassetts were not keen to sell, but the Eatons, with majority control, insisted on exiting. With fifteen suburban papers, including large weeklies in Mississauga and Brampton, Inland had been competing against Torstar's community paper group of fourteen weeklies called Metrospan.

Metrospan's roots were in the Toronto suburb of Don Mills, where journalists Ken Larone and Russ Eastcott started a weekly called the *Don Mills Mirror*. It had an early circulation of 3,500 and was supported by Shoppers Drug Mart's Murray Koffler, who was prepared to pay three cents for each *Mirror* delivered. Shortly thereafter, *Mirrors* also sprang up in Downsview, Willowdale, Scarborough, and North York, all suburbs of Toronto. Outside the city, weeklies were also established in Mississauga, Burlington, Aurora, Richmond Hill, Oshawa, and Woodbridge.

At this time, community papers were in their very formative stages. Their underlying rationale was to offer advertisers saturation distribution—later called total market coverage—for their in-paper ads and flyers. Hyper-local news coverage was displayed in these papers, which were distributed free to every household. Classified ads were also offered free of charge in order to build up readership. Often, the papers were distributed by volunteers. For smaller and regional advertisers, these weeklies provided a very welcome alternative to big dailies, like the *Star*, with their dramatically higher advertising rates.

To Bee and his soon-to-be chief financial officer, Murray Cockburn, the opportunity to bring these two companies together was too enticing to forgo. At this point, Metrospan's earnings were quite limited, constrained in part by the group's competition with Inland. The idea of Torstar controlling the *Star* as well as the vast majority of community weeklies around the city might have appeared worrisome to competition regulators, but it was nothing short of captivating to Bee and his CFO. Cockburn was then dispatched to investigate whether Western Broadcasting's owner, Frank Griffiths, might be prepared to buy back Torstar's shares. He was, and with the proceeds, Torstar paid $13.5 million to buy Inland. The new company would be called Metroland, and its first president would be the hard-driving John Baxter, Inland's former boss.

Over the next four decades, Metroland would expand dramatically to become Torstar's most profitable division, with community papers in close to one hundred markets. Under the leadership of Baxter, and later Murray Skinner and Ian Oliver, Metroland became one of the most respected and successful community newspaper groups in North America. It has always prided itself on its local editorial quality, along with its relentless competitive ethic. For Torstar, ownership of Metroland provided a competitive advantage unknown, if unimaginable, to most North American dailies. I can well remember, much later, the *Denver Post*'s legendary publisher Dean Singleton asking me incredulously, "How did Torstar manage to pull this off?"

Bee would later tell me he never imagined how successful Metroland would become. Yet there is no doubt he fully understood the competitive sensitivities the deal would produce. Under his direct orders, a short two-paragraph story ran in the *Star* on the deal with amazingly no mention of Torstar's ownership. The very next day's *Globe and Mail* carried a long front-page story specifically outlining Torstar's control of the new company with its total circulation of nine hundred thousand—almost 40 per cent of the Toronto-area total. As a result, alarm bells also rang at the Kent Commission, where, only weeks before, Bee had heralded diversity of ownership. Asked by special invitation to return, he was subject to what one news report called "the toughest grilling a media owner has yet experienced." Bee argued vehemently that the merger of weekly chains still left the Toronto market with a wide choice of newspapers and other media. He did allow, however, that "we may have erred in underplaying the story and I must accept responsibility for that."

With all these corporate moves, Bee had successfully transformed the corporation from a family-dominated single newspaper into a modern conglomerate. The company name was now officially changed to Torstar, and a separate corporate office was set up on the sixth floor of One Yonge to deal with non-newspaper businesses. Cockburn, who would develop into one of Bee's closest advisers and would later represent the Honderich family on the Torstar board, was now firmly entrenched as chief financial officer. There was also the separate corporate development office, where Megarry and Black explored potential acquisitions. Meanwhile, the *Star* continued to prosper. Over the next decade, weekday circulation grew from 377,000 to 492,000, and Saturday sales rose from 489,000 to 781,000. Advertising linage jumped by 25 per cent.

Amid all this growth and prosperity, Bee began to think of succession. Certainly, his record of accomplishment spoke for itself. It seemed the high school dropout with absolutely no business training had an uncanny knack of making the right strategic decision at the right time. Associates would say he could be very unpredictable, although he would always do his homework thoroughly. He also had a record of assembling talented advisers around him. Yet it wasn't as if he were trying to create a "team" environment. The final decision would always be made by him—and only him. When it came to personnel or negotiating through ticklish situations, he could also be ruthless. His record of sudden and unexpected dismissals of senior editors or associates is legendary. Sentiment rarely, if ever,

Joseph E. Atkinson, founder of the Toronto Star *and its publisher for fifty years (1899-1948). His values and beliefs formed the Atkinson Principles, the intellectual foundation on which the paper operates to this day.* (Toronto Star *File Photo*)

Beland Honderich's predecessor as publisher, Harry Comfort (H. C.) Hindmarsh. (Toronto Star *File Photo*)

The historic Toronto Star *Building at 80 King Street West, circa 1961. Joe Shuster, who was a former newsboy at the* Star *and the co-creator of* Superman, *used it as a model for the* Daily Planet. (*Norman James/*Toronto Star)

As captured for the Kitchener Record, *the Baden Honderichs gathering and boiling sap for the manufacture of maple syrup. Pictured left to right are Delford Honderich, Calvin Honderich, Walter Dietrich, and Beland Honderich.* (Kitchener Record *photo*)

Beland Honderich (in the foreground, second row, extreme right), the young, nattily-dressed, ambitious reporter for the Kitchener Record *awaits the arrival of the King and Queen of England, 1939.* (Kitchener Record)

Honderich family values from generation to generation. (Both photos courtesy of the Honderich family)

*Beland Honderich when he was the
Star's financial editor, 1950.*
(Toronto Star *File Photo*)

A Star *publicity photo of Beland Honderich being greeted by his wife
and children, John and Mary, as he returns from yet another reporting
assignment abroad, 1949.* (Toronto Star *File Photo*)

Beland Honderich, the intrepid foreign reporter, the year and exact whereabouts unknown.
(Toronto Star *File Photo*)

The end of World War I as announced on the front page of the Toronto Daily Star, *1918.* (Toronto Star *File Photo*)

Breaking the Gerda Munsinger story, 1966. (Toronto Star *File Photo*)

The Star's *switchboard operators were legendary. They were known to track down anyone anywhere. This photo was taken in 1960 at the* Star *building on 80 King Street West.* (Toronto Star *File Photo*)

The Star *newsroom at King Street West in 1930. A pneumatic tube system was installed between the copy desk and City Hall.* (Toronto Star *File Photo*)

Beland Honderich stands beside a model of the Star's *25-storey office tower with directors William J. Campbell and Ruth Atkinson Hindmarsh, 1969.* (*Norman James/*Toronto Star)

The Star *newsroom, 1970.* (Toronto Star *File Photo*)

A "typical" reporter's desk.
(*Rick Eglinton*/Toronto Star)

Christopher Reeve portraying Clark Kent and Margo Kidder as Lois Lane in the movie Superman, *shot in the* Star *newsroom.* (Toronto Star *File Photo*)

John with his parents upon graduating law school in 1971. (*Courtesy of the Honderich family*)

John and Katherine on sabbatical. (Courtesy of the Honderich family)

Honderich family Christmas ski holiday, 1986. From right to left, Robin, Emily, John, and Katherine. (Courtesy of the Honderich family)

Family celebration. From left to right, Beland, Mary, David, and John Honderich. (Courtesy of the Honderich Family)

Martin Goodman, 1965.
(Toronto Star *File Photo*)

Charles Templeton, the Star's *former executive news editor, in the 1960s.*
(Toronto Star *File Photo*)

Left to right, Beland Honderich, Senator Keith Davey, and Peter C. Newman, the Star's *editor-in-chief, 1970.*
(*Reg Innell*/Toronto Star)

Star *national affairs writer and political columnist, Chantal Hébert, 2016.* (*Chris So*/Toronto Star)

Pierre Berton at his desk, 1987. (*Ron Bull*/Toronto Star *File Photo*)

Christie Blatchford in 1978. (*Frank Lennon*/Toronto Star)

John Honderich getting a book signed in 1993 by Star *sports writing legend, Milt Dunnell, who was also one of Beland's closest friends.* (Toronto Star *File Photo*)

Star *reporters Rosie DiManno and Kevin Donovan question Toronto police chief Bill Blair, 2013.*
(*Bernard Weil*/Toronto Star)

Star *managing editor,*
Mary Deanne Shears, in 2003.
(*Ron Bull*/Toronto Star)

Long-time Star *photographer, Boris Spremo, in 1966. He*
set the gold standard in news photography.
(*Frank Lennon*/Toronto Star)

John Honderich with Alain Dubuc of Montreal's La Presse. (Toronto Star *File Photo*)

GREAT WAR COVERAGE, GANG.... BUT WHERE'S THE METRO ANGLE?

Always focused on the city of Toronto, 1991. (*Aislin*/Toronto Star)

*John Honderich welcomes Liberal leader Lyn McLeod, Premier Bob Rae, and Conservative leader Mike Harris to the newspaper-sponsored debate in 1995. (Andrew Stawicki/*Toronto Star)

*John Honderich and Prime Minister Brian Mulroney are all smiles after the Toronto Blue Jays clinch the American League pennant. (Boris Spremo, CM/*Toronto Star File Photo)

*With South African president Nelson Mandela, his wife Graca Machel, editorial board editor Haroon Siddiqui, and foreign editor, Jimmy Atkins, in Toronto, 1990. (Ken Fraught/*Toronto Star)

Showing Prime Minister Justin Trudeau a photo of his father taken by the Star's *Boris Spremo.* (*Rick Madonik/*Toronto Star)

John Honderich handing out free newspapers at Union Station in Toronto.
(*R.J. Johnston*/Toronto Star)

Torstar Annual Meeting. From left to right, Murray Skinner, president of Metroland;
Jagoda Pike, publisher of the Hamilton Spectator; *John Honderich; and Donna Hayes,*
publisher and CEO of Harlequin. (*Dick Loek*/Toronto Star)

Gathering with Star *staffers on the day John was awarded the Order of Canada, 2003.*
(*Richard Lautens/*Toronto Star)

*Three generations of Honderichs singing in church: daughter Emily, John, son Robin,
and grandson Sebastian.*(*Rick Madonik/*Toronto Star)

interfered in his judgments. But virtually all his decisions—be they to create Metroland, acquire Harlequin, or understand the need to set up a press council—all reflected a deep and sophisticated appreciation of what would make Torstar stronger. It would always be his driving mission. Nothing would ever get in the way of it.

In '76, however, Bee surprisingly decided to appoint a new president, turning to William "Bill" Dimma, former dean of York University's school of business. Under this arrangement, Bee remained as publisher of the *Star*, as well as being chair and CEO of Torstar. Goodman had been made president of the newspaper division, with Denis Harvey succeeding him as editor-in-chief. To those close by, it was an intriguing sight to see Bee, the epitome of a hands-on manager, relinquish control to someone else. Not only that, Dimma's management style could not have been more different from Bee's. He believed totally in a collaborative style, calling many meetings and taking much longer to make decisions. Ultimately, he lasted only two years in the job, leaving feeling somewhat embittered.

Dimma's short tenure was emblematic of the experience of many senior managers who worked directly for Bee. In the '70s, for example, there were six different managing editors, among them Borden Spears, Ted Bolwell, John Brooks, and Hartley Steward. Each was in place for a maximum of two years. As Bolwell, who left the *Star* to become editor of Rupert Murdoch's *New York Post*, said later, "He [Bee] gives people responsibility without authority and has created a climate where talent is stifled." In another interview with *Maclean's*, he went even further, declaring, "The *Star* is unmanageable while Honderich is publisher." Another editor, quoted anonymously in *Media & Advertising*, added, "As it goes down the line, his [Bee's] suggestions and insistence on certain things can be inhibiting and frustrating to an innovative person."

The record shows that once a senior manager got on the wrong side of Bee, the end of their tenure wouldn't be far off. Bolwell, for example was a hard-nosed, no-nonsense editor who had high expectations of his staff. But he could be stubborn, a trait that inevitably led to confrontation. Brooks came from the promotion department to head the newsroom, with virtually no experience in editorial. His most famous line expressed his hope that reporters would feel professionally fulfilled so that they could leave the newsroom each day "with smiles on their tummies." In the case of Dimma, his management style and modus operandi were so completely different that conflict was almost inevitable. In making senior management appointments, Bee rarely took outside counsel, a practice that led to some very questionable promotions.

In '78, Megarry was hired away to become publisher of the *Globe and Mail*, being replaced by Paul Zimmerman, who had been president of the Canadian division of *Reader's Digest*. Bee hired him because of his experience in direct mail, an area Bee felt could be part of Torstar's future. Zimmerman's lack of editorial knowledge, however, meant few viewed him as a natural successor to Bee. On the newspaper side, Goodman's influence grew, his ability to work with Bee now firmly entrenched. And on the sixth floor, Cockburn became the go-to executive—the one others went to before trying out a new idea on Bee. Reflecting later on how he had dealt with my father, Cockburn said, "I think Bee's reputation caused people to try too hard to anticipate his thinking and to try to satisfy him. This was not a manner in which I felt comfortable living. I found it best to do my homework, then tell him what I felt even if I thought he might disagree. The homework part was important, because Bee did his homework faithfully."

All in all, the '70s proved to be a decade of triumph for Bee. The diversification proved a success, the paper was flourishing, and succession plan was established.

What could possibly go wrong?

13

TRANSITION TIME

The '80s would mark the sole time frame when Bee and I worked in the same building for the *Star*, he as publisher and I as a spanking new deputy city editor. Our paths rarely crossed, the publisher's office being appropriately located in the spacious corner office of the sixth floor while my small refuge was back in the far reaches of the fifth-floor newsroom where city reporters worked. But he was the ultimate boss and his periodic walks through the newsroom continued unabated. He would tell me later how, as publisher, he missed being more involved in editorial, feeling that he did not want to undercut the managing editor of the day. It would not be until later that I understood the irony of that reflection. However, it was a sentiment I never forgot. Of course, I had heard epic tales of a newsroom coming to a virtual halt upon his entry. As I had imagined, those tales were grossly exaggerated. But all accounts of his iron control and constant demands were reinforced immediately. The acronym HCI—"high corporate interest"—was most often affixed to those stories coming from above. Translation: Beware, this comes from Bee! This was a practice, I should acknowledge, that persisted through my time at the helm.

The shock to both the newsroom and the paper came in '81 with the tragic death of Marty Goodman, a victim of pancreatic cancer

at age forty-six. It all seemed so unfair. Goodman was unquestionably a giant of a newspaperman—a reporter, editor, and president
full of gusto, drive, and an unquenchable thirst to do more. Everyone
knew his story. A graduate of the Columbia School of Journalism,
he joined the *Star* in '58 as a general assignment reporter, covering
city hall, labour, and finance. He was named a Nieman Fellow at
Harvard in '61, an experience so etched in his family's memory that,
upon his death, an annual fellowship was established in his name to
give a Canadian journalist the same chance.

Goodman's rise at the *Star* had been nothing short of meteoric.
He was Ottawa bureau chief in '65, city editor the following year,
managing editor two years later, and editor-in-chief three years after
that. His journalistic passion was national unity. "I cannot believe
that ordinary Canadians want to see this society ripped apart," he
would say. And he would ensure great play was given to national
symbols and heroes such as Terry Fox to make people feel more a
part of Canada. During my time as economics reporter in Ottawa,
I was often at the other end of his requests—make that "orders."
They were relentless and numerous, for another of his manias was
that newspapers did a lousy job of covering economic issues. He read
voraciously and had an encyclopedic knowledge of current events. I
remember when, as Washington correspondent, I was upbraided by
him for using a quote that had appeared in the *New York Times* the
day before. Luckily, I was able to tell him I had been at the Senate
hearing after that, where the same quote was used. But as everyone
in the *Star* newsroom knew, "Marty is always watching."

His other great passion in life was baseball. He was pitcher for the
Star fastball team, where his competitive edge was as sharp as his
newsroom editing. Indeed, when he was undergoing chemotherapy
for his cancer, he instructed doctors to make injections only in his left
arm. That right arm still needed to pitch. Veteran sports columnist
Dave Perkins—"Marty's catcher"—recalls Goodman laying out his
plans for the *Star* to buy the New York Yankees. It seems he took the

proposal twice unsuccessfully to the board of directors. Ultimately, George Steinbrenner bought the club for what now seems a paltry sum of $13.5 million and turned it into a billion-dollar investment. "It could have been us!" Perkins recalls Goodman saying often.

There is absolutely no doubt that Goodman, had he lived longer, would have been *Star* publisher upon Bee's retirement seven years later. Not that he and Bee always agreed. They didn't. Every morning he went to work at 7 a.m., a knot in his stomach, wondering if the paper had met Bee's expectations. Yet, seventeen years younger than Bee, he dominated the newsroom in a way none of his predecessors had, and more importantly, he had figured out a way to work constructively with Bee.

They seemed cut from the same cloth, both working manically, putting in the same long hours; both with the same passions for economics, politics, and national unity; and both with printers' ink running through their veins. Indeed, I remember thinking quite intently that Goodman was the son Bee never had. Newsroom veterans at that time recall how protective, in an odd way, Bee was of Goodman. Of course there would be criticism, but Bee always showed nothing but the highest confidence in his editor. In the background, Bee had also done all the legwork—including preparing the paperwork—to have Goodman become part of the voting trust. This would have been an extraordinary privilege not accorded anyone else, and it illustrated the lengths to which Bee was prepared to go. Little wonder, then, that when he first learned of Goodman's prognosis, he wept openly. They were so similar in so many respects.

I was never jealous of him, being instead highly impressed with his credentials as the boss. It was also my distinct impression that Goodman was the final arbiter in decisions related to my role at the *Star*. We had a good professional relationship. At every meeting, he would always pepper me with questions about how I was doing and what I thought about particular political issues. I shared his obsession with national unity, and I had just assumed he would be my boss for a long time. And that was fine.

Whenever Bee was asked about the notorious turnover in senior management in the newsroom, he would often say Atkinson had found his trusted second in Harry Hindmarsh—and he was looking for the equivalent. To me, and virtually everyone else, Goodman was "Bee's Hindmarsh." And so, unsurprisingly, his death struck Bee very deeply. As mentioned earlier, the last time my father saw him, Goodman expressed remorse for never being able to fully please him, an extraordinary deathbed confession for an executive to make to his boss. That comment hit Bee particularly hard. Quietly, he had also arranged that the insurance payout on Goodman's death would be doubled. At the funeral, which attracted more than a thousand mourners, Bee appeared particularly burdened as one of the pall-bearers. In the eulogy, Goodman was remembered as a "brilliant speeding comet, touching our lives and leaving an empty space."

After Goodman's death, Bee was determined his memory should be enshrined in the city he so loved. After much study and negotiation with the city, the *Star* later funded a 56-kilometre multi-use trail that runs along the shores of Lake Ontario. It bears his name, fulfilling Bee's ambitions for a meaningful remembrance.

With Marty's passing, a new reality emerged: there was now no obvious editorial successor to Bee. Again, Bee went the unconventional route, turning to the *Star*'s great humorist and daily columnist Gary Lautens to head the newsroom. Lautens had been hired to replace Pierre Berton, and his top-of-page-two column became the most widely read in Canada. He wrote in brief but evocative spurts, often comparing each column to a fir sapling: "I hold it up and shake it thoroughly until every loose needle is shaken loose." However, he had no experience whatsoever in running any news department. To help Lautens, Bee turned again to veteran editor Ray Timson. He had proven multiple times his ability to live up to Atkinson's original newsgathering mantra—"get it first, pursue every detail, and play it big." When Timson asked you how you were covering a story, you knew you were under the gun. If he was satisfied with your reply, he'd grunt and leave. If not, that long forefinger would descend, pointed directly at your forehead, with gruff words and an intent stare to accompany it. So, there they were, Timson and Lautens—quickly earning the moniker "Knuckles & Chuckles."

On the business side, Bee went outside newspaper ranks to recruit two heavy hitters in the business consulting field—David Jolley and David Galloway. Along with one-time political guru Jim Coutts, they had founded Canada Consulting Group, a managing consultant firm later bought out by the Boston Consulting Group. Galloway was dispatched to run Harlequin, Torstar now being its sole shareholder. Jolley, with no journalism experience, was brought in to run the newspaper group as a successor to Goodman. Both were savvy and shrewd operators intent on learning the ropes and improving financial performance. What Jolley didn't know about newspapering he was determined to master, aided considerably by his new personal relationship with the discerning Ellie Tesher, then a reporter for the *Star*'s life section and later an advice columnist syndicated throughout North America.

It was in that same life section that a perceptive young reporter, Leslie Scrivener, would be the first to embark on a story that captured the hearts and imagination of the entire country. The subject was Terry Fox, the one-legged cancer survivor, and his lonely Marathon of Hope across Canada. It would be Scrivener's always inquisitive editor, Bonnie Cornell, having seen a TV snippet, who descended on Scrivener, saying, "Find out if this guy's for real." That was about noon, and by mid-afternoon the *Star*'s legendary switchboard operators had located Fox, with the help of the RCMP, in the home of the mayor of Come By Chance, Newfoundland. Scrivener recalls that she and Fox hit it off right away. "I was a believer right from the start, violating all rules of journalism," she says. Telephone land lines were the only means of communication, and they agreed to chat every Thursday.

At the time, the twenty-two-year-old was only 148 kilometres into his cross-country run, and Scrivener recalls him as open, chatty, and charismatic during the phone calls that provided the grist for her weekly reports. As he made his way through the Maritimes, the mediastream intensified, and by the time he made it to Toronto, it was a tsunami. When a recurrence of his cancer forced Fox to stop in Thunder Bay and fly home, Scrivener went to his hospital bed in Port Coquitlam, B.C. On a second visit, Fox asked her to write his story, given her huge role in his success. Deeply touched, she agreed. She then took a leave of absence to write the book, which ultimately sold over fifty thousand copies.

The other huge story at the time—one in which I became deeply involved—was the spate of alleged baby murders in the cardiac ward of Toronto's venerable Hospital for Sick Children. The stories of the thirty-six babies who died mysteriously between July 1980 and the following March had shaken the city to its core. Right from the outset, the hospital had insisted the deaths weren't a result of any criminal conduct. But the world-renowned Centers for Disease Control and Prevention, the U.S. public health agency that had been brought into the investigation, repeatedly insisted foul play could not be ruled out. And it pointed to autopsy results showing levels of a prescribed drug thirty to forty times higher than those it deemed safe. To question an established institution like Sick Kids was not easy. Yet the *Star* constantly led the way with its hard-hitting investigative pieces under my direct boss, the paper's first female city editor, Mary Deanne Shears. A peppery fireball from Newfoundland, Shears had a capacity to galvanize the newsroom in times of crisis that was second to none. The paper never let up, much to its credit. One nurse, Susan Nelles, was eventually charged with four counts of murder, but the case was dismissed when evidence showed she was not on shift for one of the murders. An almost year-long public inquiry, most of it televised, gripped the city and the media as various theories were expounded. While strong doubts persist, no one has ever been charged. The mystery remains.

As deputy city editor—the entry management job in the news-room—I oversaw the paper's dozen or so beat reporters, who covered everything from labour to health, transit, medicine, the environment, and education. As such, I was able to work with the more seasoned reporters, some of whom eventually made their mark as distinguished chroniclers in their field: Louise Brown in education, Marilyn Dunlop and Lillian Newbery in medicine, Ross Howard in environmental affairs, and Rick "Badger" Brennan in transportation. I was particularly satisfied when one of the features I proposed to Dunlop—and edited—won a National Newspaper Award.

Having been out of Toronto for a decade, it was a huge help to get a special quiet boost from my dearest aunt and confidante, Ruth Spielbergs. An amazing character, and Bee's oldest sister, Aunt Ruth had an amazing web of contacts and a mass of information about the city's social network. She produced weekly summaries of suggestions and city observations—always numbered—that became known in the newsroom as "Spielbergs's notes." Bee would often inquire—never gently—whether each note had been pursued. Her judgment and powers of observation provided me with many tips to take to story meetings. In short, she got me reconnected to the city, for which I am forever grateful.

On a broader scale, at that time the *Star* introduced a bevy of new columnists who quickly became household names, bringing more awards and notoriety to the paper. The indomitable Michele Landsberg started a groundbreaking column on women's and gender-equity issues that garnered a huge and loyal audience. On the political side, Richard Gwyn, with his characteristic insight and investigative skill, chronicled the birth of the Canadian Charter of Rights and Freedoms and the rebirth of Pierre Trudeau as PM. Later, Carol Goar added her perspective on national issues. And noted humorist Joey Slinger brought his acute sense of irony and the ridiculous to a regular column. Finally, there was a new-wave sports columnist, Wayne Parrish, who brought his fine descriptive writing to a realm heretofore replete with traditional jock prose. All five of these *Star* luminaries were named best in their field in Canada at some time or other during the early '80s.

On the production side, one of Goodman's last huge initiatives was turning the *Star* into a morning newspaper. For ninety years, the *Star* had been an afternoon daily, flourishing like many other metro dailies as the "evening read." That had been the tried-and-true road to success. Yet, with the advent of more competitive news reporting and a desire to get the news fastest and first, the arguments for a morning newspaper grew. The *Star* was far from the first to make the switch, being preceded by several major U.S. metro dailies. Reader surveys, analyses of when people had most time to read, and studies of when they wanted the news all pushed in one direction. Planted firmly against this momentum was the institutional bias, often strongly held, to stick with what had worked. For Bee, it took time and the repetition of the mounting data before he became convinced. Finally, the call was made—and the *Star* has never looked back.

Meanwhile, a seemingly small reporting error on the business pages suddenly catapulted my career upwards in a direction not foreseen. It came just eighteen months into my new job and just as I had finally discovered the joy of being an editor—seeing others' work published. The moment was in May '84, as Torstar was releasing its financial results and holding its annual meeting. This had always been (and still is) a particular point of tension at the *Star*, for any deviation whatsoever in the reporting is simply unacceptable. Unfortunately, the usually very dependable Jim Daw, who rose to become one of Canada's foremost auto industry reporters, got some figures wrong. Blame was ultimately placed on the business editor, John Bryden, and he was dismissed, forcing management to find a replacement on the spot.

And there I was, a graduate with a B.A. in economics and the former economics reporter in the Ottawa bureau, working on the other side of the newsroom. It would be a very short discussion with

Timson. The job was a promotion and there was no time for chat. So, a day later, my appointment as financial editor was carried in a short page three story in the paper. Having never even considered the job a week before, I was quoted as being excited "because business news is an exciting part of the city and the *Star* is talking to the people who make it exciting." The irony that more than four decades earlier Bee was appointed to the same position was not lost on either of us. The big difference was that my duties were exclusively in business while he had had the joy of being able to fly around the world on great stories. But I remember him comparing the huge gap in our economics training before I took this job. He was very proud.

For me, the new job represented both a huge challenge and a huge opportunity. I now had a staff of about twenty to oversee, a separate section to design and run, and a new field to cover. At the outset, it seemed very daunting, with a whole raft of new skills required. Not only that, the advertising department had introduced a new pricing system that was attracting pages and pages of technology career ads. The once sleepy business section would now often run to thirty-six or forty pages, producing additional news holes to fill. Perhaps most strikingly, I was left entirely on my own, with precious little oversight or supervision. Most emphasis was still on the news file for the front section, as it should be. My goal was simple, just as Timson had laid out: produce the best business section possible that fits the needs of the *Star* audience.

The challenge for any *Star* business editor is that both the *Globe and Mail*'s Report on Business and the *Financial Post* have made business coverage the essence of their trademark. There is simply no point in trying to compete at their level. That said, there is a wide swath of business news that is relevant to *Star* readers—content once inelegantly described as "business news necessary for the manicurist in Mississauga." Personal finance information, comparative interest and mortgage rate charts, small business stories, emphasis on high tech, and competitive coverage of major business stories all became the order of the day. In addition to me, the business section contingent included a respected columnist named Jack McArthur and a personal finance expert in Pat Fellows. In my role as editor, prioritizing stories and arranging coverage would be paramount, followed by a trip to the design department to draw up the look of the next day's business front. In late afternoon, my routine took me to the daily news meeting, where I would outline the big stories and make a pitch for any story I felt deserved front-page consideration. The final task was deciding on page layouts and overseeing final editing of copy. Those were the basics of running a separate section.

In very short order, I came to love it. Working with talented reporters and editors, shaping out new angles, having fun with new designs, and participating in the verbal back and forth—sometimes caustic—of the daily news meetings all became my fix. So did engaging with the often controversial Diane Francis, who started her business writing career at the *Star*. This is where she wrote her first business column and started profiling Canada's great entrepreneurs and tycoons, a talent she subsequently expanded into a series of best-selling books and a regular column at the *National Post*.

Even with a smaller business staff than our competitors', we strove to compete, if not beat them, on some major business stories. The collapse of Alberta's Northland and Canadian Commercial banks was one. Another was the phenomenon of shareholder rights' crusades, particularly at Canadian Tire. Perhaps the most dramatic was the bare-knuckled hostile takeover of the venerable Union Gas company, led by former Ontario treasurer Darcy McKeough, by upstart Unicorp, led by Jim Leech, who later transformed the Ontario Teachers' Pension Plan into one of the world's largest. Both principals called to complain about particular *Star* scoops during the battle. I delighted in the fray, not really digesting that this would later become a regular component of my job.

Another dramatic business story, albeit one closer to home, came in August 1985, when Canada's newspaper world was jolted. Out of the blue, Torstar and Canada's largest newspaper chain, Southam Inc., struck a deal for a $216 million share swap. Not a whisper or peep preceded the announcement. For Bee, this represented a long-dreamed-of chance to expand Torstar's newspaper base. While the *Star* was by now the dominant paper in Canada's largest city, it lacked a footprint in the rest of the country. Similarly, Southam operated fifteen dailies across the country but lacked a Toronto presence, a critical factor for national advertisers. In close *Star* circles, bringing these two entities together was always called the "Southam dream."

At the time, rumours started circulating that a mystery buyer—either Paul Desmarais or more likely Conrad Black—was accumulating Southam shares with an eye to a hostile takeover. Since the Southam-owning families held only 23 per cent of the company's shares, they were clearly exposed. So the ever-elegant and shrewd Southam chair, St. Clair Balfour, quietly reached out to Bee, the two having forged a deep mutual respect over many years of newspapering. After a frantic set of negotiations at the *Star*'s offices over one weekend, an agreement was reached. Insiders still remember the negotiators' frustration that *Star* secretaries still used electric typewriters, which meant slow corrections. As a result of the deal, Torstar gained a 22.4 per cent voting interest in Southam, while Southam took a 30 per cent interest in Torstar, albeit with non-voting shares. This meant that the Southam/Torstar group now controlled 45 per cent of Southam, effectively making it takeover proof. The deed was done—however, there were two big problems.

First, required notice had not been given to the Toronto Stock Exchange, and second, Southam minority shareholders had not even been consulted, let alone allowed to vote. Both Bee and Balfour insisted secrecy was essential in order to stop the corporate raider from making a pre-emptive bid. But securities law had been clearly breached, and thus the Ontario Securities Commission launched an investigation. It later concluded the swap amounted to "an unacceptable arrogation to directors of unlimited power to do with a company as they deem appropriate." The stock trading privileges of all twenty-three directors of both companies were consequently suspended for a year.

As a business editor who would be called upon to organize news coverage, I was literally dumbfounded when I showed up for work on the Monday following the deal. As a family owner, I was thrilled that the "Southam dream" was becoming a reality, but Bee, as would often be his practice, had conspicuously failed to give me or the family any notice. So there I was, mouth wide open, unable to give editors or reporters any idea about what had transpired. Most, I am sure, didn't buy my ignorance. I was totally embarrassed. It was obviously a huge story for the business section. More significantly, there was the deliberate breaking of the securities law. What did this mean for a newspaper that habitually preached from its editorial page about the rule of law?

I didn't hear from Bee for several days. But he was not the slightest bit regretful about his actions. "We had to do it this way," he declared, dismissive of both the brouhaha and his failure to give me any warning. This was a response I would come to expect, despite my protestations. As a reporter, I was never in a position where my lack of knowledge of the corporate machinations of Torstar made any difference. But as business editor in the *Star* newsroom, responsible for coverage of major business stories, it was crucial that I be informed. It was not that I felt Bee deliberately excluded me. Rather, what rankled was that it simply didn't occur to him to notify me or to consider the position I would be put in. And yet there I was, a part of Torstar ownership and a senior editor in the *Star* newsroom. It would not be the only time.

I had another issue. The paper's business columnist, Jack McArthur, told me he really wanted to write about the transaction. And it was clear, as we discussed it, that he would be taking a somewhat critical point of view, writing later, "There's a mixed bag of misgiving about several aspects of the deal." My quick reaction was that he should do it, editorial integrity being essential for both the paper and my section. If I stood in the way, I would be open to all sorts of criticism. I sought out Timson and told him of my plans. "I'm leaving this to you" was his reply, followed by his trademark stare. I stayed the course—and in the process, delivered a clear message to my colleagues. A point had been made.

It would be about this same time that my wife Katherine and I started talking about taking a mid-career sabbatical year in London. Bee couldn't believe it, asking incredulously, "Aren't you afraid of losing your place in line?" Even the mere concept of a sabbatical was simply not something he could fathom. At the time, it was certainly seen as unconventional, for precisely the reason Bee expounded. Yet that reticence didn't stop us from making plans, after which I gave my notice, requesting the standard year's leave of absence allowed to others. At forty, I felt a year away of study and writing would do wonders, saying at the time I wanted "to recharge my batteries." I had seen others do it and return fulfilled. Katherine was anxious to develop her writing career abroad. Furthermore, we both felt it would be a wonderful experience for our young family to live in one of the world's great cities. I arranged to take a few economics courses at the London School of Economics, received a NATO fellowship that led me to northern Norway, and won a scholarship from the European Community that took me to Copenhagen, Rome, and Paris. Stories to the *Star* would issue from each stop.

As I left in mid-1986, I celebrated a totally satisfying two-year stint as business editor, leaving with no promise or idea of what might come next. Timson wished me well, nothing more—but nor did I expect anything more. My position had to be filled, and who knew what the scene might be the following year? This uncertainty is standard fare for newsrooms. As it turned out, my limited knowledge of econometrics restricted the number of courses I would follow at the LSE. Instead, I spent a great deal of time writing a book about one of my long-standing passions—the Arctic. As a law student, I had worked two summers for futurist Richard Rohmer on his concept for a plan for the orderly development of what he called the Mid-Canada Corridor—that wide swath of Canada above the developed south and bounded on the north by the tree line. That job allowed me to take several tours to the glorious Arctic. And in Washington I had watched the lead-up to President Reagan's announcement of the Strategic Defense Initiative, a plan that would necessarily militarize Canada's Arctic. Published by U of T Press, *Arctic Imperative* allowed me to advocate on a host of northern issues. Writing that book, as it turned out, made for a very satisfying experience. As did spending uninterrupted time with Katherine and our two children, Robin, five years old at the time, and Emily, three, exploring the various byways of London's Primrose Hill district. For most of the year, the *Star* seemed very far away.

14

A SECOND EDITOR

The intriguing proposal came in an early May '87 telephone call from Ray Timson: why don't we meet halfway in Bermuda, he said, "to discuss next steps"? I had been prepared to fly home from London if needed. But the elegance of a private rendez-vous in the coral pink Southampton Princess, the grand dame of Bermuda's hotels, was inescapable. And I could tell Timson was quite delighted with the prospect of a short busman's holiday. So, Bermuda it was. And there, over savoury meals and languid walks, the surprise offer emerged. He asked me to return to the paper as editorial page editor, as part of a reorganization of the senior editorial team. I was surprised, to say the least. There had been no forewarning, no discussion with Bee, as had been the custom. What made the offer particularly attractive was that I would be succeeding my long-time colleague and friend Ian Urquhart, who was being promoted to managing editor. So, no one was being moved artificially to accommodate my return. Under the plan, Timson would become executive editor, my boss.

The formal announcement came in late August, in a traditional page three story titled "Three Senior Editors Get New Posts at *Star.*" What caught the more nuanced reader's attention was the careful wording of the change, announced by "Publisher Beland Honderich." There was no mention of any family connection between us, only the need to insert the title "Publisher" two times in front of Bee's name—so as to distinguish him from the other Honderich in the story. I found it all totally appropriate, given the circumstances, and was delighted with my new assignment. My only concern, especially after the tragic passing of Marty Goodman, was Timson's health. I had nagging doubts, as during our Bermuda walks he seemed to run out of breath all too quickly.

Bee was also clearly delighted with my new appointment, and to my great surprise, his opinion on the value of my sabbatical completely transformed. He talked about how it was such a "worthwhile" way to spend a year away, intensely studying a particular subject and then writing a book. Why not set up an annual fellowship to allow senior Canadian journalists of repute to do precisely the same? he asked. I was immediately taken with the concept, and we jointly took the proposal to the Atkinson Foundation. After a short negotiation, we agreed the Foundation, the *Star*, and the Honderich family would each contribute annually to fund a $100,000 year-long fellowship for a Canadian journalist to pursue a research project on a topical public policy issue. It was expected the winner would come up with policy suggestions, and the winning topic, not unexpectedly, would be consistent with the Atkinson Principles. And its name—the Atkinson Fellowship in Public Policy—became synonymous, for more than three decades, with one of the most sought-after fellowships in Canadian journalism. For each of those years, I was chair of the selection committee, an annual joy I would never miss. Ultimately, the list of articles, books, films, and podcasts produced a treasure trove of research on some of Canada's most important and complicated public issues. Topics included everything from Indigenous affairs to euthanasia, women and alcohol, aging, Arctic affairs, our mental health system, and urban planning. The list of winners included André Picard, Scott Simmie, Judy Steed, Ann Dowsett Johnston, Tanya Talaga, and Stephanie Nolen. Both Bee and I never stopped feeling a quiet pride with this initiative.

Our other major joint project came shortly thereafter, when Bee decided he wanted to do something significant to help the disadvantaged in Toronto. The sparkplug for a possible initiative was the ever-inventive Veronica Lacey, then director of education for North York. She took us both on a tour of the four high schools in the city's Jane-Finch neighbourhood, notorious for its racial strife and crime. Why not provide a fellowship for a deserving student from each school to pursue a higher education? she asked. We loved the idea, adding that each winner would also have a chance to work one summer at the *Star.* The program was endowed and "Honderich students" have been filling summer jobs at the paper ever since, with the list of successful university graduates inching upwards every year. A great treat for Bee and me became attending the annual celebration of the winners at York University. Again, this initiative was the source of much joint pride.

As I took my new seat in the editorial page editor's corner office, I knew a firestorm was awaiting. The national debate on the proposed free trade agreement with the U.S. was in full swing, with the *Star's* categorical and unequivocal opposition firmly established. Indeed, our intensive coverage had already become a story itself. Then Prime Minister Brian Mulroney would regularly cite the *Star* as an example of the powerful interests arrayed against him. Without question, the *Star* dedicated more resources, more column inches, and more analyses of the subject than any other media outlet. Our economics editor, the respected David Crane, was working non-stop to provide detailed special sections on all aspects of the proposed deal. There was hardly a day when the debate didn't make page one. We had become, unquestionably, THE anti–free trade newspaper in Canada.

Our controversial coverage was also encapsulated in a memorable exchange between Canada's chief trade negotiator, Simon Reisman, and the *Star's* irascible, no-nonsense Washington bureau chief, Bob Hepburn. At a delicate point in the talks, Hepburn asked the totally legitimate question as to whether changes in the vital Auto Pact were envisaged. Reisman immediately shouted at Hepburn, "The *Toronto Star*, that rag! That damn thing is a very poor excuse for a newspaper, and I have no respect for it, or you." Then, as he stormed off, he turned and yelled, "You know what you are? A hack!" The exchange was covered coast to coast, with pieces also appearing in both the *New York Times* and the *Wall Street Journal*. In the *Journal*, Bee was quoted as saying, "I don't know Mr. Reisman and I don't think twice about what he said."

In my new job, I was responsible for the editorials, the letters to the editor, and the op-ed page. Under the regime established by Bee, the editorial page was where we expressed our opinion, consistent with the Atkinson Principles. Those views would also shape what stories we opted to follow and develop on the news side. However, in covering the news, we had an obligation to be accurate, fair, and balanced. Right from the outset, I felt the letters and opinion pages had to reflect both sides of the free trade debate. So I began a concerted push to ensure some balance in these sections.

Yet our editorial position, in editorial after editorial, was solidly against. I was so personally committed to the cause, I agreed to appear regularly to debate *Globe and Mail* editor William Thorsell. In many quarters, the free trade debate was also portrayed as a fearsome face-off between Canada's two largest newspapers, the *Globe* being strongly in favour. So it seemed only appropriate to engage my counterpart in person. Thorsell and I would enjoy these engagements tremendously. Only six weeks into the job, I also decided to write a page one editorial entitled "Our Sovereignty Is Threatened." Under criticism that the *Star* was being hysterical, I told the CBC, "If you can't get passionate about your country's future, what can you be passionate about?" Page one editorials—rare at any newspaper—had been used very sparingly in the past. I decided to change that, particularly for the purpose of trumpeting new crusades—a tradition that continued until I left. Behind the scenes, Bee and I also decided to come together, in another joint effort, to quietly finance the cartooning efforts of playwright Rick Salutin, whose anti–free trade comics were causing quite a stir. That support was never made public.

On review, the overall negative bent of the *Star*'s trade deal coverage is beyond doubt, and the paper was taken to the Ontario Press Council over its so-called "biased" coverage. However, editor Crane did an exhaustive search of all stories and showed how both sides of the debate were represented. We noted all *Star* columnists were allowed to express a different view—and that several did. We also stressed that the *Star* was a "crusading newspaper whose aim has always been to stimulate debate." That idea had very much become my credo—the *Star* must always be seen as a crusader, a point I felt it was important to emphasize. The press council ultimately dismissed the complaint.

During this time, I was also able to witness first-hand Bee's fabled and withering treatment of Canada's political leaders. The *Star* invited then Liberal leader John Turner to an editorial board meeting to discuss free trade. He was not being very specific when Bee interjected sharply with a hard, direct question to "Mr. Turner." "C'mon Bee, just call me John," Turner replied, in his slap-on-the-back manner. Bee repeated the "Mr. Turner" intro, and Turner again asked to be called "John." Bee paused, then declared dismissively, if not slightly irritatedly, "Just answer the question, Mr. Turner." The chill was instant. Turner never recovered. And Bee ended the meeting by saying, "Don't come back until you have something more constructive to say." This was certainly not my style, but no one in that room had any doubt about who was in charge.

Prime Minister Pierre Trudeau didn't fare much better. Bee met privately with him only once, over lunch in the *Star*'s sixth-floor dining room. They were disagreeing sharply over the issue of wage and price controls when Bee decided he'd had enough. Trudeau's principal secretary, Jim Coutts, reported to me that the balance of the meal was spent in near total silence—not exactly the type of treatment a PM might expect.

It would be during the year after the free trade debate ended that Bee made perhaps his most significant and penetrating speech about journalism and publishing. The timing of his declaration was hardly accidental. It would also be the only time he reached out to me about a speech, aware of the import of what he was about to say. He was eager to hear my reaction, and I proudly ended up in the front row, totally in agreement with his remarks. The occasion was the presentation of his third honourary degree, at Carleton University in Ottawa. There, in no uncertain terms, he directly and pointedly dismissed the notion of objectivity as "a fiction" and laid out his overall philosophy of publishing.

"Newspapers, I am frequently told," he said, "should be objective. They should publish the facts in their news columns and confine their opinions to their editorial pages. This is a nice theory, but it is not only false, it also discourages full and frank pubic discussion." He continued, "No self-respecting newspaper deliberately distorts or slants the news to make it conform to its own point of view. But you cannot publish a newspaper without making value judgments on what news you select to publish and how you present it in the paper. And those value judgments reflect a view of society—a point of view if you will—that carries as much weight, if not more, than what is said on the editorial page. . . . If newspapers were truly objective, they would all select and publish the news in much the same way. Instead, there are vast differences in the way different papers handle the same stories. . . . The major reason is that publishers and editors view the world from quite different perspectives."

The speech caused quite a stir in journalism circles—and still does—particularly over Bee's dismissal of the sacred crystal chalice of "objectivity." Yet Bee's ultimate vision of a caring, crusading newspaper and how it should operate has been the intellectual bedrock on which the *Star* has succeeded. It is the *Star*'s essence, its raison d'être. It has given the newspaper an identity—one that separates it broadly from virtually all its competitors. Ask readers anywhere in Canada about the *Star* and they will know what it stands for. The original motto, "A Paper for the People," often epitomizes the replies you hear. This is a paper that likes to stand up for the little guy and minorities. It likes going on crusades. Its political leanings are progressive, most often Liberal. It is a newspaper with character. It was a tradition I was committed to pursue and build on.

Six months into my new role, another firestorm broke out, setting the stage for several decades of troubled relations with Toronto's Jewish community. The sparkplug was an editorial applauding then Foreign Minister Joe Clark's recognition of the Palestine Liberation Organization as the legitimate bargaining arm of the Palestinians. Canada was the last major country to do so. Margaret Weir, a former diplomat turned editorial writer, was sent to cover the speech and write the editorial. She was dismayed when Clark was booed off the stage, with the largely Jewish crowd at the Canada–Israel meeting rising to sing the Israeli national anthem. Weirs called Clark's message a "timely one," adding, "It was also a necessary reminder to members of the Jewish community in Canada that they are citizens of Canada, not Israel." That last sentence raised the old anti-Semitic canard of dual loyalty. While that was not what Weirs intended, the sting was certainly felt. Hundreds of complaining letters were written, demands for an apology arose, and the paper and its editorial page editor were labelled "anti-Semitic."

Throughout my career, this tension between the *Star* and the city's Jewish community was a constant. We were the only Toronto newspaper then to have a foreign correspondent stationed in Israel, yet every correspondent or columnist who wrote on the Middle East invariably came up for criticism, sometimes quite virulent. Our editorial policy positioned us very squarely in the mainstream of North American dailies, but in Toronto we would always be seen as more pro-Palestinian, more critical of Israel than other dailies, in sharp contrast to the always pro-Israel *National Post*. It even got to the point where Benjamin's Park Memorial Chapel started a boycott of the paper, accusing us of anti-Semitism for running a *New York Times* chart comparing Israeli and Palestinian deaths in one of the *intifadas*.

Ultimately, I probably spent more time, wrote more letters, and took more calls on this issue than any other. Our efforts to reflect the debate never stopped. Studies were commissioned on our coverage. Opinion pieces were requested to inform readers of delicate issues, such as dual loyalty. The sting of being labelled an "anti-Semite" never lessened, but nor did my determination to provide fair coverage on the issue. That became the driving force much later, when the erudite Haroon Siddiqui became a regular columnist, the *Star*'s first Muslim in such a role. His sometimes strong rebukes of Israeli policy acted as a lightning rod within the Jewish community. When asked about his column—as I often was—I would reply, "Isn't Toronto big enough to have one Muslim columnist?" Certainly I thought so.

It would be just one short year into my new role that, once again, a reorganization catapulted my career. As he had planned to do for some time, Bee stepped down as publisher, with his seventieth birthday nigh. And, once again, he opted for an unusual replacement structure—two executives to occupy the office of chief executive. They were David Galloway to run Harlequin and David Jolley to run the newspapers. Under the plan—which drew considerable commentary elsewhere—the two would rotate the title of president and executive vice president each year. Bee also announced to the board he would remain as chair until his seventy-fifth birthday. In the same statement, he added that the appointment of a new editor, not named, would be made by the board. No names or candidates were listed.

Leading up to this, Timson took me aside, confiding that he wanted to get out of the daily grind. While he didn't cite his health, I felt this was a big factor. As Jolley, the new *Star* publisher, had no editorial experience, Timson outlined a new committee of the Torstar board that would oversee editorial at the *Star*. Under this arrangement, the new editor would regularly report to this committee. And if there was a fundamental disagreement between editor and publisher, the editor could lodge a direct appeal with the committee.

Then the huge news directed at me: "We"—not defined—"want you as the next editor." Again, I had had no prior discussion with Bee, but this time I went directly to see him. He insisted the choice had been Timson's, that I had impressed him in my new job, and that a strong editorial leader was essential to the new publisher. Of course, I had no doubt of Bee's involvement, even though officially I was told a separate directors' panel committee—minus Bee—had the final say. Such an appointment always required his approval. Yet he did seem genuinely pleased. The appointment was formally announced by Jolley in a page one story, with me declaring, "This paper has been the conscience of this city and province. It has been in the forefront, challenging and asking for reform and looking for better ways to help the common man in society. That is a tradition I am determined to pursue."

Not surprisingly—or even unexpectedly—the cries of nepotism emerged from both within and without. The *Financial Post* had run a series titled "The Heir Apparent," in which a former unnamed *Star* managing editor said my appointment as editor "would be nepotism of the first order, but he's probably as qualified as anyone on the paper to handle the job. So, there would not be the shrieking of derision within the industry." In *Maclean's*, the often biting Allan Fotheringham wrote that my rise was "about as secret as the recipe for boiled eggs." Internally, the remarks never came directly, but I knew they were there. My strategy was simple: get on with the job and let the results speak for themselves. I repeated that to myself often.

It would be four months later that Timson retired. As veteran wordsmith Jack Brehl wrote, "You can take Timson out of the newspaper, but you can't take the newspaper out of Timson." A legend by any definition, Timson served a thirty-year stint at the *Star*, encapsulating a stunning career. He dried dishes in Gerda Munsinger's Munich apartment, watched John F. Kennedy be nominated for

U.S. president, and later covered the Texas trial of Jack Ruby, the man who shot Kennedy's assassin. He wrote gripping stories on the trapped miners in the Springhill, Nova Scotia, mine disaster, and walked with freedom fighters in the U.S. South. Timson's passion for horseracing, earned as a dyed-in-the-wool east-end Torontonian, meant his eye for a good thoroughbred was about as sharp as his eye for a good story. The biggest story of his career? No doubt, he would say the 1969 moon walk. And he could recite word for word his exact lede on that story: "Like kids at Christmas who couldn't wait for morning, two Americans romped across the face of the moon. . . ." Timson was truly one of a kind—and the finest news editor I ever worked with.

As the new editor, I was intent on making a mark as soon as possible. While working as deputy city editor, business editor, and editorial page editor, I certainly had a front-row view of what was required. Each of my predecessors—Lautens, Timson, and Urquhart—had a unique style. I was determined to carve out my own, more befitting the times and consistent with my personality. There would be openness, consultation, and compassion. I knew full well how Bee's newsrooms had run. Mine was to be much, much different. Indeed, I think one of my driving ambitions was to show just what "different" looked like. One of my first actions, for example, was to scrap Bee's prohibition against the use of the word "gay" in describing the homosexual community. Bee had never accepted the modern use of the word and had banned it. For good measure, I also moved quickly to have our benefits package made accessible to gay partners.

To me, being editor of a newspaper is somewhat akin to conducting a full symphony orchestra drawn together to play Mahler. There are so many disparate elements and egos that must be harmonized simultaneously to produce a great result. The production of a large metro newspaper is often called the "daily miracle." No one editor or person could possibly know how each element of the paper comes together— be it the weather map, the crossword, the comics, the advice columns,

the horoscope, the sports agate, the TV listings, the editorial car-
toons, the wire service copy, etc. The list goes on and on. To succeed,
an editor must delegate and rely on department editors. And nowhere
was this more important than the huge Saturday paper.

Generating more than half of the paper's total advertising revenue, the *Saturday Star* had separate sections over the years for autos,
travel, condominiums, lifestyle, political and feature commentary,
foreign news, careers, and house sales. All our reader surveys showed
how popular these sections were, with travel usually taking the top
spot. My sense was that these sections had often been neglected by
management. I started with a different approach. The *Star*, for
example, was the first paper in North America to adopt "Wheels"
as the name for its car and truck section. Devised by then foreign
editor Dennis Morgan, who moved to be the section's first full-time
editor, Wheels would command my attention for any number of
reasons—be it the need to keep prize columnist Jim Kenzie happy,
to ward off complaints about negative car reviews, or to make sure
there was enough space to carry features. The same process and
attention would be required for the other Saturday-only sections.
The main news sections, however, would always be my first priority.
This is where we would make our mark, and I knew exactly how I
wanted this to happen.

Borrowing one page from Bee's initiative in the '60s, I decided to
bring on board a host of new pre-eminent voices to the paper. In
many posts, we already had top-notch reporters and columnists. But
in other areas, I felt we could do better and perhaps inflict some
competitive harm on our competitors. To that end, I lured three
superb talents from the *Globe and Mail*: columnist Tom Walkom,
feature writer Judy Steed, and Judy Stoffman as our new fashion
editor. From the *Sun*, I recruited Marion Kane and freelancer Jim
White to revamp our food section. The fact that Kane was able to
lure the legendary Julia Child to come north for a dinner and publicity round won her my loyalty forever. Finally, on the political side,

we signed the *Globe*'s veteran page six columnist Geoffrey Stevens as a Sunday columnist, and the epitome of sophisticated political commentary, Dalton Camp, as a Saturday columnist.

On the cartooning front, I managed to convince the *Montreal Gazette*'s notorious and brilliant cartoonist Terry Mosher, who draws under the pen name Aislin, to try out Toronto. The experiment lasted for two years, but in the process he flashed his brilliance on the subject matter of Ontario's somewhat boyish-looking premier, Bob Rae. Nor did he forget his bag of tricks in Quebec. By tradition, I learned, his first cartoon usually had some "off-colour" aspect to it. Thus, when he submitted a cartoon featuring Premier Rae along with Quebec premier Robert Bourassa, I instantly took it to eighteen other staffers to see if they noticed anything amiss. A unanimous "no." Only after it was published did we notice, belatedly, that at the end of Bourassa's prolonged nose might be a used condom. Yet not one subscriber complained.

The other area I was intent on bolstering was foreign and national reporting. To me, the mark of an outstanding newspaper has always been its ability to have its own correspondents out in the field, reporting on important stories. The need for Canadian voices to be telling faraway stories from a Canadian perspective is, in my view, self-evident. Furthermore, as the principal newspaper for one of the most diverse cities in the world, these stories provide welcome fodder for impromptu water cooler chats.

It would take a while, but eventually we would establish bureaus in South Africa, Moscow, India, central Europe, and Mexico, adding to our existing complement of Washington, London, Jerusalem, and Hong Kong. The insightful dispatches, from, for example, our renowned correspondents Bill Schiller in Johannesburg and Steve Handelman in Moscow represented some of the finest foreign reporting anywhere. They brought to life the dramatic re-emergence of an open democracy in Nelson Mandela's South Africa and the first threads of freedom in Russia under Mikhail Gorbachev's glasnost.

Just as important was the need for Canada's story to be told. Our national press agency, Canadian Press, provided the nuts-and-bolts news. But for more in-depth, insightful coverage, an on-site, permanent reporter could provide so much more. We had always had correspondents in Quebec City and Vancouver, in addition to our large parliamentary bureau in Ottawa. Under the new regime, we would eventually add bureaus in Edmonton, Montreal, and Halifax. At a time when our country's unity was being tested, this became very important.

We also opted to forge a new hiring path by asking quadriplegic Barbara Turnbull to join our staff, not quite sure at the outset how it would all work. A part-time clerk at a convenience store in a Toronto suburb, Turnbull was shot in the throat during an armed robbery, leaving her paralyzed from the neck down and confined to a wheelchair. As determined as one could ever imagine, she earned a journalism degree at Arizona State University, where she was the valedictorian of the graduating class. She took up our offer to join the newsroom, showing over the next twenty-five years a verve and life perspective inspiring to all. In the process, we also helped develop the tools to enable her to do her job as a reporter. For the newsroom, her presence and spirit were a constant inspiration.

Another addition to the roster was perhaps the most daring and acclaimed war correspondent in recent memory. Paul Watson preferred, as he told me directly under some intense questioning, to spend his holidays covering wars or hotspots. He knew the risks. He accepted them totally, as did his family. A "two way"—newsroom-speak for reporter/photographer—Watson would head out fearlessly, camera in hand, to ferret out great stories. The front pages of the *Star* during this time were resplendent with his dispatches from Eritrea, Romania, Serbia, Mozambique, Angola, Syria, and South Africa. He was one of the very first Western journalists to enter a genocide-striken Rwanda, and his desperate escape from a bombed Baghdad was recounted in vivid detail.

But Watson wrote his most celebrated piece in 1993, while covering the bloody civil war in Somalia. Most of the Western press had fled, given the gruesome attacks on journalists, but Watson insisted on staying, being the only one left. And he was on the ground in Mogadishu when the body of a fallen U.S. air crewman was dragged through the streets by an unruly mob. Risking his own life, he was able to take an action photo that literally was published around the globe. Credited with being the prime reason for U.S. withdrawal from Somalia, it was also a spark for the Oscar-winning film *Black Hawk Down*. For this heroic shot, the *Star* was awarded the coveted Pulitzer Prize for spot news photography, making it the only Canadian newspaper ever to receive this honour for its news coverage.

Sitting beside Watson in Columbia University's stately auditorium as we accepted the prize will go down as one of my greatest memories. We minted a special newsroom coin for the occasion. Despite the acclaim, Watson became haunted about the feelings of the widow of the downed airman. We discussed it privately several times, as he recounts in his appropriately named memoir, *Where War Lives*. Watson would ultimately win four National Newspaper Awards, including one on the child sex trade in Asia, another on the anarchy in Somalia, and another on the murder of a Somali teen by Canadian soldiers. His exploits are simply legendary. Sadly, after returning to the *Star* following a stint with the *Los Angeles Times*, he resigned from the paper in 2015 over a disagreement about a story of his on Arctic expeditions.

While expanding the paper's news horizons was gratifying, I was also confronted early on by unexpected crises. The first came in '89 when celebrated book reviewer Ken Adachi was exposed for plagiarizing three paragraphs from *Time* magazine. The evidence was clear cut, and it was published by the *Globe and Mail*. It was his second such offence, and he had been warned in writing that any recurrence would necessitate dismissal. Stoic and not offering any excuse, Adachi opted to resign under my strong urging in a sombre, short meeting in my office. What no one expected was Adachi's decision to commit suicide soon after. The newsroom was stunned. I was personally devastated, and even more so when several treatises on plagiarism were discovered on his office bookshelf.

The second shock came about the same time that the travel industry decided to boycott the *Star*—removing all travel-related ads—until we stopped publishing "negative" stories in our highly read travel section. There were three such stories that industry reps outlined in meetings with publisher Jolley and me: one detailing vacationers' complaints about food and accommodation at a Dominican Republic resort; another, the humorous experiences of *Star* editor Geoff Chapman in hurricane-struck Cancun, Mexico; and the third, an explanatory piece on a new travel complaint branch set up in Ontario. None of those should have run in the travel section, we were told. We were just as explicit in response, arguing that prospective travellers deserved to be told the truth. In my view, we had to hold firm.

There could be no compromise, or our editorial integrity would have been impugned. And to emphasize our seriousness, I ordered that the boycott be covered in front-page stories in which I was quoted saying, "The editorial integrity of the *Toronto Star* is not for sale." Ultimately, we stood strong, and the ads all returned six months later. We did, however, lose more than $7 million in ad revenues in the process. Those were days when we could afford it—and I was proud for the newsroom to label me the "Seven Million Dollar Man." As the *Financial Times* cheered, "If other newspapers would follow Honderich's example, there would probably be far fewer disillusioned Canadian tourists."

The glory days of record advertising, however, were coming to an abrupt halt as the recession of the early '90s set in, with our revenues plummeting by a staggering one third. Jolley ordered layoffs across the company, a move hard to criticize given the precipitous downturn. The economy was in steep decline, with economic despair the dominant mood of the day. Thus, the order came to cut fifty jobs in editorial, more than one tenth of our newsroom staff. It was a tortuous task, particularly for a newsroom not used to austerity.

Understanding the morale was sagging badly, I became totally involved in the process, with a goal of trying to mitigate wherever possible. Indeed, I made sure to speak personally with every staffer affected, which was a practice I continued throughout my career. I made it a point to say "My door is always open," speaking quietly with countless staffers who sought me out. Being a mentor and career adviser was, in my view, an essential part of the job. I also sought out every possible solution in tough times. Supporting me in that effort, our deputy book editor, Doris Giller—after whom the prestigious Canadian literary award is named—voluntarily resigned as she lay in hospital dying from cancer. That magnificent gesture resulted in the saving of one job.

Tensions rose even further, however, when Jolley demanded another twenty-five editorial layoffs. While advertising was still in decline, I was furiously opposed to further cuts. Layoffs in a union environment like the *Star* are dictated by seniority, under the rule often called "last in, first out." Thus, the first to go must be the mostly young, fresh hires. In the previous layoff, I had done virtually everything to protect this crop of talented hires, whose reporting had become the backbone of the paper, by instituting reductions in other areas of the newsroom. But with more cuts demanded, these young stars were now in jeopardy. I argued to Jolley that we would be compromising the future editorial well-being of the *Star* if we proceeded. To buttress my case, I compiled the seniority list, which revealed that, among others, burgeoning investigative ace Kevin Donovan and the oh-so-talented yet complex Rosie DiManno were at or near the bottom.

Up to now, Jolley and I had worked quite well together. But I drew a line at these cuts, and so activated the special appeal process by which I could make my case directly to the Editorial Advisory Committee of the Torstar board. This would be the first and only time the committee was used in this way. As board chair, Bee was a committee member, and he made it very clear to me privately that he would stand behind Jolley, arguing, "The publisher is entitled to have his orders followed." I showed up for the meeting determined yet fully expecting a speedy dismissal.

Just as the meeting was to begin, however, there was a rustling at the door of the wood-panelled Torstar boardroom. In walked an ashen, very sickly Alex MacIntosh. Not seen for months because of his brutal battle with cancer, Alex had been Bee's closest confidant, if not consigliere, as company lawyer and director. He had literally come from his deathbed to argue his point. Both Bee and Jolley were clearly shell-shocked by his appearance, already reckoning Alex was not there to back them up. His turn to speak came quickly, and reading from the material I had thankfully couriered to his home, he declared it would be a "grave mistake" to proceed with these cuts. In his characteristic gravelly, monotone voice, he summoned up every ounce of strength to argue my case. I was overwhelmed, almost to the point of tears. So was the committee. Alex quite literally saved the day, and Donovan and DiManno both went on to become superstars at the paper. I would never see him again, but I would be forever grateful.

Adding to the turmoil of the times was a worsening labour scene. The *Star* was one of the last large dailies on the continent to maintain its own delivery fleet. Most others had outsourced circulation delivery to independent contractors. With declining ad revenues and the $400 million expense of the new printing plant in Vaughan, *Star* management felt it was time to do the same. That rationale certainly made sense to me. While the nostalgia of those maroon and *Star*-blue trucks ran deep, the prospect of saving tens of millions of dollars while young journalist jobs were at stake was too powerful to resist. The Southern Ontario Newspaper Guild, which represented circulation as well as the newsroom, recognized changes were inevitable but feared outsourcing would lead to job losses elsewhere. So members decided to take a stand at the *Star*.

What unfolded was a five-week strike that *Toronto Life* magazine described as a "wounding game of labour–management brinkmanship," noting, "the paper lost money, readers and advertisers, and the employees sacrificed five weeks' wages without getting much more in the way of job security." The paper's other six unions had little sympathy for the strike, as their members stubbornly kept the paper running. In the newsroom, there was a total staff of twenty-two that was able to run a smaller sized paper. It was a herculean effort, which drew on every ounce of my leadership and management skills. The strike took a particularly nasty turn when Jolley, unbeknownst to me, decided to fire several strikers for roughshod behaviour. Not only did this move prolong the strike by several weeks, it meant the process of reconciliation in the newsroom would become even more difficult. As editor, and a family owner to boot, I was often the target of caustic comments. I always made a point of crossing the picket line every day in full sight and often stopped to speak with editorial employees.

The strike was settled a few weeks before the *Star*'s one hundredth birthday, but within the confines of One Yonge, there was little appetite for celebration. I would write the centennial editorial, quoting renowned Toronto historian William Kilbourn, who had written, "Win or lose, the *Star* has been goading, cajoling and haranguing Torontonians into action or reaction, enthusiasm or fury, for 100 years now." A few days later, we also officially opened our state-of-the art Vaughan printing plant by running off a colour reproduction of the original 1892 front page. With six lines of new MAN Roland Colorman presses and new futuristic robots, which automatically loaded newsprint on the presses, the *Star* was now mechanically set for a brighter, more colourful future. Sadly, the prognoses for growth in advertising and inserts that had provided the foundation for the plant's overall design in the roaring late '80s no longer appeared valid. Indeed, they would never prove true.

Without a doubt, this time was my lowest as editor. The fallout from the bitter strike, the layoffs, and the worsening economic scene all contributed to a deep sense of malaise. An article in the *Ryerson Review of Journalism*, under the title "Lost at Sea," quoted several *Star* editorial staffers who talked about a lost sense of mission. Any goodwill gained from the new hires, new foreign bureaus, and new presses seemed long gone. So did appreciation for our crusade for a new vision for Greater Toronto. I knew I had to provide a spark.

The first step was to accelerate the push on our city crusade. The debate on this issue centred on the patchwork quilt of inward-looking local governments, competing transit systems, and affordable housing deficits that constituted the Greater Toronto Area (GTA). Three decades before, the city had been celebrated for its integrated Metro style of government and regional planning. Sadly, as the GTA population skyrocketed, necessary changes were not made. Later in the decade, noted urbanist Anne Golden would craft a definitive plan to unite the GTA, but in the early '90s there seemed little political will to act. Thus, we started with another front-page editorial and produced a host of stories under the rubric of "Making Our City Work." For the next several years, articles appeared throughout the paper, always under the "Making Our City Work" banner.

Ultimately, the crusade built up so much momentum we were able to sponsor a debate on the future of the GTA with Ontario's three political leaders—Premier Bob Rae, Liberal leader Lyn McLeod, and Conservative leader and later Premier Mike Harris. Harris agreed but then wanted to drop out. I told his staff we were determined to proceed, warning I would happily proceed with an empty chair with his name on it. Harris did show up and did well in the Royal York Hotel ballroom, where eight hundred people crammed in to watch.

Another major initiative came in a top-to-bottom redesign of the paper to take advantage of more colour and the better reproduction capabilities of our new presses. Redesigns are always a huge internal rallying point, as reporters, editors, and designers battle furiously over such delicacies as font, typeface, borders, margins, and mastheads. Hopes are usually high that a new look will bring in droves of new readers, yet more often than not, those hopes are dashed. Change too much, however, and the consequences can be dire. As a group, newspaper readers tend to be stubbornly loyal to what they're used to.

Perhaps the most daring and ultimately most impactful initiative was born of my decision to engage in a written letter-style dialogue with my counterpart Alain Dubuc, editor of Montreal's *La Presse* newspaper. The spark for this idea came in an accidental conversation with one of my university professors, the great economic nationalist Abe Rotstein. "How can you get your readers to engage with Quebec?" he challenged. The separatist drums were beating again, and it seemed a second referendum was probable. I called up Dubuc, whom I hardly knew, asking whether he was open to a periodic written dialogue. There would be no limit on topics, other than that our overarching umbrella would be the Quebec–Canada relationship. After some back and forth, we agreed on a format. Each of us would write letters to the other, with each missive appearing on the same Saturday, in English in the *Star* and in French in *La Presse*. We also agreed we would avoid talking on the phone. This was to be a true letter exchange—rather nineteenth century, I often mused.

The exchange lasted for four years, right up to the October referendum in 1995. In his "Dear John" letter to me, Dubuc would unleash on a multitude of topics. He would never hold back, instead consistently spelling out precisely how Quebecers felt on a particular issue. Similarly, in my "Mon cher Alain" letters, I felt I had the latitude to be as blunt and forceful as he had been. It was often a vigorous exchange, sometimes very heartfelt, sometimes amazingly insightful, and sometimes just joyous. We both reported an amazingly positive response to this exchange. Indeed, I will never forget a happenstance trip to Montreal during which I was recognized several times, the most memorable instance including the epithet "maudit Trudeauist" (wretched Trudeau follower).

As a result of the letter exchange, I was invited to speak twice during the 1995 referendum debate, an honour I cherished. The first address was to a professional audience, and the second, the week before the vote, was at Montreal's Canadian Club, where Dubuc and I did a bilingual reprise to the delight of the five hundred in attendance. The *Star* had also prepared a special eight-page section full of letters to Quebecers, expressing a fervent desire for them to stay in Canada. Sadly the "no" committee vetoed distribution of the 350,000 copies, arguing one letter on the back page of the section was too negative. Enraged, I decided the *Star* would hire six buses to take Torontonians to Montreal for the final national unity rally the following week. Some in Quebec City later pushed that we be charged for interfering in the campaign. Those charges never materialized.

It seemed this initiative acted as a statement that the *Star* was back and setting the agenda. That impression would prove critical, as events would shortly reveal.

PART III

15

CONRAD BLACK
AND PREPPING FOR WAR

It would be a late afternoon on a lazy November Sunday in '92 when the phone rang. Working at home, I had come to expect regular calls from the office. Answering them was part of the job. This time the decidedly excited voice on the other end of the line was my old boss, now news editor, Mary Deanne Shears. Never one to hold back, she began in trademark bombast: "So Honderich, what 'n hell is going on?"

To which I replied quickly, "What are you talking about?"

Sensing I might be trying to be cute, she persisted, "C'mon John, you know what I'm talking about."

Bewildered, I repeated, "I don't have the foggiest idea what you're talking about."

She paused slightly, then said, "Are you serious?"

To which I repeated, "I don't have a clue."

She paused again, this time longer, then almost shouted, "Your father has just sold all of Torstar's Southam shares to Conrad Black!"

There I sat, caught completely off guard—editor, Torstar family owner, and son—taking in an unexpected and dramatic move from Bee that would ultimately shape Toronto's newspaper scene and my life for the next decade.

Not that I hadn't heard the grumblings about the Southam investment, so hurriedly cobbled together six years before. I had. And the
devastation on the Torstar balance sheet, caused by the recession of
the early '90s, was unmistakable. Two days after the *Star*'s centennial, David Galloway heard from Black in London that he was prepared to pay $259 million for Torstar's 22.6 per cent interest in
Southam. That would be a 17 per cent premium on the shares then
trading at $15.38. Two days later, from his Palm Beach condo, Bee
phoned his long-time colleague and Southam boss St. Clair Balfour,
informing him of a special Torstar board meeting in two days' time.
Balfour sensed trouble, correctly guessing what was afoot.

As part of the 1986 share swap, both Balfour and Southam president Bill Ardell were made directors of Torstar. At the Sunday board
meeting, Bee immediately asked Ardell to step outside since he had a
conflict of interest in such a sale. Balfour wasn't asked to leave; nor
was Galloway, who, as part of the swap, was Southam's vice president.
For Torstar's directors, there was a clear ethical dilemma: the shares
were bought to protect Southam from takeover, yet now they were
selling to Canada's most notorious takeover artist. There was an animated debate, but ultimately the sale was approved, though not unanimously, with Balfour abstaining. Bee would later defend the sale,
arguing, "We had to sell these shares for the stockholders."

To my mind, the sale was foolhardy. I had absolutely no doubt the
decision would boomerang, with Black returning to attack the *Star*
in some manner, armed with a cross-country newspaper chain at his
back—though one critically lacking a Toronto voice. In a sharp
letter to Bee several weeks later—letters having become our principal means of communication on delicate issues—I wrote, "There is
no doubt Black will take over Southam. . . . His longing for a Toronto
outlet will increase and he will come after the *Star*. It will take time,
but he will be back to haunt everyone at One Yonge. You may not
be around, but I likely will, and Black has the deep pockets to pose
a real threat." I further told him that I was furious to have been

humiliated once again by a total lack of advance warning. In a short call after the announcement, Bee told me he "didn't have time" to contact me. That reply only compounded the injury. Only months before, he had dumped a pile of tax documents on my desk for me to sign, again without warning or explanation. Now this. No longer would I serve on family boards, I wrote.

I have always been both fascinated by and extremely wary of Black. Our paths first crossed at a private soiree at which legendary singer Dinah Shore was the headliner. Right from the start, we would usually engage in newspaper banter, barbs, and braggadocio. Intensely proud of his reputation as a voracious newspaper reader, he would normally declare he couldn't be bothered reading the *Star*. His most delicious slam came years later when he professed, "I personally can't read one paragraph of the *Star* without getting glottal stops or apoplexy." Better than being bored, I might have replied. For several years, my wife and I were occasional guests at his Park Lane Circle dinners, with his recitation by heart of A.E. Housman poems being my most memorable recollection. Those invitations ceased once his more hardline second wife, Barbara Amiel, arrived on the scene.

As was his wont at that time, Black sued the *Star* over a column by Rosie DiManno. Entitled "Black Sheds His Bad Boy Image," the column was intended to paint a picture of a more resurrected Black after a decade of legal turmoil. Yet, in the process, DiManno naturally referred to his contentious dealings with Massey Ferguson and the Dominion Stores pension fund, and to his conversion to Catholicism by Emmett Cardinal Carter. His demands for an apology were quickly rejected, and our repeated counter-demands for a recitation of the errors elicited nothing concrete. Black once bragged his libel suits were "a profit centre." But I was not about to back down. This became a matter of principle, which, coincidentally, is the title of Conrad's memoir. Two years and tens of thousands of dollars in legal fees later, we worked out a compromise, with the *Star* printing a four-paragraph recitation of the facts of the Dominion

Stores pension history. The words "regret" or "apology" would never appear. Nor was a penny paid in damages.

Parenthetically, the only suit I ever filed for slander involved the former TV commentator and later senator Mike "Duffster" Duffy. The often over-the-top Duffy proclaimed in a broadcast that I had personally intervened to stop publication of a poll showing Mike Harris's Conservatives gaining in the '95 Ontario provincial election. The assertion was a bald-faced lie, and I even sent Duffy a registered letter from the highly regarded pollster Michael Adams—once dubbed the Mother Teresa of pollsters—repudiating his claim. But he refused to budge. Feeling my reputation was at stake, I decided to sue, motivated by the phrase I would often use when advising others—"You only have one reputation!" Eventually, Duffy's TV network sought to close the file. My demand was simple: an abject apology from Duffy—written by me—would have to be read on air. Indeed, that was done, and for good measure I reproduced the apology and a large photo of "Duffster," which took up almost all of page three of the paper. A point was made.

Meanwhile, as Black gradually built up his newspaper empire in Canada, there would be another huge change at Torstar in '94. The rotating CEO structure was not working as Bee and the board had hoped, so Jolley was let go, leaving Galloway as the sole CEO. That, in turn, meant the publisher's role was open. There were three senior vice presidents under Jolley—marketing's Tom Murtha, production and finance's Neil Clark, and me. My immediate reaction was to stay put. I had been editor for six years and felt there was so much more to do. What did I know about circulation, advertising, or production? The sting of nepotism also reverberated once again loudly in my head. Too many had told me openly it was only "inevitable" I get the top job. It never seemed inevitable to me. It was as if I wanted to prove them all wrong

Yet Galloway came to me directly, indicating I was the overall choice for the role. My first reaction was one of reluctance. Then

Clark, so dedicated and thoroughly professional, came to my office declaring he was not in the running and that I was "plain and simple—the choice of the staff." My wife Katherine, however, was steadfastly opposed, arguing heatedly it would decrease my time at home and my more public role would conflict with her writing career. Our relationship had already been going through tough times, with her resentment of the *Star* and the time it demanded growing daily. It would be a torturous period, especially as I heard about some of the outsiders now under consideration. I was sure I could do better. Trying to reconcile those competing pressures while coming to terms with my own ambition meant that for weeks I was in a state of emotional turmoil. For Bee, the job had always come first. His balance scale had always tilted towards the office. There was no obvious example there for me to follow. Instead I turned to a few close colleagues—with the brilliant and discerning John Ferri proving particularly invaluable. Ferri would always argue that I should follow my instincts, insisting I should overcome my concerns of nepotism. In retrospect, it was not at all how one might have imagined someone striving to be boss. Yet, in many respects, it represented a culmination of my experiences as "son of."

As was his custom, Bee stayed out of my deliberations. "It is your decision to make," he would say once again. Ultimately, I decided I did want the job. Indeed, the more I thought about it, the more I felt this was the right decision. And I became more certain that if I turned it down, I would regret it deeply forever. I knew this would have huge implications for my relationship with Katherine, and it did. I told Galloway of my decision, and shortly thereafter the board of directors met to confirm my appointment as the sixth publisher in the *Star*'s history. I prepared very upbeat remarks, concluding with "This is a company with a rich tradition of leadership and a century of achievement. To continue that tradition and build on those achievements is a daunting responsibility. However, I welcome the challenge."

I left and the vote was taken. As I was told weeks later by the rather chagrined new board chair, Dr. John Evans, directors were shocked when one director voted against. That one was Bee. Not an abstention, but a "no." An abstention I would have understood. But a "no"? We never discussed it. Never. Nor did I ever hear his reasoning. But it stung—deeply. Indeed, in an ironic twist, the day after the vote, unaware of the voting composition, I wrote a note thanking Bee for his support and asking him out for a celebratory lunch. Years later, I would receive a call from Peter Newman asking if I was aware that my father had voted against my appointment. Did I have an explanation? he asked. An explanation was never forthcoming from Bee. Neither he nor I ever raised the subject. But from that point forward, I never again sought out his opinion on editorial changes to the paper. I had done so in the past, but no longer.

As the appointment was announced, scores of excited employees jammed my office for an impromptu champagne celebration. I was overjoyed with the reaction. That evening, however, I returned to a darkened house and a very, very long walk with the dog. With not much gusto, the nepotism angle also resurfaced—this time in *Toronto Life* magazine. Under the cover headline "Could Anyone but a Honderich Run the *Star*," the reporter postulated that Bee had cleverly orchestrated my appointment. Interestingly, there would not be one person going on record to support the theory. Board chair Evans, several others, and I all rebutted the argument. By now, it seemed my record spoke for itself.

About the same time, father–son relations would go through another twist as Bee's official retirement, after almost fifty-two years' total service, was to be made public. I wrote him a note arguing a story in the paper marking his outstanding career would be "appropriate." That was also the view of every editor, staffer, and senior executive I spoke with. Bee replied that he would prefer to retire "quietly" but added he would speak to a reporter "if you insist." I did, and veteran editor Gerry Hall was assigned. Bee, however, tried once again to stop the story, and I appealed directly to Jolley to approve its publication. It would be one of Jolley's last decisions as publisher and he agreed wholeheartedly the story should run. Bee would later write he was "sadly disappointed" his wishes had not been respected.

In my new role, my responsibilities increased dramatically, as I was now overseeing advertising, circulation, production, digital, and technology. As part of the executive team, I had been exposed to the major issues in each area—but now, I was in charge. My first step was to start a weekly Monday morning executive meeting at which the division heads were to be present. I insisted all were free to speak their minds. At first, they weren't sure if I meant it. But CEO Galloway would later say he could "sell tickets" to listen in on those meetings, which he heard were often vibrant, if not downright raucous. More importantly, a team spirit was grown.

Any thought of new initiatives ran smack into the financial realities of the business. The recession had wreaked its damage and the company was set in '94 to actually lose money. Ad revenues were off by a third from their peak, and newsprint prices had skyrocketed to double the price per tonne. Even worse, we were experiencing the first vestiges of the internet cutting into our classified revenues, a devastating trend that would only accelerate. I decided a dramatic reset was in order. It would be my first major move as publisher. Under the rubric of "SOS: sink or swim," we began a cross-company intense strategic exercise, under the guidance of David Pecaut and Joan Dey from the Boston Consulting Group, to come up with a new way of doing business. "The goal is to secure our future," I declared in a speech. "It is time to sink or swim. I have no intention of sinking." All seven of our unions were invited to join the process and they did.

After months of intense study, a draft of a new strategic plan emerged, with sixty-eight specific recommendations cutting across all departments of the paper. Changes were proposed for everything from a new commission sales system to a new blanket wash system for our presses, to a reduction of churn in circulation, to a revised press replating schedule, to the creation of a new business division, to an increase in commercial printing, to a dramatic increase in national advertising. In editorial, no item was too small. Should the food section be moved to Sunday? Should we bring back a new consumer service? Should we continue with our zoned sections? Should the *Star* use more stories from our community papers? How could we make the newsroom more diverse? Ultimately, many changes were implemented and new ways of operation took root. Coincidentally, this process took place at a time when both the economy and advertising rebounded strongly, resulting in a return to healthy profits. Over the next decade, we were able to record seven of the top ten years of financial performance at the paper. In my view, the SOS process played a huge role.

In editorial, I also decided a change in newsroom management was in order. Previously Bee had made such changes as a matter of course and with a frequency that often left heads spinning. And once an editor was replaced, he—and it always had been a "he"— would be sent packing. It was a practice I was intent on changing. Ian Urquhart had been managing editor of the newsroom for six years, a job often described as one of the most demanding in Canadian journalism. Again, it was my view that the ideal span for anyone at the helm of the *Star* newsroom was five years, but no longer. A fresh approach and new ideas were preferable after that. As a result, I instituted a five-year rule for any incoming managing editor. My new pick was *Star* veteran Lou Clancy, who was my national editor during my time in Ottawa. We shared the same approach to news, staffing, and life in general. I was confident we would work exceptionally well together—and we did.

The second change involved the outgoing managing editor. In virtually every case, these were talented editors who had worked their way tirelessly through the ranks only to see their careers ended abruptly. Could they not do something else at the paper? Urquhart presented the perfect test case. He had worked diligently as editor of the editorial page, national editor, and Ottawa bureau chief. We discussed possible options outside the newsroom, and after a brief university stint, he became our Queen's Park columnist, providing the must-read analysis of Ontario provincial politics for the next decade. It became a precedent I would use wherever possible.

The third change involved myself—and this one I have Bee to thank for. He always regretted "losing touch" with the newsroom, as he often put it. While his distance from it as publisher never stopped him from waltzing through or demanding changes, he was sensitive to upstaging the editor. I was determined my fate would be different. To this end, I entered the job of publisher as "editor" and decided never to cede that title in practice if not in fact. No announcement or big deal was ever made of it, nor did I ever use the title again. But, right from the outset, I would make it a daily practice to do a late afternoon visit to the newsroom to check on the next day's paper—just as I had done as editor. And I continued to be intimately involved in all staffing, strategic, and crusading issues. I would even periodically attend the weekly feature meetings as a "guest." And succeeding managing and executive editors all had to get used to receiving my fistful of papers with green pencil markup, highlighting mistakes, suggesting news follows, posing queries—and yes, even paying compliments. As a result, I could honestly say I never felt I "lost touch" with the newsroom.

And that proximity certainly came into play in '95 as the *Star* began planning for the trial of the serial rapist and murderer Paul Bernardo. Never before had the city, or for that matter the province, been so gripped by a gruesome criminal trial. Following on the heels of the sensational O.J. Simpson trial in the U.S., it was as if the long-established rules for coverage of a trial were being rewritten. Legions of reporters were expected, and even columnists were preparing to attend. That latter prospect resulted in a surprise telephone call from Mr. Justice Charles Dubin, head of Ontario's Court of Appeal. He wondered if we would be sending a columnist, to which I replied that Rosie DiManno would indeed be attending, along with her columnist colleague Christie Blatchford. He expressed concern, warning me that the writers must not form opinions or cross the legal line of contempt—a line more often mired in fog rather than clarity. He added, ominously, that he would be watching carefully.

His warning meant that for the entire trial, our legal counsel, Bert Bruser, and I would pore over DiManno's columns with her, line by line, for possible missteps. Was she forming a legal conclusion? Was she being fair? Was she going too far? To say those discussions sometimes got exercised doesn't quite capture DiManno's resolve. The practice of having legal counsel show up in our newsroom dated back decades. I would take it a step further, however, persuading Bruser to set up shop full time in the newsroom. As our drive towards more investigative reporting intensified, Bruser, who was a graduate of the Columbia School of Journalism, brought a combination of sage legal advice and natural journalistic skills that proved invaluable. He also became my most loyal and truest confidant. Ultimately, our coverage of the Bernardo trial was massive—but legal. In a private lunch much later, the affable and media-savvy trial judge Mr. Justice Pat LeSage said he had no complaints. And columnists have now become a mainstay of court coverage.

A few months later, a totally unexpected request arrived on my desk. Would I care to have a quiet, off-the-record lunch with the newly minted premier of Ontario, Mike Harris? If so, I was to pick the place and make it as discreet as possible. I opted for the small dining room in the out-of-the way Radisson Hotel on Toronto's waterfront. We met and Harris didn't waste any time. Armed with a study that promised $300 million in savings, he said he wanted to "move forward" on governance of the Toronto region, which the *Star* had been so loudly crusading for. "The whole region?" I asked. "No, only 416 [central Toronto]," he shot back, "because I promised 905 [suburban Toronto] at your debate I wouldn't move." Indeed, he had done precisely that at the *Star*'s '92 Royal York Hotel debate. He went on: "Unless I have the *Star*'s support, there is no way this will fly. It's what you stood for, but can I count on your support?" Harris and I were hardly natural political bedfellows, the *Star* having editorialized against his election. Yet here he was, a native of North Bay, determined to tackle a thorny Toronto issue that so many others had studiously avoided. His resolve was admirable. And while a total regional plan would have been preferable, the *Star* had been wholly in favour of creating an enlarged city of Toronto. Indeed, I had penned a front-page editorial entitled "A New Vision for Our Supercity" at the beginning of '95. "You can count on our support," I committed.

What followed became known as the "Megacity debate," in which ferocious opposition from the city's existing six boroughs poured forth. Most of the populace was opposed, with non-binding referenda resulting in "no" votes. But Harris was determined, as was the *Star*. We took to the battle with both editorials and ongoing features on the values of an integrated city. This is what the paper had championed for years, so our position was hardly a surprise. Yet the level of vitriol and ill feeling engendered was constant. At every social gathering, I could count on being accosted, most often in less-than-polite language. Ultimately the city was integrated, making the mayor of a united Toronto one of the strongest politicians in the country, elected directly by more citizens than any other politician in the land. Parenthetically, former Toronto mayor Barbara Hall, a fierce opponent, bet me $20 that Toronto's fabled neighbourhoods would be weaker ten years after amalgamation. I eagerly took the bet, arguing exactly the contrary. I was delighted when, a decade later, she voluntarily paid up.

The following year, the *Star* achieved its greatest editorial success ever, winning nine of fifteen possible National Newspaper Awards—a feat never achieved in the awards' history. What was so gratifying was the spectrum of winners—everything from spot news to critical writing, layout, feature photography, and column writing. For the third straight year, Rita Daly, Jane Armstrong, and Caroline Mallan won the Special Project award for the paper. Sports photographer Bernard

Weil won for his iconic shot of Canada's Donovan Bailey winning the 100 metres at the Atlanta Olympics. Business reporter Jonathan Ferguson won for his groundbreaking investigation into Steve Stavro's takeover of Maple Leaf Gardens. And our celebrated foreign correspondent Paul Watson won his fourth NNA for a series examining the horrors of Asia's sex trade. It was a night never to be forgotten.

It would be in mid-'97 that word leaked out—quite deliberately—that Conrad Black was indeed going to launch a new national daily, based in Toronto. To put this in perspective, over the previous half century only two other national newspapers had been launched—*USA Today* in the U.S. and *The Independent* in Britain. Moreover, success by any measure meant this new paper would be forced to make its mark in the huge Toronto market, where more newspapers were published than in any other city in North America.

While most observers concentrated on the other national paper, the *Globe and Mail*, as the primary target, I argued to one and all that, in order to succeed, the new paper would have to siphon off *Star* readers in Toronto. While our editorial philosophies would obviously be different, readership surveys showed a significant slice of readers were open to all papers. Those same surveys revealed we had significantly more readers with incomes above $100,000 than the *Globe*. Furthermore, we had the lion's share of exclusive readers who read only the *Star*. That huge number of exclusive readers, in turn, translated directly into our dominant advertising base. To me, the stakes were huge: our dominant position would be at risk. In his entertaining and encyclopedic book on the upcoming war, *Ego and Ink,* journalist Chris Cobb wrote that I was the first publisher to use the "newspaper war" metaphor, noting, "With his dramatic mix of war and sporting metaphors, Honderich made it clear he considered the *Star*'s dominance to be under attack, and that failing to prepare accordingly would be sleepwalking to disaster."

From my private conversations with *Globe* management, I came to learn that no expense would be spared in the upcoming fray. While we had more reporters, the *Globe*'s editorial budget ballooned to $48 million—$8 million above the *Star*'s—at the height of the war, according to Cobb. As part of our preparation, we organized a three-day retreat in Muskoka at the Clevelands House Resort to plan strategy. What emerged was a three-page document entitled "The Conditions for Winning," combined with an action plan of seventy-seven specific items covering all divisions. In many ways, I was using the same approach to motivate cross-company action that I had used in the SOS campaign. The Torstar board was also fully behind the approach, allocating $10 million extra to fight the war.

On the editorial side, the plan called for another more colourful *Star* redesign to be introduced six weeks before the launch of Black's paper, the name of which was still a mystery. To bolster our reputation as the voice and soul of Toronto, we also decided to create a separate new section every weekday, called GTA. To herald this launch, we commissioned a new branding campaign around the slogan "It's where you live." Coverage of the outer suburbs of Toronto was a key component of this new section. It was at this retreat that we also committed to do more investigative reporting and to expand coverage on what we called "our new visible majority." The benefits of those two initiatives would be felt for years.

One of my principal assignments was to ward off attacks on our "stars," which I fully expected. Sure enough, Black's soon-to-be editor, Ken Whyte, started a full court press to entice Rosie DiManno to join "this exciting new national adventure," as he described it. Whyte had chosen well, for the loss of DiManno and her signature Toronto column would have been devastating to the *Star*'s reputation, not to mention its effect on staff morale. A long and tortuous negotiation would ensue, much of it spent over red wine. But Rosie stayed.

Another critical area to buttress was our coverage of women's issues. For years, readership studies had revealed the *Star* was read equally by men and women, with women often the slight majority. None of our competitors was even close in its appeal to women. Again, our heritage tells part of the story. J.E. Atkinson's wife, Elmina Elliott, started the first redesigned women's page, writing under the pen name Madge Merton. She wrote on women's suffrage, pensions, and minimum wage. Described by Atkinson's biographer as being "a somewhat austere cast of character," she objected strenuously when her husband introduced the first page of comics. To her protests, he supposedly said, "My dear, I'm not running a Sunday school paper." To which she replied, "I rather wish you were." Through the years, a host of usually strong-willed women—Lotta Dempsey, Jessie McTaggart, Helen Palmer—forged their way in the male-dominated newsrooms. Editor Bonnie Cornell had recently reshaped the Life section into something more modern and hard-hitting, featuring the cutting-edge column of Michele Landsberg. We decided also to add feminist icon Doris Anderson to the roster. Promotion of this entire area of our coverage was given new priority.

The most unusual raids—believe it or not—involved attempts to lure away the *Star*'s eight switchboard operators, led by the inde-fatigable Linda Turner. Known in the newsroom simply as "switch-board," they were legendary in their ability to find anyone, anywhere, and at any time. They also delighted in tracking calls, ferreting out sensitive information, and playing the role of sleuth. Whyte knew only too well the exploits of "switchboard" and what their loss would mean to *Star* newsroom morale.

Consider these tales. Our scrappy Mexico reporter, Linda Diebel, needed to speak to someone for a story on Guatemalan coffee work-ers. She had a name but no telephone number. Switchboard tracked him down in London, U.K.—in a telephone box on a subway plat-form. Foreign editor Mike Pieri enlisted switchboard to find our grizzled correspondent Gerald Utting, lost in Uganda trying to inter-view Idi Amin. Switchboard found Utting's whereabouts in a blood-spattered Uganda prison, and put one of Amin's henchmen on the line for Pieri. Veteran columnist George Gamester wanted to speak to the world's most famous dancer—Fred Astaire. Switchboard found him playing rummy with his agent. Gamester also loves to tell the story of how he enlisted switchboard to track down a Cuban man with no phone, whose son had brought home a bottle he found washed ashore. It contained a note written by a Toronto man who had dropped it in the Atlantic Ocean twelve years before. Of course, switchboard found him. Such exploits were legendary and endless. Ultimately, I would spend many hours making the necessary adjustments, allowing us to keep all, save one. As newspaper war chronicler Cobb wrote, "It speaks volumes about the degree of sensitivities that the publisher of Canada's largest newspaper was to keep such close tabs on the movements of his switchboard operators."

In the summer before the official launch, Black made a brilliant strategic move to solidify his new paper's prospects. He bought Canada's established and highly regarded *Financial Post* from Sun Media. As part of the transaction, Sun Media acquired four profitable established dailies in Southern Ontario—the *Hamilton Spectator*, the *Kitchener-Waterloo Record*, the *Cambridge Reporter*, and the *Guelph Mercury*. For Black, the advantages were huge. In one fell swoop, he had eliminated a financial competitor while acquiring an established brand on which to shape his new paper. Not only that, but in return for selling the four dailies, he received $150 million from Sun Media— an ample war chest with which to wage the upcoming war. The *Post* also brought with it established reporters and columnists, allowing the paper to build a national weekday circulation of 100,000 and a Saturday circulation of 200,000. Suddenly, the credibility and prospects of the yet unborn paper rose dramatically. Rumours immediately began to swirl that the new paper would incorporate the established *Post* brand into its name. And, of course, it did.

Back at Torstar, we were in shock. The transaction caught us totally by surprise on more than one front. First, our fears of a fierce newspaper battle were wholly reinforced. But second, and more importantly, Torstar's strategic position in southern Ontario was unquestionably compromised, threatening our regional advertising and circulation dominance. Torstar had always gone to the lucrative southern Ontario market boasting of its much higher circulation, advertising, and promotional positions. That, in turn, had resulted in our securing a huge share of advertising at superior line rates. After the deal, Sun Media was able to boast—plain and simple—that it was bigger. With its four new dailies plus the *Toronto Sun*, the *London Free Press*, and a few small others, its combined daily circulation in the region rose to 580,000. The *Star*, by contrast, stood at 515,000. As Sun Media CEO Paul Godfrey declared, "We have always said we were in this business to grow, not remain static, and again we've proven it." The reality of those numbers was not lost at Torstar. Something had to give. The status quo was simply unacceptable.

As launch date for the *Post* neared, activity at the *Star* became frenetic. With our redesigned paper, our new GTA section, our new promotion campaign, and most importantly, all our stars in place, we were as ready as we could be for the *Post*. And, on the strategic side, we were about to make another move that would jolt the newspaper world, particularly in Toronto.

War on two fronts was about to begin.

16

TWO WARS

The headlines blew out in rapid-fire succession. On October 28, 1998, the *Star* front page read: "Black's New National Daily Draws Kudos, Complaints." The very next day, the headline blared: "Torstar Bids $748 Million for Sun Newspaper Chain." To say the buzz in Toronto's media circles whipsawed dramatically doesn't quite capture the shock or amazement. It was to be a hostile take-over bid involving two long-time, crosstown rivals whose style, size, and approach to journalism, not to mention their political and phil-osophical leanings, were about as diametrically opposed as one could imagine. No one doubted this battle would command front-row attention for the next while. For newspapers, who have always had a legendary delight in picking at the entrails of each other, this would be as delectable as it gets.

Meanwhile, the *Post* launched with much fanfare and hype, replete with exclusive interviews with such Canadian icons as Wayne Gretzky and Alanis Morissette, and a minor political scoop from Alberta. The *Star*, by contrast, had launched a hard-hitting series by Michelle Shephard on gang violence in schools. *Post* editor Ken Whyte penned a statement of intent for the new paper, which appeared to take dead aim at the *Globe* and made a side swipe at the *Star*. "We've had national business papers, and Toronto papers presuming to speak for the whole country, but we've never seen a paper founded to serve the nation as a whole," he wrote. There was predictable negativism on our side. But the *Post*'s stable of writers, its capacity for dramatic display, its access to superb foreign stories, and its eclectic story selection all combined to forge a formidable competitor. We knew we were in for a real battle.

As for the Torstar bid for Sun Media, the headline masked months of behind-the-scenes manoeuvring between the two companies, both intent on protecting their competitive position. For Torstar, the chart, "Who Owns Canada's Newspapers," accompanying the announcement on page one, told the story. Torstar had but one paper—the *Star*. Sun Media had fifteen and the Thomson empire had six plus the *Globe and Mail*, while Conrad Black had fifty-seven. For quite some time, CEO David Galloway had privately been warning that Torstar needed to seek out partners or deals in order to survive. Trying to make it alone—with only one paper—was not a tenable long-run strategy. That concern turned to near panic when Black suddenly sold those four Ontario dailies to Sun Media in return for the *Financial Post*, thus giving Sun Media greater regional circulation, advertising, and promotional power than the *Star*.

It was in fact the *Sun*, in the person of one-time *Star* sports columnist and now Sun Media vice president Wayne Parrish, who made the initial move to me several months before the *Financial Post* deal. He and I had kept up over the years, sharing the same passion for journalism and inside newspaper dope. At a cozy afternoon drinks in the cushy lobby bar of the King Edward Hotel, we talked of a possible merger of the *Sun*'s Canoe website with the *Star*'s toronto.com. At the end of the discussion, Parrish asked, almost parenthetically, whether we had ever considered bringing the two companies together. If we were interested, he added, Galloway should meet with *Sun* CEO Paul Godfrey. I dutifully took the message back, and shortly thereafter, Galloway paid a visit to Godfrey. At that meeting, Godfrey would say later, Galloway promised never to "go hostile." After that, Parrish and I met several times, hashing out terms of a possible merger. Indeed, the very morning the *Financial Post* deal was revealed, Parrish telephoned to reassure me our talks should continue. Ultimately, the sticking points were Godfrey's insistence on being board chair and his desire for Torstar voting stock. On October 5, I paid a personal visit to Parrish's executive office—bow tie and all—explaining how Torstar could not meet these demands. Later, it became known that my visit did not go unnoticed by *Sun* staffers. It would be a short twenty-four days later that Torstar launched its hostile bid.

Right from the outset, the media coverage and reaction, particularly from *Sun* reporters and columnists, was brutal. Despite our insistence the *Sun* would operate independently from the *Star*, the writings from their staff were universally and virulently negative. Day after day, *Sun* headlines screamed "Hands Off Our *Sun*" or "The *Star* Can't Destroy Our Spirit" or "Bow Tie Boy *Sun*-Burned." Godfrey was particularly aggressive in attacking Galloway for breaking his alleged "no hostility" promise. He also rallied local advertisers very assertively to express their concerns to the federal Competition Bureau. In fact, the bureau would later advise us offline that their required approval for our proposed deal was highly problematic. Both Godfrey and Parrish also denied that my six chats with Parrish were in any way about a merger, their staff and board being enraged their bosses had been cavorting with the enemy. Of course, I had detailed notes of each meeting and decided to go public with the particulars. That only intensified the crossfire. Years later, Parrish quietly apologized, admitting he was "forced" to deny what had unfolded.

Ultimately, Quebecor media czar Pierre Karl Péladeau came forth with a $983 million all-cash bid for the *Sun*, effectively leaving Torstar in the dust. Hailed as a daring white knight by those same *Sun* staffers—"Quebec Titan Rides to *Sun* Rescue"—Péladeau and Quebecor CEO Charles Cavell went to the atrium in *Sun* headquarters to celebrate their new acquisition. Both Péladeau and

Godfrey boasted to the ecstatic gathering about the size and dazzling future of this new company. What Godfrey and Parrish weren't told, however, was that a few hours later, Péladeau phoned Galloway asking if Torstar might be interested in buying some of its newly acquired Ontario papers. As it turned out, the cost of being a white knight was a bit too rich for the Quebecers, thus driving them to reduce their debt load. The notion that such dealing might infuriate their new *Sun* colleagues, I am confident, never crossed their minds.

The first negotiation among Péladeau, Cavell, Galloway, and me took place in one of those antiseptic yellow suites, named after a province, in the Royal York Hotel. Cavell had prepared a road map of Ontario, with all of Quebecor's papers marked with red pins and all of Torstar's daily and community papers marked with blue pins. Noting that most of Quebecor's red pins were in western Ontario, Cavell slammed his arm down on the map, proclaiming, "You can take these," pointing to three dailies east of his shirt sleeve: the *Hamilton Spectator*, the *Guelph Mercury*, and the *Cambridge Reporter*. Quixotically caught under his arm was the prize of the *Kitchener-Waterloo Record*. Galloway asked about the *London Free Press*, but there was no budge. I pushed about Kitchener-Waterloo, aware of the dramatic potential of this market and very mindful of my family connection. After a rather short negotiation, we secured ownership of the *Record*, much to our delight. It might be said the Quebecor duo's knowledge of the overall Ontario market was sparse at best. Godfrey was never part of these talks. "He doesn't have to be involved," Péladeau told us dismissively. Instead, he would be summarily summoned to Montreal the night before the $350 million deal was announced.

It would be expensive, but in one fell swoop the acquisition of four new dailies meant Torstar's dominance in the region was restored. In a bitter twist of irony, it was also not lost on commentators that these four papers were the same ones Black ceded to secure the *Financial Post*. Both the Torstar board and I were ultimately very pleased with the final outcome, our strategic goal now assured. Nor was it lost on us that securing Competition Bureau approval of our bid to take over the *Sun* had become next to impossible. Galloway, on the other hand, felt he had lost the battle. In accordance with its reputation, Quebecor threatened at the last minute to scuttle our deal. We had agreed, as part of the original deal, to help with circulation delivery of the *Sunday Sun* but had balked at doing the same for the weekday papers. Up to that point, the *Toronto Sun* was only available for sale at boxes. Providing home delivery for the weekday *Sun*, we felt, was not a competitive advantage we were prepared to hand over. At a hastily called drinks session at the Four Seasons Hotel bar, the notoriously hard-nosed Cavell dispensed with pleasantries to tell me the deal was off unless we delivered the weekday *Sun*. I replied, in kind, that this was not possible. He threatened again. I stood up, declaring, "I think this conversation is over." But the deal went through, with Torstar standing firm.

For the next couple of months, I had the rewarding job of bringing the four new papers into the Torstar web. When Sun Media had bought these same papers a scant six months before, their executives had shown up in fancy limos, showily displaying the power of the *Sun*. That approach had evoked critical local comment and I decided to do things much differently. On a snowy January day, I headed out early—alone—insisting I would drive to each paper. And at all four locations I held a town hall declaring each paper would continue to be responsible for its own content, with no forced editorial directives from Toronto. The afternoon meeting in Kitchener was particularly poignant given Bee's early stint at the *Record*. Hardly anyone at the meeting was aware of the historical connection—or, for that matter, seemed particularly interested in it. Meanwhile, Sun Media staff were beginning to learn what their new Quebec owners had in store for them. At the formal announcement of the new deal in Montreal, Godfrey had to deliver the distasteful news that 180 *Sun* staff were being laid off immediately, including the paper's editor and chief financial officer. That would be only the beginning. Quebecor would exact many more cuts, ensuring the *Sun* would never be the same bustling, boisterous competitor. Indeed, as many *Sun* staffers would later confide to me, the paper would probably have been much better off under *Star* control. That had always been my view.

With the corporate fireworks now over, we could turn our attention to battling the *Post*, which was brimming with confidence after all its positive reviews. My main objective was to do everything to show we were maintaining our dominance in readership, circulation, and advertising. For each of these three categories, there would be periodic reports throughout the year, recording the ups and downs. Any twist or unusual swing would undoubtedly spark great media coverage. As I would say over and over, "The first rule of war is to win." It was essential we maintain that storyline. I also instituted the practice of printing periodic "Dispatches from the Newspaper Wars" for internal consumption, fully aware they would leak outside. At every board meeting, chair John Evans would always ask if we had lost any stars. And I was always able to reply in the negative. Not that some editors and reporters did not cross over. A few did—but none of our stars.

Globe publisher Phillip Crawley and I also committed to stay in close touch, our common enemy being the *Post*. Following celebrated stints in New Zealand and at the *South China Morning Post*, Crawley had been recruited to succeed the affable but less forceful Roger Parkinson as CEO and publisher of the *Globe*. Throughout the years, Crawley and I had always worked well together on newspaper boards, particularly that of the Canadian Press. I admired his competitive spirit and newspaper savvy, each of us having raided the other's stable from time to time. Yet you only had to visit Crawley's office to know what a competitor he was. There on his wall was the photo of a rather short man in rugby gear, staring ahead defiantly on a north England pitch. As Black would soon discover, Crawley also knew how to wage a newspaper war.

Ultimately, it would be superior journalism that would make the difference. The *Post* was definitely a high-quality competitor, offering a broad range of stories and commentary displayed in full grandeur. Crawley opened the coffers to expand his coverage and spark the *Globe* to new heights. At each paper, the mission was the same— be more creative and invest more. As Black told Cobb with trademark sarcasm, "The *Post* gelignited the fetid little media log-rolling and back scratching society in Toronto." Amid all this hype, where could we make a difference?

For me, continuing to provide groundbreaking investigative journalism was the answer, along with reaffirming our role as the sole voice of Toronto and region. With the advent of cable and digital news, newspapers were already struggling to stay on top. We used to say we were already out of date the moment we put the paper to bed on the presses. Not only would radio stations read our stories first the next morning, but subsequent news events and updates would always appear first on websites and electronic media. We used to call this phenomenon "rip 'n' read," meaning the best news source for most local radio stations would be a subscription to the *Star*, which then could be ripped into snippets and read on air—sometimes word for word.

While newspapers may no longer have had the edge on breaking news, that never stopped us from unloading the full resources of the *Star*'s newsroom on big stories or disasters. The tragic death of Princess Diana in a Paris car crash, for example, sparked huge special sections and page after page of heart-rending stories. For the 9/11 attack on New York's World Trade Center, we decided to rush out a special afternoon edition of the paper, complete with dramatic photos and as much detail as we had. Indeed, Rosie DiManno managed to sneak across the border and begin filing from New York. Whether covering wars, disasters, breaking news, or great sporting events, Rosie always made it her business to be there. For this particular special edition, we had to recall our pressmen to work another shift. Volunteer staffers were also sent out to distribute the free paper downtown to commuters heading home. It would be our most widely distributed single-copy edition ever.

While such efforts reaffirmed our traditional role of going the extra mile, it was not enough. I felt strongly we had to offer surprises—stories and investigations you would not find elsewhere. And if those stories revealed malfeasance, neglect, or wrongdoing, so much the better. The Michener Award for public service journalism is indisputably the highest journalism prize in the country. Established under the auspices of a former governor general, it is open to all media in Canada, and it celebrates stories, broadcasts, or podcasts that make a significant difference, such as a change in public policy. I felt all our investigations should aspire to this level. And I am proud to say that when my tenure as publisher ended, the *Star* had been nominated for thirteen consecutive Micheners.

That list of nominees illustrates the breadth and import of those investigations. In '97, we received a nomination for a series on the tragedy of youth unemployment for which more than one thousand young people were interviewed. It was cited by then Finance Minister Paul Martin has having influenced the contents of his 1998 budget. The following year we won the award for Scott Simmie's searing and very personal look at Ontario's fragile mental health system. The next year, the nomination came for a groundbreaking series on the daily struggles of children—the most innocent victims of poverty—surviving on welfare in Toronto. A year later, a series by renowned investigative reporters Robert Cribb, Laurie Monsebraaten, and Rita Daly won a nomination for a series on how Ontario's medical regulatory system failed to discipline doctors who harm patients. Throughout her career, Monsebraaten earned widespread acclaim for her ongoing stories on Toronto's social welfare system, epitomizing the paper's continuing commitment to the Atkinson Principles. In my final year as publisher, the *Star* received two nominations, one for "Broken Homes," a disquieting series revealing deficiencies throughout

Toronto's low-income housing projects, and a second for a series by Moira Welsh on the abuse and mistreatment of seniors in the province's nursing homes. Welsh was another stalwart whose constant scrutiny of nursing homes brought many investigative scoops.

Perhaps the most significant Michener win, and one of which I am particularly proud, was a 2002 series by a team of *Star* journalists and researchers led by Jim Rankin on racial profiling in the Toronto police force. For years, studies and inquiries had intimated the widespread prevalence of profiling, but hard evidence to back it up had not been found. As a long-time crime and police reporter, Rankin came across a police press release that accidentally referred to a suspect described as having "yellow" skin, which Rankin learned was a skin colour code for people of Southeast Asian background. That in turn led to the discovery of internal police databases that recorded skin colour, including one that documented all arrests and charges laid. After spending a year and tens of thousands of dollars to get access to the database, with the police fighting us every inch of the way, Rankin and *Star* database specialists spent a summer examining and analyzing the data, and brought in an expert on statistics, who backed up their methodology prior to publication. They found absolute proof that police systemically discriminated against people of colour, particularly Black Canadians, on minor drug charges and motor vehicle offences. The series caused a huge uproar. The city's police board and mayor all came to the paper to protest. Police chief Julian Fantino accused the *Star* of using "junk science," and the police union sued us for libel all the way to the Supreme Court of Canada. We won convincingly and unanimously at every level, and, more importantly, racial profiling in police was now taken as fact. We had proven it.

When it comes to investigative reporting at the *Star*, the name Kevin Donovan most often comes to mind. Donovan first earned his spurs as a special war correspondent in both Iraq and Afghanistan. Behind the cheery smile and seemingly easygoing demeanour lies one determined, take-no-prisoners reporter whose focus on getting the story is unmatched. While his escapades are many, during the newspaper war he cut his swath through Canada's charities sector, exposing many for spending more on fundraising and office costs than on good works. Throughout his career, Donovan, although not trained as a lawyer, has also been prepared to go to court himself to argue fine points of law. Indeed, his success rate in legal battles is high. He would later earn international acclaim for his investigation of Toronto's notorious mayor, Rob Ford. After that, his tenacity in searching for clues in the still unsolved murders of drug company magnate Barry Sherman and his wife Honey earned him headlines everywhere.

The search for new voices continued throughout the war. Gone was my previous term "pre-eminent hire," replaced by the new "marquee hire." On the political front, perhaps one of my proudest acquisitions was Chantal Hébert, the franco-Ontarian whose political analyses and searing commentary had made her a fixture on the federal scene. Hébert told me she was the first native francophone ever to be hired as a columnist by an English-speaking newspaper, a particular point of pride for us both. On the provincial front, we lured from the *Post* the indefatigable Robert Benzie, whose subsequent pursuit of Ontario premiers has been relentless. As a guest columnist, we took on veteran Graham Fraser, whose knowledge of Quebec political life is encyclopedic. On the business side, we enticed both Jennifer Wells and David Olive to join. On the arts and entertainment side, we hired noted culture columnist Martin Knelman, feature writer Oakland Ross, and playwright and theatre critic Richard Ouzounian. For investigative reporting, we hired David Bruser (son of long-time *Star* lawyer Bert Bruser), who went on to win four national investigative awards.

Another major tenet of our strategy was to reinforce our obvious advantage as the paper of Toronto. The new executive managing editor and former *Ottawa Citizen* editor, Jim Travers, took to this challenge with trademark gusto. An exceptionally talented journalist,

Travers was brought in to replace Lou Clancy, who stepped down after a successful stint running the newsroom. And in accordance with my new policy of finding new positions for departing senior editors, Clancy was granted an academic leave of absence before heading out to run the newsroom at the *Record*. The centrepiece of our local strategy was the creation of a separate GTA section, chock full of stories that appeared nowhere else. Travers also developed a much broader Ontario paper, with stories from around the Golden Horseshoe. As Travers told Cobb, "We were always going to be the Voice of the Leafs, the Voice of the Jays, Voice of the Raptors and Voice of the Argos. They [competitors] could never match us in terms of the size of the staff and size of the coverage." Sadly for Travers, his difficulties in adapting to the *Star* newsroom and culture, combined with ongoing health issues, brought about a need for change. Again, in accordance with my new policy, he returned to Ottawa as our parliamentary columnist, joining Hébert to form an unmatched duo for insightful federal commentary.

To carry on the editorial battle, I turned to my one-time boss, newsroom veteran Mary Deanne Shears, known throughout the newsroom as MDS. The first woman ever to head editorial, MDS brought to the job her trademark drive and a withering disdain for perceived slowness or incompetence. She had joined the paper as a reporter and had worked her way up through the editing ranks, excelling in every post she occupied. Famous for her fuchsia or canary yellow hair, she could energize the newsroom in a flash. And as far as she was concerned, getting the news today was not fast enough.

Shears had been totally involved with Travers in planning for the war, and so didn't miss a beat in her new job. She also expanded another priority in our coverage, putting a greater emphasis on exploring the ins and outs of the city's diverse communities. Both as editorial page editor and editor emeritus, Haroon Siddiqui was appropriately relentless in reminding us that visible minorities would soon become a majority of the city's population. His prompting spurred self-interrogation: Did the paper reflect this? Did our photos reflect this? Did we cover these communities? Who should cover them? Certainly, neither of our major competitors in the war spent much, if any, time on such issues. It was also important that we remember the *Star*'s history on what was once called "multiculturalism." Bee often told me it was the paper's open coverage of the city's new Italian immigrant community that proved critical in the battle with the *Telegram* back in the '60s. In '86, feature reporter Olivia Ward won a Michener for her eight-part series on "ethnic minorities," after spending three months interviewing 1,400 new Canadians. We had a history and tradition of being the paper for new Canadians. We could never do enough.

To add to these initiatives, I decided, building on previous Toronto crusades, that the paper should launch a new crusade for a "new deal for cities." Citing the ongoing crises in affordable housing and in funding for transit and social welfare systems, I penned a page one editorial urging Canadian cities be given more powers and respect. Any new deal must involve fundamental changes in government structure and finances, I declared. No longer should large metropolitan cities be deemed mere "creatures of the provinces"—as had been past practice—but rather they needed to be seen as distinct power centres with legitimate needs requiring attention. The crusade ran for several years.

Most importantly, it caught the particular attention of three notable federal politicians—Prime Minister Paul Martin, Reform leader Preston Manning, and soon-to-be NDP leader Jack Layton. As president of the Federation of Canadian Municipalities, Layton had championed the cause, borrowing on his experience as a Toronto councillor. I always found the future NDP leader to be one of the most creative policy thinkers on the public scene. We collaborated often and the *Star* editorially supported his unsuccessful 1991 mayoral run. My relationship with Manning was a completely different story. Our paths had never crossed—our political outlooks being rather divergent—but he called asking to see me to discuss the "cities crusade," and we spent several hours in thoughtful conversation.

Martin and I had discussed the cities agenda often, and he understood the issue to its core. That interest culminated in a private lunch at the fashionable North York restaurant Auberge du Pommier, where Martin asked whether I would run for the Liberals in the next federal election. As I would tell him later, "The earth didn't move." I explained I had always resisted running for office, for I felt I could do much more to shape public policy as publisher of the *Star* than as a member of Parliament. It would be the same answer I provided to Liberal strategist Senator Keith "the Rainmaker" Davey—whose father coincidentally had run the *Star*'s pressroom—in response to his periodic requests to run. Neither of them took issue with my logic.

Parenthetically, in my position as editor and publisher, I had always made it a practice to reach out to every newly elected prime minister, premier of Ontario, and mayor of Toronto to set up a separate, direct line of communication. The purpose was not to allow interference in the *Star*'s reporting but rather to provide a forum to discuss issues privately, should that be necessary. Responses varied across the spectrum. Of the prime ministers, Brian Mulroney easily called the most, though I had many conversations with Martin and Chrétien too. On the other hand, I never met or even spoke once with Stephen Harper. Of the Ontario premiers, Dalton McGuinty and Kathleen Wynne called most often, with long-serving premier Bill Davis carrying on the relationship the longest. My communication with mayors was, as might be expected, much more regular, with Mel Lastman, for example, calling often. By far the most emotional encounter was an unexpected personal visit by a sobbing Lastman who begged unsuccessfully to have a story on the arrest of his wife Marilyn for shoplifting killed, even though police had already made the arrest public.

Meanwhile, in the newspaper war, the battle for circulation was only escalating. The *Post*'s first publisher, celebrated newspaperman

Don Babick, later acknowledged that the paper was seeking one hundred thousand subscribers or readers in the GTA. They didn't have to be paying purchasers, but rather should be regular readers verified by readership surveys. Only with such an audience could the *Post* support its advertising rates. In the trade, this is known as getting eyeballs. And Black's agents left no stone unturned in flooding the Toronto market with free copies. In airport lounges, for example, the *Post* and *Globe* had to outbid each other to have their papers displayed exclusively. In his book, Cobb estimated that almost a quarter of a million free copies of the *Post* were handed out across the land. He noted that, particularly in Toronto, the giveaways were everywhere, "making the effort of actually purchasing [a paper] an act of extravagance, stupidity or charity."

Nor can it be said the *Post* was the only competitor resorting to such tactics. Both the *Globe* and *Star* were equally ferocious in keeping their readership numbers up. I was determined that every readership and circulation survey show the *Star* as holding its own. And the stories in each of the papers reporting on such surveys always seemed to accentuate each paper's positives and its enemies' negatives, prompting much derision in journalistic circles. But maintaining our front-runner momentum was critical. So we too flooded coffee shops, gas stations, car washes, donut shops, and university and college campuses with free copies. We were open to all ideas, and so was the *Globe*. Ultimately, it is estimated this battle would cost the three dailies more than $1 billion, a truly staggering amount. But if Black's strategy was that his opponents would wither under the attack, he was to be sorely disappointed.

It would be late August 2001 when the bombshell dropped. Black was selling all his papers, the *Post* included, to Canwest Global's Izzy Asper. Many *Post* staffers felt fundamentally betrayed, their dedication to this new national dream now smashed on the shoals of financial reality. Black's debt load was unsustainable and the costs of fighting the war too great. Furthermore, those readership and circulation surveys had not budged much. The *Globe*, in particular, under Crawley's strategic guidance, had rebounded strongly after the *Post*'s initial bounce. The *Star*'s dominance in the GTA market was unchallenged. In a chance encounter later with *Globe* owner Ken Thomson, I asked whether he thought Black's fundamental error had been underestimating Thomson's determination to fight. Thomson paused, then replied, a slight smile on his face, "I have rather thought so."

With the newspaper war now subsiding somewhat, everyone was looking forward to more normalized competition when a shock decision from the Ontario Labour Relations Board threw us into an instant panic. The union representing the paper's 2,200 paper carriers—who delivered papers every day for a few hours in early morning—sought a declaration that the carriers were "employees," thereby entitling them to union representation and a collective agreement. Our lawyers expressed their confidence that these "part-timers" would not qualify, leaving us totally complacent and unprepared. Then the decision dropped. Not only did the carriers win, but their union started the clock ticking to a strike deadline only a month away. Only twice before in North American newspaper history—in Winnipeg and San Jose, California—had carriers gone on strike. In both cases, they won double-digit pay hikes when those papers were unable to get papers to subscribers' homes. After a rushed round of deliberations, we decided to fight. It was nothing less than a bet-the-business decision. However, another huge increase in our circulation costs would not only put us at a competitive disadvantage but also endanger our overall financial position. Indeed, that was the principal argument I used to the Torstar board in justifying our strategy. Fighting unionism and these particular workers might seem inconsistent with the Atkinson Principles, but our very existence in the crowded Toronto market was at risk.

The first step was ensuring all seven unions were with us. If they struck, particularly the pressmen, success was not possible. To complicate matters, the union representing the carriers was also our largest, representing more than a thousand employees in advertising, circulation, finance, and editorial. I led a blitz of meetings in which we ultimately secured promises of co-operation from all seven unions. In short, they recognized what was at stake. Meanwhile, under the tutelage of one-time photo editor Brad Henderson, a veteran of operational planning during other strikes, we came up with an action plan. There were no precedents to follow. We had to come up with our own.

The strike hotspots became forty-three plaza parking lots around Toronto, where trucks would normally drop bundles of papers in the early-morning hours for carriers to deliver. We assigned three *Star* management employees—only men, to the distinct consternation of a few women managers—to each plaza, where they attempted to persuade the strikers to return to work. Their efforts paid off, and although we did hire outside carriers, some of the original 2,200 opted to continue working for the paper. There were scuffles every night and police would often be called to intervene. It would take three weeks, but we finally prevailed. The heroism and determination of those managers was the deciding factor.

There is no doubt this strike represented my greatest challenge as publisher. Motivating the troops and making daily strategic decisions while running the paper and overseeing outside communications took every ounce of energy I had. Like the other managers, I would also hand-deliver late papers to subscribers on weekends. In one much recounted incident, a *Star* subscriber in a north Yonge Street condo told me she wouldn't accept the paper "unless it comes from the guy in the bow tie." Raising my *Star* cap, I told her laughingly, "You're talking right to him!"

While the turmoil seemed non-stop, it did not end at the office door. Life at home became more and more tumultuous in the years following my appointment as publisher. Katherine wanted nothing to do with anything involving the *Star*. If any conversation in social circles veered to talk of the paper, she became instantly off-put. No *Star* gathering was ever held at our home. It seemed we had grown very far apart. A relationship involving two high-profile writers— one a novelist and the other a newspaper publisher—is bound to be riven with competitive tension. In courtship, I had pledged to be equally involved in raising the children, but that became more and more problematic as the demands of being editor and publisher mounted. Though I was fully committed to supporting Katherine's career as a writer, I rarely sensed a reciprocal effort.

Five years earlier, we'd had a trial separation that lasted most of the year. One of the final sparks for that decision occurred the very night U.S. president George H.W. Bush launched his assault on Baghdad, eventually starting the Persian Gulf War. A critical marriage counselling meeting had been set for that same evening. I had stayed at the office until the very last moment, keenly aware we had several war correspondents in the field. As I drove to the session, I heard on radio the Baghdad blitz had begun. I immediately turned back to the office, driven by my gut feeling that, as editor, I must be as close to the scene as possible. Such work-related choices became more and more regular, leading to even more disquiet on the home front.

During that trial separation, I worked on my own with a counsellor to deal with unresolved anger issues, much of it related to my earlier-life relationship with Bee. Upon returning to our home, Katherine and I did try to work out rules of engagement. They helped, but ultimately the battle over my decision to become publisher and the consequent work pressures took their cumulative toll. It was my decision to leave, but I had learned my lesson carefully from four decades before. We gathered both kids, now fifteen and fourteen, at the kitchen table to reveal the news and the plans going forward. It was essential that they hear it from me directly. And they did.

Near the end of 2003, I felt it was time to celebrate a successful newspaper war well waged. We rented a large space in Toronto's historic Distillery District and invited staff, directors, major advertisers, and Toronto's newly elected mayor, David Miller, whom we had endorsed, to celebrate. Attached to the walls were charts showing how we had maintained both readership and circulation levels throughout the five years. In a very upbeat address, I also made a point of emphasizing how we had maintained our dominance in the Toronto market while remaining true to our social justice roots. It was a glorious celebration.

Back at the paper, however, the strategic push was on to build up other parts of the business to help support the *Star*. Having concentrated so much of our energy on the paper and the war, we now needed to turn our attention elsewhere.

17

METRO IS BORN

We certainly didn't begin with a master plan to create a cross-Canada network of transit papers, though a decade later, that would be the outcome. Like other unimagined breakthroughs, the initial rationale for the first *Metro* in Canada was decidedly less ambitious. As part of the SOS strategic review, the decision was made for the *Star* to look for new outside opportunities, building on our brand. Similarly, we were always looking for ways to solidify our position in the crowded Toronto newspaper market. With *Metro*, there were both defensive and offensive elements that led us to the final decision. Protecting the *Star* always topped the list. Staying one step ahead of our competitors in the ferocious Toronto newspaper market ran a close second. Ultimately, the saga of *Metro*'s birth revealed both the challenges facing newspapers at the turn of the century and the often dramatic steps taken to confront that precarious future.

As a somewhat grizzled newshound, with now a quarter century in the business, I saw my greatest challenge as coming to grips with the potential decline of the *Star*. The internet had already begun exacting its toll on the paper's advertising revenues. A host of small, niche publications had sprung up, snatching sectors of ads. And internationally, a new phenomenon—transit-only tabloids—was emerging. When newspapering has been in your blood a long time, it's almost as if its ongoing existence becomes axiomatic. Up to this point, conversations between Bee and me on the subject had been surprisingly scant. Protecting the *Star* was, of course, his paramount concern. Yet I was fully aware of those haunting accounts of senior executives in dying industries clinging desperately to the past as the future slipped away. Even though the energy and vitality we had recently shown in the great newspaper war with the *Post* were palpable, the warning signs of seminal change were more compelling.

Year after year of industry research showed a consistent and worrisome decline in newspaper readership, particularly among younger cohorts. Alternatives to newspaper advertising were cropping up everywhere. For example, I could remember my days as business editor, when we ran business sections with up to twenty-four pages of careers advertising. At the peak, that category alone brought in almost $75 million in annual revenue. Now it was fast seeping away to the internet. Indeed, this was the force that drove *Globe and Mail* publisher Phillip Crawley and me to bury a century-old rivalry and unite to create the online jobs site Workopolis. Similarly, the bulwark of daily newspaper ad revenue, classified ads, was following a downward path. Every day, we used to be able to count on at least thirty-five to forty full pages of such ads. "Don't ever forget that pays for a lot of your reporters," the ever-wise composing room superintendent Al Surminsky would constantly remind me. I never forgot. The days when department stores such as Eaton's or Simpsons "owned" the back page of the first section had long passed, along with any regular advertising from local food chains. Glossy inserts had become the vehicle of choice for many advertisers, who preferred the total market coverage guaranteed by our community papers.

In the early 2000s, every strategy session began with a discussion of the threat posed by the internet, both to readership numbers and advertising. If we didn't worry about it, Torstar director, fellow voting trustee, and Duke economics professor Cam Harvey would. Something of a digital guru, Harvey consistently and persistently warned about the "readership cliff" newspapers were about to confront. Many a board session was spent trying to convince him otherwise. There might be a cliff, but it would be more than a few years coming, we would argue. Up to then, we had been right. But Harvey's warnings never ceased.

The turning point for me came in a business case presentation on the fabled U.S. magazine *Sports Illustrated*. The original magazine was beginning to suffer from the same loss of readership and advertising that had plagued large metropolitan newspapers. The trend was unmistakable and consistent. So the magazine's executives came up with a new strategic plan, whose essence was to spin out new magazines, CDs, and products all linked to the gold-plated brand of the original. The development of a host of products, most notably the swimsuit issue, was the outcome of this strategy, bringing a new era of prosperity to the company. How could a similar approach work for another gold-plated brand—the *Toronto Star*? The logic of such a strategy seemed inescapable. So the first step for us was to create a business ventures division, dedicated to creating new but related businesses.

Finding the right person to oversee this division was critical. And that person just happened to be Andrew Go, my right-hand man in advertising. An ethnically Chinese native of the Philippines, Go would in all likelihood have spent his life running his family's newspapers in Manila had the family not run afoul of former president Ferdinand Marcos. Driven out of the country, Go ended up in Toronto, where he was eventually brought on by Bee, a hiring of particular pride for both. Go is a brilliant salesman and strategist who had an uncanny knack for always coming up with "win/win" solutions to problems. This creativity, combined with his entrepreneurial flair, propelled him through the ranks of advertising to the top spot. We had always worked well together, first while I was business editor and later during my time as editor. We collaborated in the early '90s to launch *eye* magazine, Torstar's entertainment weekly designed to combat the growing advertising power of *NOW* magazine. He became *eye*'s first publisher, a title he enjoyed immensely. It was under Go's urging that I became the first editor ever to address the advertising department at its annual kick-off event. Given the white-bread, conservative, button-down cliquishness of ad sales types, Go was never "one of the boys." But to me he was always "Andrew"—smart, reliable, strategic, and totally trustworthy.

Thrown into his new role, Go immersed himself quickly and returned to our weekly executive meetings with new ideas. His first triumph came with an innovative partnership deal hammered out with *Sing Tao* newspapers of Hong Kong. We had often talked in strategy sessions about entering the "ethnic" newspaper market in Toronto, but we had never quite figured out how or where. With this deal, we were propelled instantly into a leading position in the thriving and highly competitive Chinese-language newspaper market. *Sing Tao*'s Canadian newspapers, as well as those of its principal competitor, *Ming Pao*, were owned 100 per cent by their Hong Kong parents, in flagrant violation of Canada's laws restricting foreign ownership of Canadian newspapers. This was just the critical bargaining lever Go needed to open up negotiations with Sally Aw, the mercurial and crusty matriarch of *Sing Tao*.

A multi-millionaire many times over, Aw treated her foreign papers like she was a protective mother hen. Unbeknownst to us, her senior managers in Hong Kong had been habitually dumping thousands of copies of their paper into the South China Sea, in a desperate attempt to inflate circulation numbers. Aw later denied any knowledge of the dumping; however, several of her associates would ultimately end up behind bars. In her negotiation with us, her major concern was loss of control. But Go never gave up. He kept reminding her about the Canadian law and was also able to offer the *Star*'s editorial content as a carrot. Since *Sing Tao* and *Ming Pao* were engaged in fierce competition for hegemony in the Toronto market, the prospect of superior local news content was appealing.

My role was primarily one of schmoozer, reassuring Aw that we were intent on being first-rate partners. Over one multi-course lunch at her corporate headquarters overlooking Hong Kong's old airport in 1997—happily coinciding with the formalities of the Hong Kong handover—we toasted a new relationship. I thought we were set. Yet it would be another six months and $20 million before the deal was finally sealed. "We basically walked in and were able to come out full partners," Andrew would later boast, cracking a telltale wry grin. A decade later, our *Sing Tao* partnership would become the undisputed number one Chinese-language newspaper group in the country, with papers in Toronto, Vancouver, and Calgary. And the financial return on that initial $20 million turned out to be very handsome, to say the least.

It would be at another of our weekly Monday morning executive sessions in late 1999 that Go first raised the prospect of the *Star* launching its own free transit paper. The immediate howls of protest, mine included, that such a paper would obviously cannibalize the mighty *Star* were almost predictable. After all, wasn't our number one priority still fighting the great newspaper war? Wasn't Toronto still one of North America's most competitive newspaper markets, with four dailies? How could there possibly be room for one more?

Go, however, was not to be deterred. He returned a few weeks later with the tale of how a brash new Swedish company, *Metro*, had completely turned the Swedish newspaper market upside down with its free transit papers. Indeed, in the super-competitive market of Stockholm, *Metro* had rocketed to second place in circulation in a remarkably short period of time. Moreover, *Metro* had brazenly boasted of plans to expand worldwide, with Philadelphia being its first point of entry in North America. *Metro* openly broadcast that it would move first to cities with well-integrated subway and transit systems. That, Go argued, meant that Toronto had to be high on its list. Then, to complete his case, he imagined a "fighting brand strategy" in which the *Star* used both its mainstream paper and a new transit paper to appeal to different segments of the advertising market. Such a combo, he argued, would not only provide a huge competitive advantage for our advertisers but also allow us to take direct aim at our feisty competitor, the *Sun*. While there was some overlap in readership between the two papers, the *Sun* had for years made the legitimate advertising argument that it reached a different market. A trendy, free transit paper, Go continued, would provide just the vehicle for us to destroy that argument.

Within our executive group, the pendulum started to swing rapidly. The more we heard, the more we accepted as inevitable that *Metro* would look to Toronto. Were we prepared just to stand by or did we want to control our destiny? How much circulation would we lose if *Metro* had exclusive rights to distribute in our subway system? Would we suffer just like the large paid dailies in Stockholm? The more we analyzed, the more it became clear the very future of the *Star* could be in play. And what about this intriguing strategy of trying to sell around the *Sun*? Certainly, the more I heard, the more convinced I became. Find out more—and fast, I said.

Which is precisely what Go did—only his delving would shortly rock us to our foundations. Not only was *Metro* interested in Toronto, but one of its senior groups had already furtively entered the city, studied the subway system, and wrapped up a $1 million deal to secure exclusive newspaper distribution rights within it. Their execution was brilliant. Right under our noses, they had secretly locked up our subway system. No longer were we dealing in speculation. "Our reality has just changed," I told the group. What next?

Again, it was Go who suggested we approach *Metro* to see if we could join forces with them in Toronto. At first blush, the idea seemed far-fetched. After all, *Metro* was openly contemptuous of mainstream dailies, citing them as competitors to be devoured. But Go took the initiative, and much to our surprise, he found them receptive to a negotiation. By early March of 2000, following months of intense and often tortuous exchanges, we appeared on the verge of a deal. Floyd Weintraub, the seemingly amiable U.S. rep for *Metro*, would often call extolling the fact we would be "making history" as the first mainstream daily ever to do a deal with *Metro*.

But first, I decided to pay a visit to *Metro*'s Stockholm headquarters. It became clear each side needed an opportunity to size the other up. Certainly, that was essential for me. And serendipitously, the World Association of Newspapers was holding a special one-day conference in London for the mainstream press on how to combat the "*Metro* threat." I would combine these into a dual-purpose trip. At the time, the dichotomy of learning first how to fight *Metro* and the very next day sitting down with them to finalize a deal struck me as curiously quixotic. But any twinge of conscience evaporated instantly when I arrived in March for the opening session of the London conference. Sitting front and centre were senior executives from both of our major Toronto competitors, the *Globe* and the *Sun*. Representing the *Sun* was Pierre Francoeur, the taciturn but loyal lieutenant for the Péladeaus of Quebecor. There for the *Globe* was the ebullient Andrew Bishop, head of production. Among the many cities from around the world, Toronto stood out as the only one with three competing reps. It was obvious that we would not be alone in our interest of *Metro*.

The session opened up with the fabled British media proprietor Lord Rothermere, head of Associated Newspapers, relating how his team had outfoxed the Swedes by securing the distribution rights in London's Underground system. They called their paper *Metro*, virtually copied the Swedish template, and opted for no editorial opinion and the free giveaway model. Rothermere confessed he had been astounded by the response, and then declared, "*Metro*s are here to stay. Either you do it or they will do it. And, in the process, they will do everything to assimilate you." Editor Ian MacGregor then took us through all the tricks and techniques that worked in this new type of paper.

With these insights, I headed out the next morning for Stockholm. About to land, I remember feeling a distinct sense of anticipation that I might be on the verge of pulling one over on my unsuspecting

Toronto competitors. Of course, I hadn't mentioned my next destination to anyone, but when I arrived in the Swedish capital the *Metro* group could hardly wait to hear every detail of the London session. There was a nagging irony to the situation that left me feeling somewhat unsettled. Here I was, the first-ever "traditional" newspaper publisher coming to hammer out a deal with the company whose much-reported aim was to be owner of the world's largest chain of newspapers. *Metro*'s market was indeed the world, so intelligence on conference delegates, insights into the discussions there, and just general gossip were extremely useful to them. Yet ringing in my ears were the warnings the day before of a company dead set on "beating" everyone. Could *Metro* be trusted? Was it prepared to break the mould and partner with one of its traditional enemies?

The *Metro* group, I surmised, was equally preoccupied with doubts, but that didn't stop them from rolling out the red carpet. I was provided with a corner suite in Stockholm's stately Grand Hotel, where Nobel laureates and their families usually stay before the prize-giving ceremonies. Dinner was across the ice-clogged Norrström River, in the private dining room of the group's fortress-style headquarters. Over roast venison and the finest grappa I have ever savoured, we went late into the night, trading tales, arguing over editorial rules, and essentially sizing each other up. President Jan Stenbeck and I particularly hit it off, exchanging thoughts on how a partnership might break new ground. He had a real swagger to him, combined with a roguish charm dispensed in huge dollops. I returned to the hotel somewhat optimistic yet much the worse for the grappa.

Early the following morning I was picked up to do a tour of the subway system to witness first-hand the "*Metro* experience." If ever I had entertained doubts about *Metro*'s appeal, they were dispelled instantly. In each station, roughly three quarters of all commuters snatched up a copy of the paper on their way through the turnstiles. On every train, all one could see was the telltale green *Metro* masthead. No wonder *Metro* had rocketed to the number two spot in

Stockholm's crowded newspaper market. I was now a witness to the free transit paper revolution—and a fervent convert. Next up was a trip back to *Metro* headquarters, where Stenbeck had requested I stop by before leaving. What I encountered there was quite a different experience from the night before. Dressed casually in a thick sweater and corduroys, his shock of blond hair in upheaval, Stenbeck was all business. Nagging doubts and hurdles to surmount were the message from him. As he talked, I could not keep my eyes off a three- to four-metre-long poster above the bookshelves of a reclining, buxom Ann-Margret, one of Hollywood's favourite Swedish bombshells. We concluded our meeting, agreeing a deal was possible but that more had to be done. Once outside, I immediately telephoned Go, asking somewhat incredulously, "So how does *Metro* really make its money? We've got to do a check pronto." For whatever reason, the image of that Ann-Margret poster would simply not go away. This deal was far from done.

We quickly engaged a London-based corporate intelligence firm to give *Metro* a once over. That report confirmed the financial stability of the firm but raised disquieting concerns about its corporate practices and unpredictability. Global dominance was reconfirmed as the corporate goal, and the company's track record revealed a pattern of unorthodoxy, strategic use of litigation, and sudden about-faces. We considered ourselves warned. Yet, while the negotiations proved tough, we finally hammered out a partnership deal by mid-April that satisfied Canadian law and the interests of both parties. With a completed text in hand, I penned an expectant cover note to the Torstar board requesting formal approval for the deal within the next few days. Though the newspaper war was still raging, I wrote, "we still feel the advantages far outweigh the disadvantages." Our plan called for a $6 million expenditure over three years. Everything finally seemed in order.

Then, on the very day before the board meeting, a heretofore unknown *Metro* rep, Steve Nyland, insisted on a face-to-face meeting in my office. I asked Go and our CFO, David Holland, to attend, and inquired whether either of them knew what was up. They were perplexed as well. Minutes later, the strikingly blond Nyland marched in, dressed entirely in black and carrying a glistening black attaché case. Without so much as a greeting, he icily declared the meeting would not begin until both Go and Holland were told to leave. I retorted frostily, "If they're not here, there's no meeting." Nyland repeated his demand. I gave him the same response, the tone no doubt reflecting the annoyance rising inside me. Finally, and deliberately, he proceeded to lay out five new "preconditions" that must be accepted immediately or there would be no deal. The five points represented a complete repudiation of the deal we had worked so hard to finalize. And he knew it, only too well. In one short sentence, I told him his demands were "unacceptable" and declared the meeting over. What we witnessed that morning was the Swedish "unpredictability" we had been warned of, delivered in executioner style.

The very moment Nyland left, we catapulted into action. "This is war," I shouted at Go and Holland. Furious that we had been double-crossed, my first and only reaction was that we would have to bring out our own paper—and do it in six weeks' time, right from scratch. The three of us agreed and started planning. There was no doubt *Metro* would go it alone, and of course, we knew their timetable. The *Sun*'s eventual entry came as a late surprise, but having made the decision to occupy this new space, we weren't about to abandon it now. We never waivered once on the strategic rationale; nor, for that matter, did the Torstar board.

It has always been my view that the Swedes seriously underestimated our resolve, mine in particular, and felt they had the killer advantage with their monopoly access to the subway. Later, some *Metro* executives confided that head office in Stockholm had never been comfortable dealing with a mainstream newspaper. The company was much more used to fighting such newspapers, and the prospect of doing the first-ever partnership with one simply didn't sit well with those at the top. Another explanation is that the Swedes were craftily determined to get an even better deal, using the deadline of the Torstar board meeting as leverage. A plaintive telephone message from their New York rep, saying that he was "disappointed with how events had unfolded," gave some credence to this view. Indeed, months later, the Swedes would complain to CEO Galloway that I had "overreacted." To me, it was a double-cross, plain and simple. Any trust *Metro* had earned after months of tortuous bargaining had evaporated. If this was how they were going to act, how could we possibly be partners?

My first act was to drive that very afternoon to the strip-mall headquarters of Gateway Newsstands in York Region to see if we could negotiate a separate deal for TTC access. Gateway had secured exclusive distribution and concession rights within the subway system back in the mid-'90s. As it turned out, Gateway's deal with the Swedes was rock-solid and the best legal advice we received was that we would have to work around it. In other words, *Metro* started with a huge distribution leg up.

What *Metro* didn't have, however, was local knowledge and arguably the best newspaper team in the country. On the editorial side, we knew our ability to provide *Star* stories to our new paper gave us a huge starting advantage. Vian Ewart, one of the newsroom's most creative and seasoned editors, was immediately drafted to design the new paper and recruit the necessary journalists. He picked strategically from our properties, including Ian Somerville, the *Star*'s veteran art director, and Bill Reynolds, the then editor of *eye* weekly. On the distribution side, veteran *Star* circulation director Rupert Fry jumped into the fray. Fry liked nothing better than a good old fashioned circulation war. "You build it, one by one," he would always tell me. Having worked his way through the circulation ranks over more than three decades, he knew the ins and outs of the GTA market. So it came as no surprise when he discovered that the Swedes, lacking local knowledge, had locked up the subway but had fortuitously overlooked the regional GO commuter train system with its tens of thousands of riders. Hundreds of street boxes had to be ordered immediately and a choice of colour made instantly. All heads turned to me and I chose deep purple, a colour used to great effect by the Disney folk in Orlando. The last decision was to be the name. This took more time and it was the editorial team that ultimately came up with the winner—*GTA Today*.

On Monday, June 26—exactly eighty-six days after Nyland left my office—we launched. The *Sun* had surprised us all by coming out with its version, *FYI*, and beating us to launch by three days. Its creator, former *Star* managing editor Lou Clancy, would later say he had sat down in Betty's, a restaurant across from the *Sun*, and drawn up a prototype on the back of a napkin. Indeed, the first *FYI* came out five days later, surely setting a record for the fastest birth of a new paper. As Clancy explained later, "We knew there were two other free papers coming into the market, so we responded to the competitive pressures." His remark certainly captures the cutthroat spirit that engulfed the city's newspapers then.

In my somewhat breathless announcement to staff, I drew on this same spirit. "The newspaper wars just get crazier and crazier," I declared. "For now, the main focus is on the commuter market. And with *GTA Today*, we have a real winner!" For the first day, we had a press run of one hundred thousand copies and close to ninety thousand were picked up, exceeding all expectations. My daughter Emily joined me as, bedecked in purple *GTA Today* T-shirts, we handed out papers in Union Station to disembarking GO passengers. Altogether, the team distributed twenty-two thousand papers in the station. But we were under no illusions as to what lay ahead. Our operating mantra was "This will be a marathon, not a sprint." We knew it would be a war, with the city's transit system as the battleground. Our goal was simple: win the readership battle with a superior paper and use local knowledge to outwit the Swedes and force them to incur huge losses. Our constant message was that we were in this to win and that we had the full financial backing of Torstar behind us.

Our first tactic was to try to limit, as much as possible, the area in the subway where *Metro* "newsies" would be allowed to hand out papers. Before launch, we had dispatched the ever-reliable municipal reporter Bruce Campion-Smith to do an access to information request on the contract between Gateway and the TTC. The transit system did everything to frustrate our efforts, but we took the view that *Metro* could be distributed only from within the narrow confines of Gateway newsstands, not across the entire system. From day one, we had spotters roaming the subways taking photos of *Metro* newsies handing out papers. For the first several weeks, I wrote the taciturn TTC general manager, Rick Ducharme, every day complaining about the practice and demanding the TTC stop it. Our complaints ultimately had little practical impact.

On the editorial side, we knew we had a superior paper right from day one. Since *Metro* was being run out of a downtown hotel room, largely by staff from its sister Philadelphia paper, its access to local stories was limited. As chair of Canadian Press, I was able to block any attempt to secure the national news service. And every day we dissected *Metro* to see if it had scalped any stories from either the *Star* or CP. Indeed, on several occasions, we sent threatening legal letters complaining about the unauthorized use of stories. The *Sun*'s *FYI* never became a serious contender, lacking both access to any transit system and sufficient editorial investment.

One hundred days later, we were matching *Metro* paper for paper, making up for its stranglehold on the subway system with more boxes and in-store promotions. A readership study showed we were preferred on a two-to-one basis over *Metro*. We knew that on an annual basis we would lose close to $4 million, but we figured *Metro*'s deficit would top $7.5 million. Our strategy was simple: keep on putting out a better paper and make the opposition's losses painful. Past history had revealed that when losses became too large over an extended time, *Metro* was not afraid to pull the plug. Indeed, we had already heard rumours that Stockholm had been surprised by both the intensity of the battle and the amount of red ink it was absorbing. What we also had on our side was the unquestioned financial backing of Torstar—at least we thought so.

Then suddenly, without warning, CEO David Galloway entered the fray. Against the backdrop of the aftermath of the *Sun* media purchase, relations between the two of us had already soured somewhat. However, he knew only too well where I stood. I was convinced we were playing the winning hand and that, with patience and superior execution, we would emerge victorious, with *Metro* no longer on the scene. He, in a nutshell, found the losses too difficult to swallow. It was a classic short term versus long term dilemma. Did we prefer to cut our losses, join with our competitor, and share 50 per cent of any profit? Or did we want to hold out longer, expect to win, control the market, and take 100 per cent of any profit? The second option was undoubtedly riskier but the potential reward far, far greater.

Galloway and I never had that debate face to face. Instead, from that point on, I was effectively shut out of the process. And when *Metro*'s wily publisher, Greg Lutes, told Toronto's Advertising Club he was in discussions with a potential Canadian business partner, Galloway sprang into action. He called Lutes the very next day, saying, "We're at a standoff. This is what we consider our market, so we're not going to back down. This is what you consider your business, so you're not going to back down. So we're both going to lose a lot of money over the next two years. Why don't we put our two papers together?" Lutes later revealed his elation in a magazine interview. "I was absolutely thrilled when I got the call from Galloway. If you look at a situation where you can eliminate a competitor and draw on the resources that Torstar brings . . . it was a marriage made in heaven."

Negotiations between the two sides went much more rapidly than during the first round. A new editorial protocol was worked out, with the combined paper to take the name *Metro*. As Galloway later related, "I think we'd both proven to each other that we were both strong in this business." I learned later that the Swedes had told Galloway that I had refused to take a call from the *Metro* president after the fateful visit from Steve Nyland. This was categorically untrue, but since I was deliberately excluded from these negotiations, I was unable to rebut it. Galloway also called *GTA Today* editor Ewart to try to convince him of the wisdom of the merger. Ewart also strongly disagreed, arguing that the Swedes were already beaten. Galloway, however, was not to be deterred.

In the draft agreement, which was only made available to me just before a board meeting, Galloway proposed that the new joint paper have the unlimited right to print and circulate as many copies as it wished. I was appalled. One of the principal reasons for starting our own transit paper was to protect the *Star*. We knew *Star* circulation would be adversely affected by a transit paper, but ownership and control would allow us to limit the number of copies distributed. We remembered only too well what had happened to the dailies in Stockholm. I made this point rather forcefully at the board meeting. There was no rebuttal, and a chastened Galloway was forced to amend his position and to insist a circulation limit be included in the agreement. The final deal was then signed and announced—a mere eight weeks after Galloway's first call. Three months later, the *Sun* shut down *FYI*.

We will never know for sure how long the Swedes would have stayed if a deal had not been struck. Certainly, *Metro*'s Lutes later confided to me that he knew for a fact Swedish patience had just about run out and Stockholm was "shocked" when Galloway called. Ultimately, *Metro* became Toronto's second-most read paper, and a chain of other *Metro*s was established across Canada. Not only had the *Star* been protected, but Torstar would have a newspaper presence from sea to sea.

Ultimately, the second newspaper war was over. The first was still raging, but back at corporate headquarters, another internal battle was brewing.

18

THE BATTLE
OF HARLEQUIN

Of all Torstar's acquisitions, none gave Bee greater pride than the purchase of Harlequin. The very thought of a hard-bitten media mogul becoming entranced with the minutiae of romance fiction still amazes me. Yet there he was—the one-time shunned Mennonite from Baden—passing judgment on whether Harlequin book covers were too risqué. The economic impact of the purchase for Torstar was much easier to grasp. Right from the outset, Harlequin generated tens of millions of dollars in profit, greatly enhancing the value of Torstar. Both investors and the company's five owning families were enraptured with the investment. It became known as our "insurance policy," a property providing a welcome hedge against the vagaries of the newspaper business.

So, when I became aware in 2000 that CEO David Galloway was considering selling part or all of Harlequin as a key element of a new corporate strategy, I had no doubt of Bee's reaction. He was outraged, as was I. What we didn't fully anticipate was the bitter process that would ensue—ultimately leading to the demise of the CEO, my demise as a Torstar director, my near dismissal as *Star* publisher, and most hurtful of all, my profound sense of betrayal by Bee at my darkest hour.

It was in the early '70s that Bee and his team began looking at other investments to smooth out the generally roller coaster results of the newspaper business. Theirs would be a classic diversification strategy. The specific goal was to find a venture that would flatten the ups and downs of newspaper advertising in southern Ontario. The first acquisition was the Toronto-based Comac Communications, owner of many magazines. The second was Western Broadcasting, a West Coast radio, TV, and cable firm. Discussions were already underway with the firm's owner when, unexpectedly, the most important acquisition in Torstar's history literally walked in the door.

The driven and sometimes tempestuous Dick Bonnycastle, chair of Harlequin, asked to see Bee in his office and immediately offered to sell control of his company for $30 million. Neither Bee nor any of his advisers had ever thought of Harlequin as a viable option. Indeed, it turned out Bonnycastle had been acting on his own, with his family unaware of his overture. Nor was it ever clear why he saw Torstar as a natural buyer, given that other book publishers would probably have been very interested. But the advantages for Torstar immediately became apparent. First, there was no reliance on advertising. Rather, all income came from the sale of relatively inexpensive books to a huge cadre of loyal readers. In fact, the books provided relatively cheap entertainment in tough economic times. Finally, Harlequin appeared to have no competitors and was spread out across the globe. Thus, Torstar happily snapped up the offer, securing control in 1975 and total ownership by 1981.

Two decades later, however, Galloway had become preoccupied with Torstar's sagging stock price and the emergence of the new buzzword in the media world—"convergence." In full froth over the threat of the internet, traditional newspapers were seeking media mergers and alliances everywhere to protect their financial positions. Izzy Asper's Canwest had just completed its $3.2 billion takeover of Conrad Black's media empire. This, in turn, had followed on the heels of Time Warner's blockbuster merger with AOL. Owning multimedia platforms for the delivery of content became the key priority of all media companies. Providing "one-stop" shopping for purchasers of both TV and newspaper ads was the new imperative.

Galloway became an immediate and firm "convergence" adherent, a belief that fuelled his desire to find a broadcast partner. Right from the outset, I was far more skeptical. I had witnessed first-hand the significant differences in how print and broadcast reporters go about their work. And on the advertising side, it baffled me that advertisers would pay more simply because they could do so at "one stop." But I was clearly in the minority. Caught smack in the middle of this debate was Harlequin. While it clearly provided no synergies or broadcast value to the newspapers, it did produce each and every year upwards of $100 million in profit. In the two decades since Torstar had acquired control, Harlequin had earned well over a billion dollars. Not something to be trifled with, one might have imagined.

By mid-2000, Galloway had become fixated on doing something, anything. In a memo to the board, he cited market analysts who warned that Torstar's share price would languish absent "any bold new direction in strategy." Bolstered by a klatch of market "experts," he argued Torstar's share price did not reflect the true value of assets within the corporation. Taking Harlequin out and making it a separate company would "unlock" the true value of the romance giant, the argument went. Moreover, the proceeds to the newspaper group from any sale could be used to pay down Torstar's debt, and it would also provide a tidy bonus to shareholders. In the memo, Galloway knew he had to confront the "insurance policy" argument. He readily acknowledged that, in the past, Harlequin had helped the *Star*, most notably by providing funding for the $400 million state-of-the-art Vaughan printing plant. However, he argued the newspaper group was "a sizable company in its own right," able now to stand alone.

In the lead-up to the board's annual retreat, Galloway specifically asked what the Honderich position would be. Having run Harlequin for years, Galloway knew only too well Bee's entrenched attachment to the firm. After a short back and forth, Bee and I drafted a joint memo to Torstar, marking our first and only such collaboration. In a single-page statement, we argued that the underlying rationale for the purchase of Harlequin as an insurance policy was as valid in 2000 as it was in the '70s. We saw no reason to give up that protection, nor did we feel the newspaper division was as risk-free as Galloway argued. We wanted to send as clear a message as possible to Torstar: "While [splitting off Harlequin] might boost the stock price temporarily, we do not believe it to be in the best long-term interest of shareholders." We were united. Period.

It was predicaments like this that had begun making my own position vis-à-vis Galloway untenable. As publisher, I reported to him. Our understanding had always been that we would be united at the board on any newspaper issue. Any disagreements—and there had been a few—would be hashed out beforehand. Not only did this arrangement work, it seemed appropriate. But I was also an owner and Torstar board representative for the Honderich family, with a legal right and duty to speak my mind. There was an inherent conflict in balancing both roles, and up to that point, I had never felt the need to do so. However, this tension had surfaced sharply a few months before, when Galloway pursued a potential Torstar takeover of CHUM, the Toronto-based radio and TV company. I fully supported this move, but when CHUM came back with a fifty–fifty joint control proposal, the voting families unanimously rejected it. All, myself included, were opposed to giving up total control. An angry Galloway labelled me a "turncoat."

After the CHUM sortie, Galloway turned his attention to Rogers, the cable and TV giant. Over the years, the garrulous, always effusive Ted Rogers and I had crossed paths on more than a few occasions. An avid and discerning newspaper reader, he was always primed to discuss issues of the day. On two occasions, he arrived at my One Yonge Street office unannounced. The first came in mid-May 1998, with Ted having just visited his father's grave on the anniversary of his death. Edward Rogers Sr. had founded Rogers Vacuum Tube Co. and Toronto's legendary radio station CFRB—the foundation on which son Ted built Rogers Communications Co. At Ted's instigation, we had a fascinating discussion about being "the son of." On both visits, he also insisted on visiting the *Star*'s newsroom, not surprisingly creating quite the buzz each time. His towering figure was hard to miss. Whenever we met subsequently, he always stressed how much our two companies had in common. We did work out a few small joint ventures, but not much else. Clearly a much larger deal was now in play. While I had been carefully excluded from any of the discussions, it was apparent that if a Rogers deal was concluded, the ticklish Harlequin issue would evaporate.

As the Torstar board's annual October retreat neared, Galloway left as little to chance as possible. He hired an old business associate to prepare a seventy-two-page document that fully buttressed his arguments. Included in the document was a rather negative analysis of the newspaper division, prepared without even a whit of input from me or my entire staff. To say we were all taken aback, if not professionally embarrassed, would be an understatement. Cutting right to the chase, Galloway declared, "The newspaper industry is in long-term decline. Rogers is a good buyer. This is where we want to put the *Star*." This was a stunning contradiction of his words just a year ago: "Newspapers have a positive outlook for the future. Newspapers flourished over the last 30 years . . . and we see newspapers continuing to prosper." The sudden reversal in outlook also seemed odd given that we had just spent $335 million purchasing the four regional dailies from Quebecor and had launched the *Metro* newspaper.

Another dynamic at play was the composition of the Torstar board. Both Galloway and chair John Evans had recruited a bevy of new directors intent on running Torstar as a strong, independent, blue-chip company with as little interference as possible from the voting trust. While they would collectively acknowledge the special mission of the *Star*, the priority of extracting shareholder value would usually dominate deliberations. Most had joined the board with little or no appreciation of the obligation to uphold the Atkinson Principles, a predicament that would dramatically come to a head five years later. As my confidant and chief counsel, Bert Bruser, once queried, "John, would it be fair to say you have been asleep at the switch with all these new director appointments?" There was no doubt. And with Bee's old nemesis Burnett Thall now heading up the voting trust, Galloway's position appeared unassailable.

The site for the retreat was the boardroom at Langdon Hall, an hour's drive west of Toronto. As the opening gavel came down, the tension and anticipation in the room was heavy, in sharp contrast to the bucolic peacefulness of the greenery visible outside. Most of the morning was spent on presentations, but we were all aware a missive from Rogers was expected. The fact that an offer would conveniently appear on the very first day of our retreat—a deal that would have involved much preplanning—did not appear to strike anyone else as problematic or more than accidental.

Around noon, a sudden knock interrupted the proceedings. A special-delivery package had arrived for Galloway. "Perhaps a message from Ted Rogers," he mused, a grin on his face. The joy, however, was short lived. In a two-page letter, Rogers laid out a summary of a possible merger, including reference to the importance of the Atkinson Principles at the *Star*. Indeed, Rogers's proposal was fashioned along the lines of the *Chicago Tribune*'s approach when it took over the *LA Times* from the Chandler family. To Galloway's deep chagrin, however, the exchange share price was well below what he expected. Well below. He was crestfallen. Without much discussion, the offer was summarily rejected. Parenthetically, Rogers specifically asked that his letter be shown to the five owning families. But Galloway held it back and I would not see a copy until years later. But with the Rogers option now off the table, the Harlequin spinout was back on.

Given this frenzy of corporate activity, one might have expected Torstar's process for considering offers to be well defined. Indeed, it had been. A legal opinion from a blue-chip firm had concluded that whenever the board received an offer, its first necessary step must be to canvass the five owning families for their positions. If even one of the families was opposed, "no further action by the board would be necessary or appropriate." Thus, I was taken aback when, late in the afternoon, board chair Evans unexpectedly raised the process issue. Henceforth, whenever an offer came in, Evans declared, the board would automatically set up an independent committee of directors to analyze it and report back with a recommendation. The intent of the change was self-evident. The family owners would be bypassed until independent directors had been given a chance to voice their view.

The instant he concluded, I interjected. In rather animated form, I argued this revised process was diametrically opposed to the legal opinion, from which I quoted directly. Directors' heads whipped back to hear Evans's reply. He insisted his revised process would remain. But I cited again the opinion, a copy of which I had fortuitously brought with me. The usually unflappable Evans, his voice rising, remained adamant. And for a third time, I repeated the exact quote, this time waving my copy for all to see. Finally, an exasperated Evans blurted out that the lawyer, the distinguished J-P Bisnaire, had "changed his view." Furthermore, he was waiting outside and willing to answer any questions. At that point, the session ended abruptly and I fled to my room, muttering to myself, "They are trying to steal the company!"

My anger was palpable and, quite frankly, I was in no mood to join Evans, Galloway, or the others for the traditional post-meeting dinner. What I needed to do was get myself unwound and prepped for the critical discussion on Harlequin the next day. Clearly, I had missed the section in the Marquess of Queensberry rulebook on appropriate director behaviour in times of stress. My absence from the dinner was labelled "childish" and "not appropriate." I never discussed this with Bee, but I would soon learn a valuable lesson from it: never put yourself in a position where your conduct or words can be used against you, deflecting attention from the issue at hand.

The next morning, I was one of the first directors to arrive for what everyone knew would be a gut-wrenching debate over the Harlequin issue. Galloway made his pitch for the sale of Harlequin and then took the unusual step of immediately going around the board table, asking each director for his or her view. I was the first, repeating the arguments Bee and I had carefully prepared. Then all the independent directors, including Bee's long-time lawyer Ted Donegan, lined up solidly behind the proposal. Bee would not speak to Donegan again. Two voting family directors—representing the Thalls and Hindmarshes—also spoke firmly in favour. But catching Galloway clearly off guard, two other voting family directors, J.S. Atkinson's daughter Betsy and the Campbell family rep, Duke University professor Cam Harvey, signalled disapproval. The three of us together represented almost two thirds of the votes in the voting trust. And since voting trust approval was a precondition for any such deal to succeed, Galloway was stymied. He knew the math only too well, as did Evans. The retreat ended in a stalemate. As I left, the Hindmarsh director, the imperious and domineering Ruth Anne Winter, a high-end real estate broker in Oakville, made a point of accosting me. Her warning was blunt: "You'd better watch yourself." I knew exactly what she meant.

Back at the office, communications between Galloway and me became non-existent. A type of cold war set in, a situation that was clearly untenable. Attempting to make some progress, the entire Hindmarsh family sought presentations to be made on Harlequin. At one of the family's large homes in Oakville, I was asked to give a presentation, which would be followed shortly thereafter by the same from Galloway and Evans. We passed at the front door without comment. The Hindmarshes came down solidly for Galloway, and in the process they heard from Evans that my future was up for discussion.

Indeed, I would learn later that Galloway had already taken steps to lure Marty Goodman's son Jonathan to head up Torstar's media division. No one from the Hindmarsh family raised any objection.

But Galloway was still stifled, as directors Betsy Atkinson and Cam Harvey both continued to withhold their support, despite relentless pressure. Galloway then became reckless, warning long-time Honderich ally and former Torstar CFO Murray Cockburn, in a face-to-face conversation, that all independent board directors would resign if the voting trust turned down his Harlequin proposal. Furthermore, he would be suing for "constructive dismissal." This threat spread like wildfire through the families, only adding to the tension. But Bee and I never took it seriously.

In mid-October, the Atkinson family branch also called a meeting to discuss the impasse, inviting Galloway and Evans to attend. Bee was one of the trustees of the Atkinson estate and attended by phone from Vancouver. He shared his remarks with me beforehand, which were unchanged from the retreat. The other trustees were conflicted, but both Betsy and J.S. Atkinson's widow Elaine Berger were unmoved. They did not want to give up the "insurance policy" of Harlequin. In the discussion, Galloway made a point of apologizing for his threat. Sitting next to Elaine, he also quietly asked her who had the deciding vote if there was a tie. She replied that it was hers. He immediately gasped, and Elaine got him some water. The family decided the next step would be to seek an independent financial analysis of the proposal.

But there was one more item still to cover—my future. Both Galloway and Evans described my supposedly aberrant behaviour—including missing that dinner—in great detail and insisted the situation "had to be resolved." There was no doubt the status quo was untenable. My fate as director, executive, and publisher was now before them. But what was my crime? It was standing with Bee, as long-time shareholders, in bitter opposition to the CEO's plan. I fully understood that any reporting relationship to Galloway was no longer possible or feasible. Any meaningful communication between us had completely broken down. But losing everything? The trustees accepted Galloway's proposal to fire me. But one voice was notably silent.

Bee said nothing. Absolutely nothing. "His silence was such a shock," Elaine recalled later. It was as if he had quite simply forgotten about our joint letter and our commitment to stand together. I had fought for what both of us believed—fought hard. Was it too much for him to point that out? The same evening Bee telephoned to provide a recap of the day's discussion. It was only at the end of our call that he mentioned that my conduct had been discussed. He said he had decided to say nothing at the time "for it was a conflict of interest." Since he was scant in providing any more detail, I wasn't fully aware of what was at stake. I pushed him more on the "conflict." He answered that the family relationship did not allow him to say anything.

We would never speak of it again. Ten days later, Evans came to my office informing me I was relieved of my duties as a director, president of the media division, and publisher of the *Star*. It wasn't as if this was a total surprise, so I was prepared. I acknowledged quickly that I could not stay as media president, reporting to Galloway. However, I argued vehemently and passionately to stay on as publisher, insisting that my removal—amid the newspaper war and all our recent acquisitions—was not in the best interests of the company, or, for that matter, the *Star*. I committed to be as professional as possible in all my dealings with Galloway, accepting I would be reporting to someone else. And I also levelled a threat. If fired as publisher, I would not leave quietly. They would have "quite a mess" to deal with. The meeting did not last long, but Evans seemed somewhat open to my suggestion. A few days later, he confirmed his approval.

The formal announcement revealed I was giving up my title as president of the media group but staying on as publisher "to concentrate my energies at the *Star*." Though it was carried in all the city's newspapers, the underlying reasons never became public. Colleagues and reporters asked questions, but I remained circumspect. I was returning to the paper I loved most. I had dodged the bullet. At this point, I heard nothing from Bee. My sense of betrayal, however, was complete. In retrospect, I did not regret one iota fighting to keep Harlequin. I did not regret standing up to John Evans and David Galloway. I did not regret fighting hard. What I did regret was, at the end, being left to stand alone. I had always insisted on going my own way. Now I truly knew what that meant in relation to my father.

The following year, a sixteen-page financial analysis, prepared by PricewaterhouseCoopers for the Atkinson family, delivered its verdict on the Harlequin spinout. Its tone was decidedly negative, ending with the "cons." If done, it would deprive Torstar of valuable cash flow, render the company more subject to cyclical advertising trends, restrict future corporate options, and make it more difficult for the *Star* to uphold the Atkinson Principles. The conclusions were eerily familiar. The Atkinsons ultimately came down unanimously against the Galloway plan and the proposal was stopped.

In a note months later to Murray Cockburn, Bee questioned how Galloway could possibly remain as CEO in the face of such a report. He also emphasized the lack of a clear corporate strategy. And then he concluded, "John should be pleased with the report. It vindicates his position, but he has paid a heavy price for being right." All of a sudden, it had become "my" position. I had never received any such note.

The battle of Harlequin would conclude Galloway's career at Torstar. It was announced in the fall he would be leaving. After two decades at the helm, he could legitimately declare it was time to move on. There is no question the fallout from the Harlequin saga, as well as other controversial decisions on his part, had taken their toll. Most of the family owners no longer had confidence in his leadership. For some of the independent directors, there was also a sense he had become too eager to do a deal. Underlying all of this was an understandable desire for change.

19

PRICHARD TAKES OVER

John Evans was in an uncharacteristically expansive mood as he chatted excitedly about his new Torstar appointment. The scene was a celebratory cocktail party in May 2001, within the warm confines of U of T's Massey College. The new appointee was none other than J. Robert S. Prichard, Evans's long-time protégé and, like Evans, a former president of the University of Toronto. The patrician and ever-so-persuasive Evans had just successfully stage-managed Prichard's selection as the next CEO of Torstar. While there had been a structured selection process, it seemed to the other contender, Rogers honcho Brian Segal, that it was a mere formality. For years, Evans and Prichard had shared an extraordinarily close bond, forged by their respective presidential experience and a passion for the institution each had headed. There is little doubt Evans would have briefed Prichard fully on the recent internal Torstar battles, Harlequin in particular. But it still came as a surprise when he declared almost matter-of-factly to those assembled, "In Rob Prichard, we've finally found the one to take on the Honderichs."

Word of this pronouncement filtered back to me almost immediately via two persons there—I having not been invited to the party. At first, I wasn't quite sure what to make of it. Prichard and I had known each other since childhood, and I had been a somewhat frequent guest at his U of T dinners. I sensed there was a mutual respect between us and I had certainly been impressed with his tenure as U of T president, most particularly with his fundraising prowess. While he and I had crossed swords over *Star* coverage of U of T—once famously during a schoolyard croquet match when we argued over management of the university's endowment funds—it seemed we both understood our respective positions. Not only that, we seemed to share the same values. Thus, when I was invited during the "selection process" to chat with Prichard about the Atkinson Principles, I took his avowals of strong commitment at face value. Finally, Bee was most insistent that Prichard be "given a chance." Evans had personally flown to Vancouver to inform Bee of the change and the rationale behind it. The goodwill generated from that gesture would last for several years, much to my chagrin. Indeed, any time I raised a concern with Bee over Prichard in that initial period, it would usually be summarily dismissed.

From the start, however, I spoke to as many people as I could about Prichard's history, his working habits, his foibles and ambitions. There was no doubt he wanted to make his mark as a businessman. While his reputation in university circles was entrenched, he eagerly sought to replicate that success in the corporate boardroom. His self-professed business hero was Onex's Gerry Schwartz, whom he consulted constantly while also sitting on the Onex board of directors. (In fact, on becoming Torstar CEO, Prichard had insisted on maintaining four major directorships—at Onex, Bank of Montreal, George Weston Ltd., and Four Seasons Hotels—despite a potential conflict of interest on news coverage. Indeed, both Bee and I had specifically eschewed such directorships precisely because of a possible conflict.) Prichard had a reputation as a fast learner and a voracious gatherer of information. His Rolodex was the envy of every fundraiser, and his links to the city's establishment were gold-plated. His ever-so-large ego was legendary, leading then TVO honcho Peter Herrndorf to quip to me, "Are you sure there's enough oxygen down there for both of you?" But it was a casual, if not admiring, assessment from Ron Daniels, then dean of the U of T law school, that proved most insightful. "You should know that everything Rob does is strategic," he said. "No matter how small, everything is done with a strategic purpose in mind." I would later find out exactly what that meant.

At the introductory luncheon for the senior team, Prichard asked each person to come up with something unknown to the others. I spoke last and related what a spectacularly diligent and dedicated parent Prichard had been during his youngest son's intense battle with brain cancer. Prichard was clearly touched by the gesture, taking me aside afterwards to say so. The introductory briefing book I had prepared about the *Star* was as thorough and comprehensive as I could make it. Again, he seemed pleased, and I felt we were off to a good start.

That feeling, however, would be extremely short-lived. Over the next few weeks, as he dug into the workings of the business under the tutelage of the savvy former *Hamilton Spectator* publisher Pat Collins, a pattern of weekly digs and jibes began. The first came as I was to report to the Torstar board on the *Star*'s financial results, which were trending downwards because of the economic downturn. Prichard suggested I present "like a dog with its tail between its legs"—not a stance I was particularly familiar with. He also insisted he vet any memo of mine sent to staff about the bonus plan. The next week he abruptly cancelled a proposed change to our pension plan the night before its release, even though it had been months in the planning and discussed with him on numerous occasions. To top things off, I was also introduced to his jarring practice of barging into my office unannounced, even if the door were closed and I was with someone. On one occasion, he even put his feet on my desk— that would be the original Joseph Atkinson maple "partner" desk in the publisher's office.

Prichard's interference also extended into editorial, something rarely true of David Galloway. His first foray was to take issue with a column by veteran scribe Haroon Siddiqui, one of the great journalistic thorns in the side of Toronto's Jewish community. Right from the outset, Prichard declared he was very concerned about complaints from the Jewish community about *Star* coverage of events in the Middle East. It became a touchstone for Prichard, who continually asked for more "balance"—a code word for making sure Israel's perspective was always given high profile. He regularly praised and sent notes to Rosie DiManno for her periodic pro-Israel columns. Siddiqui's columns became a constant bugbear for him. Indeed, he mused about getting rid of Siddiqui, an idea I constantly fought.

These conversations turned out to be a mere preamble, however, to our battle over cost cutting, a fundamental disagreement that would dominate our three-year working relationship The first indication of this conflict came as the parameters for the following year's budget were being established. As if to set the tone, Prichard had provided all managers with copies of the best-selling memoir of General Electric's swashbuckling and profit-hungry CEO Jack Welch. Then he sat down with me to discuss his philosophy on cost. He opened by saying he'd met recently with his mentor, Gerry Schwartz, who advised him, "The only way to get growth from mature businesses is to cut." The fact that I had just presented a "steady-as-she-goes" approach to a seemingly approving Torstar board a few weeks before seemed irrelevant to him, as did the fact that we had just endured a bruising strike with our carriers and that the newspaper war was still in full throttle. "You live in an economic dream world," he mused at one point, following this with an order to cut costs by between 7 and 10 per cent. The battle lines were drawn, with the ultimate result being a saw-off. But when the final budget was approved, I learned to my complete surprise that the entire digital division, over which I had no control, would now report its results with those of the *Star*. Since this division was in its infancy and thus operating at a loss, the impact of this move was to depress significantly the *Star*'s reported profit.

This was now my reality. I had no doubt further budget skirmishes between us were inevitable.

The final dig that fall involved our lawyer and counsel Bert Bruser, who had been the paper's chief libel cop for two decades. He was widely considered the foremost libel lawyer in the country, and just as importantly, was one of my closest friends and confidants. Without my knowledge or consent, Prichard offered his one-time boys' campmate Brian Rogers five hundred hours of the *Star*'s libel work because of Rogers's lower billing rate. The very ethical Rogers was so shocked he contacted both me and Bruser, advising us that the approach had been made in secret. As a result, I sent Prichard a withering email labelling his intrusion "inappropriate, if not unprofessional." This would be one of the few battles I won.

By the end of the year, I took stock of what had happened and sought out Bee's counsel. He listened with limited sympathy, again emphasizing the point that Prichard should "be given a chance." As CEO, Bee would say, it was Prichard's responsibility to improve performance wherever possible. It was my role, he would add, to make sure the *Star* was protected and the Atkinson Principles were promoted. When it came to Prichard's pattern of digs and cracks, Bee was not approving, yet he was still not prepared to come to any hard conclusion. For my part, I felt the future looked ominous at best. Never before in my professional life had I been the subject of such taunts; nor did I feel we were working in harmony. It had gotten to the point where I felt on guard in every encounter. This seemed precisely as Prichard intended.

Not that there hadn't been positives that Prichard couldn't ignore. We had successfully launched our new transit paper; we had maintained a strong lead in the newspaper war; we had outsourced home delivery, which would ultimately produce $6 million in savings; and we were the first paper in North America to win a strike against carriers. Prichard acknowledged these efforts, but often the praise would be muted. Perhaps the best example was when Conrad Black gave up ownership of the *Post*, ending his role in the great newspaper war. This was celebrated with champagne at the *Star* and kudos from the Torstar board. When I told Prichard about the breaking development, he exclaimed, "Great news. I've got to congratulate Phillip [*Globe* publisher Phillip Crawley]. Can you get me his number?" I did and that was the last I heard on the matter. That exchange was emblematic of our working relationship.

So too was his reaction shortly after the settlement of the bet-the-business carriers' strike, for which the Torstar board had sent very hearty congratulations. In a meeting a few weeks later on union issues, Prichard told me point-blank I was "obsessed by unions" and that I had been a "hostage to union demands." I found this comment particularly galling.

The following year, 2002, carried on in a similar vein. One day in late winter, Prichard called me angrily into his office and vigorously raked me over the coals for dismissing the head of labour relations without the apparent consent of a superior. He labelled it "insubordination." After he had completed his rant, which took some time, I icily informed him the firing had taken place with the full knowledge and consent of Torstar's vice president of personnel. He said he would have to check, and after doing so he wrote a terse three-line note saying he had "accepted" my version.

The other major issue was a $1 million donation I had spearheaded to establish a newspaper centre at Ryerson University. The plan had been in the works since the early days of the newspaper war, and the rationale had been simple: Ryerson's journalism school has provided more journalists to Torstar than any other school and is located in our home city. The gift had been announced several years before, and details were being finalized when Prichard became aware of it. "That is simply far too much for that," he told me dismissively, curious words indeed from a former university president who had successfully garnered tens of millions of dollars for projects at U of T. He did everything possible to try and undo the donation, but it was too late. At the dedication ceremony, for which Prichard was "unavailable," then Ryerson president Claude Lajeunesse confided, "His backroom efforts to kill this were simply unbelievable."

But it would be the issue of cost cutting and the budget that dominated our discussions. Since the onset of the newspaper war, I had always committed the *Star* in board presentations to achieving historic levels of profitability over the long run. But while the newspaper war was being waged, I had successfully argued for five successive years that more had to be spent to protect our competitive position. Every other Toronto newspaper was doing this and the rationale had been accepted by the board, if not enthusiastically endorsed. Now Prichard started using terms such as "the process of optimization" and "increasing earnings growth over historic levels" and "achieving the same rate of earnings growth as the leading groups achieve." There was no doubt the *Star* wasn't as profitable as the tabloid *Sun*s or other metropolitan dailies, particularly those out west, but there were good reasons for this. For one, Toronto was by far the most competitive newspaper market in the country. Second, it had been my long-standing position that our commitment to the Atkinson Principles meant greater spending on editorial, thus resulting in a lower level of profitability.

As early as the summer, I started writing notes seeking clarification of what he meant. What level of profitability was he looking for? What did "optimization" mean? He replied that the issue should be "punted" until late September. I started hearing a lot of talk about "stretch" targets and snide remarks from his acolytes about the Atkinson Principles. A specific number was never given, but there was a clear expectation of increased profitability. The statement I found most intriguing was his complaint about "the lack of rigour in monitoring and reviewing financial performance compared to benchmark companies like General Electric." What a giant U.S. conglomerate had in common with a local Toronto newspaper fighting a newspaper war in the hyper-competitive Toronto market was far from clear to the *Star* team. Nor were we convinced that we should abandon the financial strategy that had brought us success in that newspaper war.

Thus, the *Star* budget that was finally presented, while significantly increasing our earnings, did not go nearly far enough for Prichard. Even though we ultimately doubled our profits in 2002, it was not the "stretch" he required. Prichard could barely hide his frustration during the board presentation, but he proceeded to make critical comments in the executive session afterwards. And at the board's Christmas dinner, he came right out and said the *Star* "needed new blood," adding that I was a "stick in the mud" and "arrogant." He knew full well these comments would get back to me—and to Bee for that matter—for our family director, Murray Cockburn, heard them all. Several directors were apparently uncomfortable with Prichard's outburst, with John Evans later saying "fatigue had got to him." But Cockburn's warning to me was unequivocal: "He's out to get you."

That was also my unshakable mindset as I spoke over New Year's with Bee. Communications with him that year had been very limited. He had been insisting on a regime of large direct annual payments to my children to teach them "how to deal with money," something I could not possibly support. We had been hopelessly deadlocked, until his wife Rina convinced him to accept a compromise.

In my conversation with Bee, he told me that Cockburn had made a point of briefing him directly about Prichard's comments, thus finally ending any sympathy my father had left for Prichard. With that in mind, neither of us saw a clear way forward. Prichard was still relatively fresh in his role and obviously had the support of the board. Bee also repeated his previous mantra that Prichard was well within his prerogative to order me to cut even more. I remained adamant that I was not prepared to compromise what I felt was the future of the *Star*. In short, we were at an impasse. We agreed that Prichard's preferred option was probably to fire me but that my position as an owner plus my record as publisher had made that problematic. On the other hand, I was sick of him grinding me down. The full breadth and devilishness of his strategy in dealing with me had taken its toll. I'd had enough.

We then discussed next steps, more particularly a successor and how to protect the *Star*. It was not as if I had not contemplated any of this. Indeed, I remember verbalizing it for the first time to Bert Bruser six months earlier, as we drove over the Louisiana bayou to visit his son in Mississippi. I was extremely proud of what had been accomplished, particularly in the newspaper war. But I had held the position for eight years and I had an idea for my successor—former *Montreal Gazette* publisher Michael Goldbloom. While not a journalist, Goldbloom had always impressed me with his progressive values, his approach to newspapering, and his deep concern for the country and informed debate. The fact he was dismissed by the Aspers over the *Gazette*'s more balanced coverage of Israel had also earned him my respect. In short, I felt the *Star*'s future would be in as good hands as possible and that Goldbloom would speak his mind in future dealings with Rob Prichard.

In early 2003, I met separately with both Prichard and Evans to say I wanted to begin the succession process at the *Star*. To say each of them was taken aback would be an understatement. I don't think either ever imagined I would leave this way—voluntarily and without a fight. The following month I signed up for a media conference Goldbloom was hosting in Montreal and invited him out for dinner on Friday night, Valentine's Day. It was the first step in a four-month wooing process that would, after an intense back and forth, ultimately bring him to Toronto as my deputy. Meanwhile, the daily interaction with Prichard and Evans was much less edgy, with one or two exceptions.

Indeed, in mid-April I met casually with Evans in his office. Without prompting, he praised me for taking the initiative in seeking a successor, adding it was "most critical" I make up my own mind on the timing of my departure. "It is critical for this organization and for you that this be done on the best of terms," he said. "Anything else would be criminal." I remember feeling most reassured.

That sense of calm, however, would be wholly disrupted a mere five days later. Prichard called, insisting we meet personally that very day in my office, which in itself was unusual. Shortly after lunch he arrived, immediately plopping himself down on the couch. And, as if to accentuate what was to unfold, he planted his feet squarely and incredibly inelegantly on the coffee table between us. I sat down, stunned by his behaviour. Had he acted this way when he was the president of the University of Toronto? He began by saying it was "preferable" if he just read out the letter in his hand. He was clearly on edge, his voice cracking at times. But then he proceeded to read the three-page letter, word for word. It was a termination agreement, plain and simple, with the timing and precise terms of separation set out. Not only that, the agreement was to be made public. Once he had finished, he stood and blurted out, "I am sure you'll agree this is far better than me coming down after a board meeting one day and telling you it's all over." Before he left, he expressed the preference that a deal be signed by June. Then he handed me the letter, turned on his heels, and left.

I sat in my chair, enraged. This was as crass an exercise in humiliation politics as was imaginable. There had been no prior warning of a desire for a written agreement, let alone any negotiation of the terms of separation. This was clearly not "a departure on the best of terms," as John Evans had said a mere five days before. To add insult to injury, John was copied on the letter. So he was in cahoots with Prichard on this as well. *My oh my*, I thought. It was as if I had been set up. For the first hour I felt nothing but anger. But then, just as suddenly, an icy calm took over. I determined right there and then I would not be cowed, nor would anyone else learn what had just transpired, except of course Bert, and a day or so later, Bee. I was not going to take this on Prichard's and Evans's terms. Not this way.

And if they thought I would act rashly, they would be disappointed. I didn't miss a meeting that week, and I did my best to act as if nothing had happened. All Prichard's emails were answered promptly and correctly. I then took a turbulent month to assess my next step.

As anyone who has gone through a termination knows, the journey is nothing short of an emotional roller coaster. There is no other way to describe it. During that month, an inner rage would often demand that I quit immediately, after negotiating better terms. The package was, quite simply, nothing close to what I felt was appropriate. At other times I discovered an inner iron determination to fight longer and leave on my own terms. After all, I had signalled my intent to leave voluntarily and had found my successor. Ultimately the latter feeling won out. Throughout it all, Bee would simply say, "It's your decision."

Exactly a month to the day later, I set up an appointment to see Evans. My intent was to be as cold and threatening as possible. I was ready for any outcome, though inwardly my preference was to stay— but only on my own terms. Surprisingly, I found him in a jocular mood as he greeted me warmly. That changed dramatically as soon as I took him through what had happened and told him I was contemplating leaving.

"What are you talking about?" he asked, seemingly incredulous.

"Read the letter," I replied icily. "You're cc'd on it."

He then brought up the compliments he'd paid me the last time we had met in his office. "Why didn't you come earlier?" he asked.

"Because you're cc'd on the letter," I repeated. "Read the letter."

After scanning it intensely, he then said slowly, "I am more than a little upset by this," adding the board would not be happy with my departure being dictated this way. He offered to immediately phone Prichard, who was travelling out west. I demurred and concluded by saying all options were on the table, including our family exiting Torstar.

It struck me at the time as inconceivable that Prichard could have written and delivered such a letter without the knowledge of the board chair, or even of the board itself. After all, I was appointed by the board. And Evans's name was in black and white at the bottom of the letter. On the other hand, I watched him read it that day and there was little doubt he seemed genuinely surprised. Indeed, his words reinforced his reaction. Ultimately, the true story may never be known, but I left his office that day emboldened and determined to write a different story.

What then unfolded was a two-month process through which I renegotiated the terms of my departure. I think it's fair to say I drove a very hard bargain, leveraging my position to the fullest. It became clear Evans was loath to see me leave in anger, fearing I would stir up a tempest he knew could become ugly. After an intense back and forth, the timing of my departure was left to my discretion. It would not be soon, but nor would it be far off. There was undeniably something surreal about forcibly negotiating my departure while still being very much on the job and with my successor already voluntarily designated. Ultimately, the greatest insult was losing the dignity of dictating the terms of my own departure, particularly the timing. I felt I deserved that. Yet the agreement certainly went partway towards restoring some pride. It was agreed I would stay on as publisher for at least eighteen months and would receive a "retention payment." Furthermore, there would be no pension penalty should I retire early, and I would receive twenty-seven months' severance. I had fought back, successfully.

In an ironic twist, at the very same time I was intently negotiating my own departure, I completed Goldbloom's entry into the *Star* as deputy publisher. Needless to say, he was totally unaware of what was transpiring elsewhere in the building. Amid all this tempest, I even attended the Torstar summer party at Prichard's farm, much to his surprise. Indeed, he sent me an email calling it "classy."

For Prichard, the next hurdle was how to explain to the Torstar board exactly what had transpired. A termination agreement with a *Star* publisher, not to mention the very firing itself, would normally require prior approval from the board, not to mention the voting trust. But I knew the board had never been formally consulted or informed, for director Cockburn would naturally have told me. Much later, I learned Prichard had spoken quietly with the two senior voting trust directors, Ruth Anne Winter and Betsy Atkinson, to get their confidential approval. Both Prichard and Evans had spent hours conferring with the two of them, knowing that, between them, they held a majority in the voting trust. Betsy later apologized to me, saying she had been "sorely misled." I felt fundamentally betrayed. But the other board members and the voting trustees only perceived that an orderly succession process was unfolding. Prichard's problem, the question he would have to answer, was: Why was it necessary to terminate John Honderich at age fifty-eight?

I assumed he would try to characterize this new agreement, as much as possible, as a natural step in the succession. As planning for the special meeting began, it became evident this was indeed his strategy. First, he insisted I not appear before the committee. Then, somehow, my written chronology was not included in the board materials, contrary to our agreement. Third, he crafted as generic an explanation as possible, to avoid revealing any embarrassing details. To that end, he wrote that our discussions had gone on for three months and had included "numerous meetings, drafts and letters." He added, "I judged it not helpful to share with you the various exchanges and drafts, believing it better to focus on that agreement."

I was furious that the board would not hear my version of events, particularly the feet-on-the-coffee-table confrontation. So I decided to speak up, and loudly. Since our agreement had specifically allowed me to submit a written report, I emailed it to all of the directors on the committee, telling them, "I neither intended nor contemplated that events would unfold in this manner. That having been said, it is essential to move on." Naturally, Prichard was furious, but he was forced to write another note to say he would reveal all of our letters, if requested. I was later told there was a "vigorous" discussion at the meeting where the agreement was ultimately approved.

Any expectation I had that my battling with Prichard would subside with this agreement was mere wishful thinking. For one thing, I had not fully appreciated what it would be like to report directly to the person who had attempted to fire me. Every time we met, I would steel myself, determined to maintain a cool, professional demeanour. Often it wasn't easy. I was determined to do everything to protect the *Star*. So, when he proposed that only the chair of the voting trust—who was then his ally Betsy Atkinson—not all trustees, be involved in the selection of *Star* publishers, I raised a real ruckus. If there was one appointment on which the entire trust would insist on having a vote, I declared, it was this one. To suggest otherwise was somehow to marginalize the trust to virtual irrelevancy.

Ultimately, if there was anybody who could provide some future check on Prichard vis-à-vis the *Star*, it was the voting trust. And as the Honderich family rep, I knew this was the one place where my voice would always be heard. Prichard, too, knew this only too well. And while Betsy and Ruth Anne Winter had quietly sided with Prichard, other voting trustees were not consulted about, and did not approve of, my attempted firing. Joe Atkinson Jr.'s widow, Elaine Berger, and the two Hindmarsh voting trustees, Lynne Hindmarsh and Peter Armstrong, along with Cam Harvey, were openly scornful and expressed their concern about what all this meant for the *Star*. Furthermore, they were flabbergasted to learn they had been left completely in the dark. The schism was deep, but on the immediate issue they were united: the entire voting trust must have a say on any future publisher. Consequently, Prichard was forced to back down.

As the weeks passed, the dynamic between us only became more difficult. It certainly wasn't helped when Prichard appointed Pat Collins as his deputy. That was, of course, his prerogative and I understood fully Collins's now-apparent eagerness to support his new boss. But the proposed announcement had him in charge of strategy, budgeting, capital allocation, and public policy issues across all newspapers, the *Star* included. It sure looked as if he would now be in charge and thus my new boss. Not only that, Collins was to represent Torstar on "appropriate" boards. The fact that I was chair of Canadian Press, Torstar's rep on the Canadian Newspaper Association, and Canada's representative on both the Audit Bureau of Circulation and the World Association of Newspapers, obviously made this objective complicated, if not directly aimed at me. In questioning the scope of this new appointment, I was joined by Torstar's two other newspaper CEOs, who also objected strongly. As a result, the job description was narrowed significantly.

Later, I also found myself wanting to pass more authority to Goldbloom and to let him shine. Thus, when the *Star*'s senior team presented its strategic plan to the board in late fall, Goldbloom did the majority of the presentation, much to Prichard's pleasure. At meetings and financial reviews, I would often urge him to handle the response. The process of my disengagement had clearly begun. So when I flew out to Vancouver over New Year's, I knew I had reached the point where it was time to leave. As I laid out my reasons, Bee didn't try to dissuade me. He was very distressed. Any respect he had once had for Prichard was long gone and he feared for the paper's future. However, the situation was simply untenable. Prichard's strategy had clearly been to grind me down, and it had worked. While I hated the thought of being labelled a quitter, the time had come. Period.

Within days of returning to Toronto, I spoke with Evans and Prichard separately about my decision. Prichard, for one, was shocked. Our agreement had me staying until at least November 2004. But here I was, eleven months early, bowing out. Evans was much more philosophic, pressing to make sure I wasn't acting rashly or out of spite. He spoke obliquely about the past and praised my record. Indeed, ever since the Prichard dismissal letter, he had gone out of his way to be civil and accommodating. He quietly spearheaded the drive for me to be awarded an honourary degree in sacred letters by my alma mater, Victoria College, and he related to several directors—knowing they would pass it on—that my departure "must be handled properly" because I had been a "critical person" for the *Star*. Furthermore, in one private chat about me with director Ted Donegan, Evans even confided that he "didn't like to be used." Whether this referred to his prior knowledge of the Prichard letter remains, for me, forever unclear.

Moves were taken to provide for my early departure. We jointly decided I would stay until the annual meeting in early May, but agreed that absolute secrecy was essential. I did not wish to be a lame duck for four months. That aim, however, was suddenly and dramatically shattered on Friday, January 24. Several *Globe and Mail* reporters started phoning key Torstar executives seeking confirmation for a story to run the following day about my departure as publisher. I was in Montreal meeting with our principal newsprint supplier when a message was left at my hotel. I was flabbergasted. How exactly had this gotten out? I barely slept that night and it was no surprise when, first thing Saturday morning, managing editor Mary Deanne Shears phoned to say there was a front-page story in the *Globe* proclaiming my demise. All hell broke loose.

I flew home that morning to meet with my senior team in my office. In a teary and very emotional atmosphere, I had to tell them the story was true. By this point, they were more surprised by the timing than the outcome. But we had been through a lot together, most notably the newspaper war. Then came the necessary drafting of press releases and statements, which Prichard and I quickly agreed should go out the following day. This would be my final battle with him.

Prichard, assuming that I would stick to the "high road," had positioned this as a "retirement." Yet never in my wildest rumina-tions had I ever imagined that. While wanting to take the high road in a general sense, I was not going to deceive or misrepresent. That would be a betrayal of my roots as a journalist. Nor, plain and simple, was this in fact a retirement. I had consulted with both Bee and Donegan, whom I trusted in these matters, and they had urged me to stay the course. Bee wanted me to be much tougher, in fact, and made reference to the Atkinson Principles. I disagreed. When Prichard read my statement, he exploded and headed down to my office for the first time since he'd read me the dismissal letter eight months before. When I refused to budge, not an iota, he cited, in a threatening tone, a potential board reaction. "I don't know what they'll do," said Prichard. Later that evening, Evans phoned to make a similar plea. It fell on very deaf ears.

Monday's *Star* had a front-page story headed "Honderich Leaves as *Star* Publisher 'With Regret.'" Written by rewrite pro Nick van Rijn, the story left no doubt as to what had happened. My statement was clear: "After almost 10 years as publisher and 28 years on staff, I am announcing that I will be leaving the *Star*. I do so with regret. For some time, there has been a corporate desire for change. As a result, I have been and will continue to work hard to bring about a seamless and effective transition. . . ."

Reaction that day both inside and outside the *Star* was beginning to mount when Rideau Hall suddenly announced the list of those receiving the Order of Canada. For my contribution as a publisher and journalist, I was on that list. As is the practice, I had been notified in advance but had been sworn to secrecy and had been given no idea of the announcement date. In reaction, I described the double-barrel news as "like a Hollywood script—an orderly departure one day and the Order of Canada the next." And that was precisely the headline on Tuesday's paper, accompanied by a photo of hundreds of staffers gathered in the newsroom for an impromptu champagne celebration. In the days after, five of the paper's columnists opined in elegant outrage on my departure, much to Prichard's chagrin. While I had recused myself from any role in the coverage of the story, Prichard had done so as well. As the days passed, I think he must have regretted that decision. There was also an avalanche of condemnatory letters, some of which were dutifully published on the letters to the editor page.

The culmination of the farewells came in an extraordinary bash in Toronto's Distillery District, with Tina Turner's signature single informing its theme, "Simply the Best." I was chuffed, to say the least. Bert Bruser, knowing Tina was my all-time favourite performer, arranged for a Tina impersonator to attend and perform the song. Both Prichard and Evans went to the party, which attracted more than six hundred people, all of whom received paper bow ties upon entry. There was a tribute video emceed by CBC anchor Peter Mansbridge, with comments from former PM Paul Martin, then Premier Dalton McGuinty, and then Toronto mayor David Miller. My two kids Robin and Emily provided some delightful family humour, and I was thrilled that all the union presidents made a point of speaking. The highlight, however, was a satiric speech by humour columnist Joey Slinger, who said quizzically, "There's been a rumour. Is it true that John has been dumped, invited out, selected aside . . .?" Prichard laughed and clapped in all the right places but departed soon after. For me, it was an incredibly emotional celebration, with countless colleagues insisting on telling me how I had played a role in their careers. There were a lot of tears.

A few weeks later, the annual meeting was held and I sat on the dais, with Michael Goldbloom beside me, for my last official function as publisher. My run was over. Goldbloom and I had worked well together, and the transition was as seamless as could be. By this point, I was very ready to move on, having secured a $1-a-year job as special ambassador for Mayor Miller. A new deal for cities had been one of my major crusades and now I was going to work at Toronto City Hall to make it happen. The farewells were many and splendid, but "lameduckdom" is really for the birds.

As I looked back that day, I had no regrets whatsoever about my decision. I loved my job and was proud of what we had accomplished. Success in the newspaper war, several groundbreaking crusades, and the garnering of thirty-four National Newspaper Awards, three Mitchener Awards for meritorious journalism, and the only

Pulitzer Prize ever won by a Canadian newspaper stood out in my mind as particular career highlights. Though I would be rejoining the board as the Honderich family representative, and my interest in the *Star* would never die, I had fully come to terms with the fact that the battles were done and my successor, the man I had identified, was anxious to take over. But just when I thought I was out, they pulled me back in.

Little did I imagine what was to come.

20

REDEMPTION

As a departed publisher, with bruises not yet fully healed, I could easily have driven off into the sunset. But my family argued strongly, Bee included, for me to take the Honderich family seat on the board. Who better to watch over the family investment? they argued. It was solely a family decision, and after some reflection, I agreed to take on the role—on a trial basis. Thus, on a hot, muggy July day, I retook my seat at the board table, not expecting anything unusual and wilfully determined to keep a low profile. Other directors were polite, if perhaps a tad wary. They understood my role as a family owner and knew I had six years of service as a director. Furthermore, memories of my role in the battle of Harlequin had long since faded. That Harlequin's profits had continued to soar didn't hurt either. Indeed, I took a particular private delight in the fact that the company's financial position was so strong. All seemed calm as the meeting began, when out of the blue, Betsy Atkinson quietly slipped a note to Cam Harvey and me, asking to meet with us right after the board meeting concluded. What could this possibly be? Harvey didn't know either.

Four hours later, in a hushed and edgy voice, Betsy informed us she was resigning immediately as both chair of the voting trust and board director so as "to spend more time at home out west." Both

Harvey and I were stunned. There had been no warning, not the slightest inkling of such a dramatic change. When pressed for reasons, she insisted it was a "lifestyle" decision. Neither of us believed that for one second. Only later would we learn of the impossible and debilitating balancing act she had tried to maintain as voting trust chair, representing the five owning families when dealing with Evans and Prichard. The breaking point had apparently been my dismissal. Betsy and Hindmarsh director Ruth Anne Winter, both of whom had supported Prichard, had come under withering criticism from their respective families when their roles in the ouster became known. Winter had already paid the price, as the Hindmarsh family had unceremoniously booted her out as their director. Years later, Betsy would apologize to me, saying she had "mistakenly" believed all Prichard had told her.

I would also learn from Betsy how intensely both Prichard and Evans had monitored every move she took as voting trust chair, proffering advice, meeting secretly in her office to plan strategy before most trust meetings, even writing agendas and minutes. While its potential ownership power was significant, the voting trust was but a shell in corporate terms. There was no fixed office, it operated on a barebones budget, and its chair received no remuneration. Trustees usually met twice a year, and most often discussions were brief. However, the trust did possess the ultimate authority to replace directors on the Torstar board. Betsy further confided that the goal of Evans and Prichard had been to limit the authority of the voting trust as much as possible. And in their view, she related, the prime obstacle was me. Ultimately, she couldn't take the pressure any longer and simply had to get out.

Who would succeed her? Certainly, Harvey could have done it. But he ruled himself out, citing his out-of-country residence and his heavy academic and speaking program. No one else volunteered. I remained deliberately silent, for taking on the chairship had never been my intent. But the other family owners all pressured me to do so. It was a unanimous effort. I was very sensitive to the fact Bee had chaired the trust for decades. Was it not time for a rep from another family? Apparently not.

Thus, a mere four weeks later, at a special meeting of the trustees, I was unanimously elected as chair, the fifth in the trust's history. In brief remarks, I committed to making sure the trust was heard at the board table and that the Atkinson Principles were observed and promoted at the *Star*. "After all, this is our core. It is what we are about," I said. For Prichard and new Torstar board chair Frank Iacobucci, however, my appointment created a dramatic and unexpected change in the ownership dynamic at the board table—one that only a few months before no one had even contemplated, let alone imagined.

Perhaps my most surprising support had come from the Atkinson family, which Betsy had represented. Having sided with Prichard, they might have been expected to oppose my election. But the two other Atkinson trustees made it clear they were strongly in favour of the move. Atkinson's perspicacious widow, Elaine, now owner of one of the world's largest perfume bottle collections, had watched my departure with great chagrin. She told me how she had witnessed first-hand the Evans/Prichard full-court pressures on Betsy. She had concluded the voting trust needed stronger leadership that would be able to stand up to the duo's machinations. That was also the view of the third trustee, one of Toronto's most esteemed counsels, John Tory Sr., father of Toronto's future mayor. "There is a lot of rough water ahead, John, and you are the only one capable of handling it," he told me. Considered one of Canada's most influential and skilled corporate lawyers, Tory had served brilliantly as consigliere for the richest man in the land, Ken Thomson, coincidentally owner of the *Globe and Mail*. Tory had been one of Joe Atkinson Jr.'s closest advisers, leading Atkinson, in his will, to specifically designate him as adviser to his daughter and widow on *Star* affairs. Though Atkinson knew of Tory's close *Globe* ties, he obviously felt any conflict was manageable. Bee, however, was not nearly so trusting. "His [Tory's] first loyalty must always be to the *Globe*," he would often say. "So, there is a fundamental conflict of interest." Bee's underlying misgivings, coupled with Atkinson's close alliance with the Thalls, the fifth family of owners, had meant he was never close to the Atkinson group. I was about to change that.

The two reps from the fourth family, the Hindmarshes, also became strong allies, particularly after watching my forced departure. Lynne Hindmarsh, widow of Harry Hindmarsh Jr., had never warmed to Prichard, having questioned his motives from the outset. While she had witnessed first-hand some of the old editorial battles between Bee and Harry Jr., she was very much rooted in the present. From her perch on her Caledon farm, where she raised sulky-racing horses and exotic birds, she watched the corporate comings and goings intently. John Hindmarsh, her cousin and a former used car salesman from Goderich, was not a man of many words. However, his quiet demeanour masked a steely determination to keep the *Star* strong. Together, representing 23 per cent of voting trust votes, they were unequivocal in their support, a loyalty reinforced by their ousting of Winter as Hindmarsh director.

The Thall family were the outliers. With their 15 per cent of votes, they had been assiduously courted by Prichard and were steadfast in their opposition to anything Honderich. The depth of the Prichard connection surfaced, to everyone's surprise, at the funeral of Burnett Thall, where Prichard delivered the principal eulogy. The bitter inter-family rivalry between the Thalls and the Honderichs had begun four decades earlier, in the battle for the publishership, and had continued unabated into the second generation. The recent decision by the family to sell all its non-voting shares, without any notice or explanation, served only to heighten tensions. By their actions, the Thalls had effectively alienated themselves from others, leaving them isolated on most major issues.

But decisions within the voting trust were based on a majority vote, which in turn was based on share percentages. Once a decision was reached, all families were legally bound by it. Thus, with my own family's 15 per cent, plus the 15 per cent from my long-standing ally Harvey, plus the 55 per cent from the Atkinsons and Hindmarshes, I started with 85 per cent support. Never forget those numbers, Bee would always remind me. It was a lesson I held on to. Always tend to those relationships, I would constantly remind myself. Do whatever it takes to keep them united. This strategy would underpin everything that unfolded for the next five years. It became critical.

At its core, the past tension between Evans/Prichard and the family owners revolved around competing visions of how Torstar should be run. Evans would often say Torstar was a public corporation, 70 per cent of whose shares were owned outside the voting trust. As such, it should be run as if it were a totally public corporation, with an independent board of directors and executives committed to maximizing shareholder value. Staunchly opposed to this vision were the five families of the voting trust. We were, after all, the only interested parties to have voting shares, the only ones who could elect directors, and the only ones unreservedly committed to upholding the Atkinson Principles. In short, while we readily acknowledged the legal obligations of a public corporation, we also saw ourselves as owners, with all the prerogatives that go with ownership. To Evans and Prichard, however, we were ultimately "a problem to be overcome," as one insider put it.

Within days of settling into my new office, the first salvo in what would be a five-year battle was launched. It would centre, not insignificantly, on what might have seemed an arcane issue—the level of commitment required of prospective Torstar directors vis-à-vis the Atkinson Principles at the *Star*. But arcane it definitely wasn't. It went directly to the heart of how the families saw the running of the *Star*. In his will, Atkinson had specifically dictated that future directors should "preserve and promote" his traditions. He also declared that the *Star* should operate for the benefit of the public, providing a full dissemination of news and opinions, "with the profit motive, while still important, subsidiary to what I consider the chief functions of a metropolitan newspaper." It was that qualification of profit that never sat well with many, Evans and Prichard being among the most notable.

Maximizing profit—or shareholder value—is often seen as the paramount legal duty of directors. At the *Star*, however, Atkinson clearly had a different view. As did I, as publisher. If we were putting out a great "metropolitan newspaper," that might result in somewhat less short-term profit, which would be appropriate. But he and I both believed that maintaining a higher-quality newspaper would lead in the longer term to greater profit. Thus, the families always considered that each director had two legal obligations: the first, to act in the best interests of the company, and the second, just as important, to "observe and promote" the Atkinson Principles at the *Star*. This was critical. Unusual, but critical. There might be tensions between these two obligations, but so be it. Moreover, the five families had recommitted to both obligations in 1957, when the court awarded ownership of the *Star* to them. As family members would often say, "We made a promise to the court."

So it was with more than a little chagrin that I read Evans and Prichard's proposed new criteria for prospective directors. Evans said they need only be "familiar with" the Atkinson Principles and "comfortable" with them to serve on the board. Prichard went even further: "It is understood the reference to profit subordination is historical in nature and that it does not modify or detract from Torstar's goal of maximizing shareholder value." To the voting trust, these new wordings were a declaration of war, a not-so-blatant attempt to rid forever any thought of a legal obligation to uphold the Principles. I was convinced none of the new directors recruited in the past decade had never even heard of this obligation. I was determined to find out. From his Vancouver base, Bee was totally onside.

After several intense months of back and forth, I insisted on making a presentation to the Board on the history of this second obligation.

Evans chose a dark-panelled study on the second floor of Toronto's ultra-establishment York Club for the meeting, citing the need for total privacy. For my hour-long presentation, I referred to 24 legal documents—from Atkinson's will, through the 1957 purchase, right up to the present. Evidence and backup for the second obligation ran throughout most of the documents. At the conclusion, I was met by total, stunned silence. The newest director, former Supreme Court justice Frank Iacobucci, was the first to declare, "This is all news to me." He wouldn't be the only one. Several wondered openly how this would affect them as directors. Indeed, Scotiabank's esteemed and erudite Sabi Marwah told me he might not have accepted the directorship had he known. Afterwards, trust counsel and long-time adviser Garth "Gary" Girvan commented on the degree of discomfort he observed, adding perceptively, "Ultimately you may have to find new directors." It had clearly been news to all of them.

In the months that followed, I met several times with Iacobucci, the then interim president of the University of Toronto, in his Simcoe Hall office. I had known Frank for decades, first as my tax professor at U of T law school. Indeed, I had a deeply etched memory of a moment when I was considering quitting law when "just call me Frank" very generously sought me out. Standing in a hallway, we had an intense chat, with Frank offering most welcome words of solace and advice. We both often referred to that moment. As if in tune with this spirit, Iacobucci—now board chair—took the lead in shepherding into print new wording for prospective directors that importantly included the second Atkinson commitment. This pleased the voting trust, who accepted our argument, if reluctantly.

What this chapter revealed, however, was the near schism at the board between, on the one hand, all the independent directors Evans and Prichard had so carefully recruited, and, on the other, the voting trust. The independents were totally loyal to the chair and CEO, and were, quite frankly, leery of the voting trust directors, particularly Cam and myself. It was at this point that I flew to Cam's home in Chapel Hill, North Carolina, where we quietly plotted next steps. We concluded it was essential that more members of the families get involved as directors. We needed more support around the board table, Cam and I being just two of fourteen. It would take a year, but eventually Elaine became a director for the Atkinsons, and one-time *Star* editorial editor Peter Armstrong was selected as director for the Hindmarshes. Now we were four.

These new voices would prove critical as attention turned to the matter the voting trust cared most about—editorial at their beloved *Star*. Following my departure, Michael Goldbloom chose veteran newsman Giles Gherson as his new editor. A former business editor at the *Globe and Mail* and editor of the *Edmonton Journal*, Gherson came with little knowledge of Toronto and was known in the industry as a respected policy wonk. Goldbloom had called on my first boss, Russ Mills of the *Ottawa Citizen*, to aid him in the selection process. As Goldbloom later confided, I had been specifically excluded at the insistence of Prichard. At the time, my primary concern was that both the publisher and editor had little connection to Toronto, with Goldbloom being ferociously attached to Montreal. Indeed, he insisted a photo of his beloved Montreal Canadiens hockey team adorn his office wall.

By mid-2005, I started receiving complaints from voting trust members about the *Star* editorial department. While both Goldbloom and Gherson talked about providing more context and background, it seemed coverage of big stories in Greater Toronto went missing. Harvey, Armstrong, and Berger all complained the paper was losing its edge. The *Globe* was continually beating it to the punch on big stories, and local news coverage seemed inconsistent at best. Most worrisome, the semi-annual readership survey showed a 10 per cent decline in *Star* readership—a huge drop. I started compiling a list of individual incidents in missed news coverage, which I shared with Goldbloom. At meetings with Prichard and Iacobucci, I would also argue, "You don't lose 10 per cent of your readership and feel your strategy is working." Prichard would always reply, "I feel they should be given more time."

At this point, we weren't calling for change; rather we were expressing great concern. But with the annual Torstar board retreat approaching, I asked for some time there to outline our concerns to other directors. This request ran into a brick wall thrown up by both Prichard and Iacobucci. The agenda was set and no time was available, I was told curtly. Amazingly, the owners of the company would not be given any time at the annual retreat to discuss their concerns about the *Star*. I arrived at the usual venue for our retreat, Langdon Hall—frustrated, yet determined. I was not to be stopped and I deliberately raised the issues about the *Star*, supported by other voting trust directors. The response was fast and equally furious. Prichard replied that he had "fullest confidence" in the editor, and furthermore accused us of conducting a "parallel process." The approach of putting our thoughts on paper and seeking the opinion of a former editor was labelled "inappropriate," missing the fact we had clearly communicated all these concerns by letter to both Prichard and Iacobucci. There was obviously a second agenda at play. It seemed to be yet another in a series of attempts to drive a deep wedge between the independent directors and the voting trustees. The atmosphere around the board table was nothing short of caustic, and the traditional dinner afterwards—which I dutifully attended— was wrapped in tension. As I drove home, I felt I'd been the target of a human battering ram.

It was literally on arrival in Toronto that I received the news—Bee was in hospital in Vancouver, having suffered a debilitating stroke. He was paralyzed on one side. The prognosis was not good. I flew out the very next day and was the first on the Honderich side to arrive. Upon rushing to his room in St. Paul's Hospital, I discovered his wife Rina and her niece, brandishing what appeared to be legal documents. As it turned out, Bee had written a new will, shifting control of virtually everything to Rina and moving many assets to

Vancouver. However, it had not been finally signed by him but rather was sitting on a lawyer's desk in Toronto. I knew I still had the power of attorney and quickly conferred with the doctors to ensure nothing would be signed.

Bee was barely able to speak and in obvious pain. Though I had consulted with him earlier about my issues with Prichard, communication between us had continued to be spotty at best and nonexistent at worst. Bee's blatant drive to seize control of all family assets had split the family, leaving my younger brother David particularly aggrieved. He had been in charge of the family's affairs for years, and Bee's abrupt abrogation of his duties cut very deep. Our family's views on philanthropy had been seemingly etched in stone. Donations were to be anonymous, restricted to projects in keeping with the Atkinson Principles, and limited in geographic scope to the circulation reach of the *Star*, where the profits had been garnered. Now Bee seemed determined to transfer assets west and even to have his name on a building. In one of our last conversations, over cigars on his balcony overlooking English Bay, I asked about the dramatic switch in his philosophy. After a long, poignant pause, he replied, "Isn't a man entitled to change his mind?" I had no ready reply. Yet the change was never to be.

It would take five very long and hard weeks before he would rest in peace. The doctors could have taken extraordinary steps, but they were very pessimistic about the results. Not surprisingly, Bee had signed a living will, specifically declaring his opposition to such steps. For the family, the decision was unanimous. We all agreed this indomitable spirit would have hated such an intervention. My only meaningful exchange with Bee in this period came during the third week, when he rasped out his memorable, "Don't let them ruin the paper." The entire clan was present for his passing; there was an immediate sense of relief that he was now free from pain.

In a note to Rina and his executors written the year before, Bee had specifically asked for no funeral. "When you have lived for eighty-six or more years there is no need for sadness or grief," he wrote. "How much nicer it would be to gather informally, without fuss, and have a glass of wine, and celebrate a life that was far from perfect but endeavoured to make a useful contribution to society." Which is precisely what we did as a family. It was a surprisingly joyous event, full of reminiscences and stories. I provided the family toast. His ashes were later spread on the hillside cemetery south of Baden, where his grandfather is buried. For months later, I was consumed with his legacy, indeed giving several interviews on his huge contribution to journalism. If anything, that drive to do everything to protect his legacy—the *Star*—intensified. It would need to.

In late 2005, Prichard made a sizable strategic bet, spending $283 million for Torstar to buy a 20 per cent interest in Bell Globemedia, the parent of both the television network CTV and the *Globe and Mail*. The idea that the parent of the *Toronto Star* now owned a piece of the *Globe and Mail* raised journalistic eyebrows everywhere. And to top it off, Prichard surprised everyone—myself included—by asking me to serve as Torstar's representative on the Bell Globemedia board. There you had it—the *Star*'s long-time editor and publisher sitting on the board that oversees the *Globe*. But the rules of engagement specifically excluded any Torstar party from seeing any document concerning the *Globe*. So whenever *Globe* publisher Phillip Crawley came to the board, I would immediately leave—each of us exchanging wry grins as we passed each other in the hall. However, I did see this appointment as a goodwill gesture by both Prichard and Iacobucci, who was now Torstar chair.

That goodwill, however, became sorely tested a short time later when Iacobucci introduced a new policy insisting board directors were specifically barred from revealing any matter discussed at the board with anyone. While board confidentiality is a given, it was a well-honoured tradition that all seven members of the voting trust, three of whom were not directors, could receive such information. It soon became clear this new directive was aimed specifically at me because of my regular memos to the voting trust on the comings and goings at the *Star.* Iacobucci said the policy resulted from new securities directives. Trust counsel Girvan told us he was unaware of any such new directives. The issue came to a head at a raucous trust meeting with Iacobucci, when Atkinson counsel John Tory Sr. argued that such a policy, if applied at the *Globe*, would prevent him from consulting with owner Ken Thomson. "This is clearly not viable," he declared, a note of disdain in his voice. We never heard about that policy again.

At the same time, the board was subsumed by a potential takeover bid for all of Torstar by a Quebec firm known cryptically as "Red." As with previous bids, Iacobucci and Prichard insisted all preliminary chats must rest exclusively with them. As chair of the voting trust and an owner, I was specifically excluded, prompting a series of terse complaints from our counsel Girvan to Iacobucci and Prichard. After several weeks, I pre-emptively reached out to Red's owners, prompting them to blurt out, "We've always wondered when we could finally speak with you." A special committee of the independent directors came out strongly in favour of the purchase proposal. But although the share price offered was very good, the five families unanimously rejected the offer. They simply did not want to give up control. The schism at the board was as deep as it had ever been.

The breaking point came a month after Bee's passing, when senior director Martin Connell, the elegant philanthropist/entrepreneur, looked me straight in the eye across the board table and said, "John, we all know the elephant in the room—the voting trust's refusal to sell to Red. Are you prepared to sit down and discuss with me ways to unlock shareholder value?" My first reaction was one of skepticism, for I had crossed swords with him on more than one occasion. He was also a close ally of Prichard. But I instantly overcame that fear and assented.

We then agreed to be blunt and honest, understanding there was no point in playing games. After two meetings with just the two of us at that same York Club, Connell said we needed someone to facilitate the process. "You choose!" And I did—John MacNaughton, the distinguished and decorated founding president of the CPP Investment Board, the agency that oversees investment of the billions of dollars in Canada's federal pension plan. A thirty-one-year veteran of the investment business, MacNaughton had an unimpeachable reputation for being honest and above board. Most importantly, we had been friends for more than four decades and I trusted him to the core.

MacNaughton drew up terms of reference, and the three of us met four times, always at MacNaughton's stately office in the Loblaws tower in midtown Toronto. What unfolded was nothing short of dramatic—indeed, setting the stage for a complete reordering of the power at Torstar. Rather than speaking of financial alternatives, our discussions were all about corporate governance, more particularly the complete dysfunctionality of the relationship among the voting trust and the board, senior management, and other directors. Connell was as open and candid as promised, as was I. At the second meeting, MacNaughton suddenly turned to Connell and, in his dry, matter-of-fact tone, asked, "Don't take this as being too aggressive, Martin, but would you agree there has been a deliberate policy of grind 'em down from the chair and the CEO vis-à-vis the voting trust, and John in particular?" MacNaughton had cut right to the core. I held my breath, but Connell replied instantly. "Absolutely— and I have been part of it." It was as if a dam had burst. I was stunned. The tone of all subsequent meetings turned dramatically, and an agreed-on set of principles quickly ironed out. For either the position of CEO or *Star* publisher, full support of both the board *and* the voting trust was deemed essential. If either body lost confidence, that would be determinative. In many respects, it seemed obvious that the owners should have a right of veto. But now it was cast in stone, embedded in Torstar governance. It also meant, most significantly, that either the publisher or CEO had to have majority support in the voting trust. From now on, my position as chair became even more critical.

The new rules came quickly into play as voting trust discontent with the direction of editorial at the *Star* reached a fever pitch. Both weekday and weekend readership and circulation continued to drop. The *Globe* had clearly set its strategic sights on the *Star*, sensing weakness. And regarding the *Star*'s internet strategy, Prichard had asked Harvey to prepare a report, which concluded, "My investigation revealed broad structural problems with both our internet produce and our strategy." In an eight-page letter in June 2006, the voting trust unanimously declared, "We have grave concerns about the editorial leadership of the paper." We specifically asked that this letter be kept confidential, but Prichard decided otherwise, defiantly distributing it to his senior team. He also declared full support for Gherson and Goldbloom, telling the executive team that management would fight the voting trust. Yet again, the battle lines were set.

For the next two months, the back and forth between the voting trust and Prichard/Iacobucci became intense. Prichard wanted the whole issue put over to the October retreat, where the board would hear a rebuttal from the *Star* team. The trust resisted, insisting it had made up its mind and wanted a change of editor right then. We had specifically structured our demand to include the editor and not the publisher. Goldbloom had obviously been my choice, and I, along with the trust, had not lost confidence in him. We simply wanted the editor replaced. However, Prichard reported back that Goldbloom was standing foursquare behind his editor and would not budge. If the editor went, so would he. We regretted that, but it became the operating dynamic.

At an August board meeting of the independent directors to consider the MacNaughton report, those directors decided to put off the *Star* editorial debate until the October retreat. To decide this with no voting trust directors present was a total affront to the trust. Our lawyer, Girvan, labelled the decision "inappropriate and likely illegal." The voting trust then met in extraordinary session and voted conditionally to replace the entire board of directors—as was our legal right—unless the situation at the *Star* was resolved to our entire satisfaction. This was as dramatic a declaration as could possibly be.

As time for the retreat neared, the personal recriminations intensified. I learned all calls to my office had been monitored by Goldbloom's assistant, and I was verbally chastised for speaking to the marketing chief about readership. Worse still, every meeting, accidental or otherwise, I had had with a *Star* employee over the past two years was catalogued and sent to a lawyer as a weapon to be used against me. The debate at the retreat was close to vicious. Several directors attacked me personally, directly impugning my integrity. Iacobucci expressed "great regret there had to be so much confrontation." However, most importantly, the result was that both the publisher and editor were replaced. As the meeting ended, Connell quietly sought me out, whispering that other directors' comments had been "entirely gratuitous and inappropriate." The following week, Prichard sought out the *Star*'s national/foreign editor, David Walmsley, who would later become editor of the *Globe*. Prichard told me he began expressing regret for the disruption in editorial but was interrupted by Walmsley, who blurted out, "You had to get rid of [Gherson]. He lost the newsroom months ago."

As the new team was introduced—my stalwart number two, Jagoda Pike, as publisher and long-time newsroom veteran Fred Kuntz as editor—reaction throughout the company was overwhelmingly positive. Pike knew the inner workings of the paper inside out after a career that saw her head labour relations and operations, culminating in her appointment as chief operating officer. Kuntz was just as well known in editorial, where he worked his way up the ranks before heading to the *Globe* in a senior editing role. My inbox was inundated with thanks, particularly from those in editorial. I had strongly backed both appointments and I offered my full support to them. Meanwhile, the moves generated plenty of ink in Toronto's other dailies, with some of them speculating on my role. The most provocative of these came from *Globe* columnist Margaret Wente, who observed, "The *Star*'s culture, into which Mr. Honderich was born, has a way of expelling foreign bodies. The *Star* man is not only back inside the building. He's back in charge."

Over the next year, the new *Star* team took hold, with the voting trust hoping the troubles were behind us. However, several early decisions struck ominous notes. I invited Kuntz to my home for dinner, offering to check in with him informally on editorial issues so as to avoid surprises. As his long-time boss and associate, I felt an "open door" policy would be preferable to the previous policy of totally excluding my perspective. Several weeks later, I received an email informing me such an arrangement wasn't "feasible." Shortly thereafter, I learned Kuntz informed all editorial staff they were not to meet with me under any circumstance. Since I had my office in the building and knew many of these individuals socially and professionally, this dictum was essentially unenforceable, if not ridiculous, as many of them told me.

It wasn't until the end of 2007 that real trouble began—and at a dramatic pace. It surrounded labour relations and Jagoda Pike's determination to make her mark. A veteran of collective bargaining, she prided herself on winning tough confrontations—and she had more than a few notches in her belt. After some early back and forth, she opted to pursue $7 million in cuts that struck at the heart of many benefits, including placing restrictions on merit pay, overtime, and Sunday pay. At a board committee, she confidently declared the *Star* could survive a four-to-six-month strike, a view not shared by any director. Furthermore, she was "taken aback" by the board's reluctance to get tough. She was clearly relishing the prospect of a battle, but this was never made clear to the board. While the details of bargaining were clearly the prerogative of management, a decision to enter a long strike required board approval.

What developed in those negotiations was a clear "us versus them" attitude. In an extraordinary move, senior union reps called me privately to warn of a debacle. Our celebrated Ottawa columnist Chantal Hébert called to say she was considering quitting given her unhappiness at the paper. *Star* business columnist Jennifer Wells did quit, citing the same reason. Management revealed they received more than two hundred employee inquiries about buyouts, representing about a quarter of those eligible. The feelings of animosity throughout the company were palpable. I warned Prichard of the dire situation and urged that the board get involved. Ultimately, it would take an emergency board meeting on the very day of the strike deadline to force management off its agenda. Prichard would later apologize to the board for not keeping directors fully informed.

By this point, my confidence in Pike had evaporated. In our periodic meetings with Prichard, it became clear she had wholeheartedly adopted his agenda for cost reduction. She made little effort to hide her disdain for my suggestions, eschewing any desire to meet privately. While we had often disagreed when working together at the *Star*, we had shared a mutual respect. That was sadly no longer the case. Her lack of experience in editorial had been a given on her appointment, but as time passed, that gap proved ever more worrisome. I had enthusiastically backed her appointment; now I was openly questioning my judgment.

That reassessment intensified when editor Kuntz introduced a controversial redesign of the paper. The major reform was to dedicate the first or "A" section entirely to local news, a step often taken by much smaller dailies. Both the editorial and op-ed pages were to be pushed to the back of the second section. And the decades-famous masthead of the *Star*, the reverse blue ribbon, would be eliminated. When presented with these plans, I raised immediate concerns. But Prichard allowed them to proceed. Both Pike and Kuntz also raised eyebrows at the board when they declared there was no longer any need to look for outside marquee hires. This remark prompted chair Iacobucci to call the attitude "arbitrary and worrisome." The duo also repeatedly referred to the *Star*'s reporters as "high-priced workers," leading new director and former Saskatchewan premier Roy Romanow to upbraid them for their attitude.

That the largest newspaper in the largest metropolitan city would adopt such a small-town design and defeatist attitude agitated all voting trustees. Both declining readership and advertising results contributed to their unease. Staff morale was cratering in all departments. The most infamous incident involved the irascible yet hugely talented sports columnist Dave Perkins. The day after he was publicly lauded for raising more than $120,000 for the *Star*'s Santa Claus fund, the workaholic Perkins was told he would be docked a day's pay for failing to provide a required doctor's note for one day's sickness. That tale ricocheted throughout the company.

While Iacobucci and Prichard were acutely aware of the problems, they pointed to a new "winning strategy" to be unveiled mid-summer. Meanwhile, I prepared a *Star/Globe* comparison chart, which revealed that across editorial, advertising, readership, circulation, and print reproduction we were being badly beaten. And particularly so in advertising. About the same time, I received an unsolicited despairing letter from our ace investigative reporter, Kevin Donovan. "I am sitting in the newsroom I have loved for 23 years," he wrote. "No pizzazz. No excitement. . . . Am I pissed off? You bet. Excellence used to be a habit at the *Star*; now it's an accident."

In the lead-up to the August board meeting, I received an outline of the new strategy: a startling $150 million for new presses, a new "*Star* lite" tab to fit somehow between *Metro* and the *Star*, a much beefed-up business section, and a commitment to stick with the "local/local" editorial strategy. Every item appeared misguided. No independent director or voting trustee would ever support the plan. At a voting trust meeting just before the board meeting, there was a consensus we had to move immediately to replace the senior team, however shocking that might be. Again, we were united—or at least I thought so.

After Pike and team made their formal presentation to the board, the plan was met with unanimous skepticism, if not condemnation. Spending so much on presses during a time of restraint puzzled everyone. So did spending so much on business coverage, the hallmark of both the *Globe* and the *Financial Post*. The redesign also drew negative marks from most of the directors. There was much muttering, creating an atmosphere seemingly ideal for my speech, which I had carefully prepared. In staccato tone, I rattled off ten areas where management had failed, including the labour strategy, the redesign, the decision to buy presses, the huge declines in advertising, the botched exit from the Audit Bureau of Circulation, the sudden departures of key employees, and the horrible morale. I concluded by stressing that this was not a "winning strategy" and that management had to be replaced immediately.

There was a poignant pause. Then, directly across from me, the no-nonsense Ron Osborne, by far the most influential of independent directors, declared, "I can't argue with any of the points you've made." Then, turning to Prichard, he asked, "What's your recommendation?" Prichard quickly replied that the team should be given more time to refine its plan, adding that if it wasn't "satisfactory" after that, a discussion would ensue on leadership. Then, feeling he had the wind in his sails, Prichard called for a vote on his appeal for time. His request was granted, with just two "no" votes—my solid ally Elaine and myself. Even owners Harvey and Armstrong went along with Prichard's delay. As a consequence, I did not have the required majority support within the trust. I fled the room, humiliated.

The seemingly rock-solid assurances of support from four voting trust directors, plus our new recruit, Romanow, had evaporated. I had always known how difficult it would be to oppose Prichard in such a charged atmosphere. But I felt betrayed—fundamentally betrayed. From my cottage porch, I wrote an email to all voting trustees, asking the question, "Are we prepared to act as owners?"

and advising them, "Sadly, I have come to the conclusion we are not. The will does not exist. Nor does the resolve. . . . Thus I have no alternative but to tender my resignation as chair of the voting trust." It was not something I came to lightly. Resignation is one of the last cards you can play. But I had had it. However, the shockwaves my decision created were widespread and immediate. Within a week, deep statements of regret were sent and I was welcomed back as chair. Most importantly, my sole condition was met. We trustees would go immediately to Iacobucci and Prichard to say we had lost confidence in both Pike and Kuntz. And since the *Star* team no longer had the support of the trust, under the MacNaughton rules this was determinative.

What then followed were three weeks of high-tension drama. In mid-August, we met with Iacobucci and Prichard, formally saying we had lost confidence in *Star* management. We argued successors had to be found for Pike and Kuntz but left that process to them. During the ninety-minute meeting, Prichard probed persistently, if not crassly, to find any cracks in our resolve. However, the united front never broke. His position, however, was firm. The board had given the *Star* team time to refine its plan. What we were doing was frustrating the will of the board. This could not be countenanced.

Elaine, Peter Armstrong, and I met with Prichard again a week later, where, with Harvey's support, we represented 85 per cent of the voting trust. Right off the top, Prichard requested a meeting with the entire voting trust so we could find a "compromise" and "dodge a bullet." We replied that this was not necessary and were discussing other alternatives when Prichard suddenly called our bluff. While he said he had "zero interest" in leaving Torstar, he declared he and Frank were prepared to resign unless the board process was respected. He added he wanted to stay three more years to the end of his ten-year term "and beyond." We also knew he was having back-door chats with John Tory Sr. about finding a compromise, despite Elaine's protests to the contrary. By pushing us to the brink, I still believe he felt he would prevail. We retired, somewhat taken aback, to consider our options.

An intense back and forth unfolded among the four families, which ultimately resulted in unanimity—we would accept Prichard's resignation. We would call his bluff. Furthermore, we were insistent that he leave sooner rather than later. What we all saw was a path forward that would finally end the battles between ownership and the board. We had had enough. We were united in our determination to act as owners. Two days later, I sent an email to Prichard stating, "We wish to confirm unanimously we respect the CEO's decision [to resign] and we accept it." Shortly thereafter, Prichard called me to discuss timing. I had wording prepared, and told him, "Rob, we listened very carefully to what you said about your own position. You spoke about your own credibility being damaged, and we accepted this. In light, we feel the six-month horizon is the appropriate one." He was extremely professional, answering immediately, "I don't disagree with that." The deed was done.

Pike was shortly replaced on an interim basis by veteran publisher and Torstar director Don Babick, whose celebrated newspaper acumen and steady-as-she-goes approach calmed waters quickly at the *Star*. I also tracked down veteran newspaperman John Cruickshank, a former publisher of the *Vancouver Sun* and *Chicago Sun-Times*, and most recently publisher of CBC News. He jumped at the offer to come to the *Star* as publisher, insisting his reliable sidekick, the effervescent and larger-than-life Michael Cooke, join him as editor. We were back in business with a serious team of top-notch professionals. Their first move was to bring back the *Star*'s old reverse blue-ribbon masthead. The owners were ecstatic.

Over the next few months, a tortuous series of meetings unfolded, leading to my announcement as the new board chair. Most of the independent directors resigned, Babick and Romanow excepted. As a result, I had the delightful task of finding a new slate, including celebrated media executive Phyllis Yaffe, strategist Joan Dea, pension specialist Alnasir Samji, former Cars.com CEO Dan Jauernig, and senior accountant Paul Weiss. None of them had any problem whatsoever with their dual obligations as directors, which included the need to promote the Atkinson Principles. I would also name my longtime associate and veteran CFO David Holland as acting CEO.

The only controversial issue became Prichard's severance. His original contract had been negotiated by John Evans, who had spared no expense whatsoever in compensating his fellow past U of T president. With a salary of $650,000, plus a bonus potential of the same, plus a company car and annual club fees, his annual compensation was close to $1.5 million—a hefty increase over Galloway's annual package. He was also given five hundred thousand stock options on signing "as an inducement to enter into a contract." And then there were the unprecedented special pension provisions, which certainly raised eyebrows internally. On signing, Prichard received five years' pension service. For each subsequent year, he would be entitled to eighteen months' service for every twelve months actually served. Finally, should he be forced to leave the corporation, he would be entitled to three years' pay, plus bonus, plus benefits.

At the often tense committee meetings to discuss severance, Iacobucci was determined to give Prichard the highest ranking for his corporate performance, even though the company had just sustained a dramatic $230 million write-down on the $283 million investment in Bell Globemedia. The investment had turned out be a complete flop. Both Iacobucci and Prichard also proposed not making the final severance public, but other members of the committee quickly rejected this course. The formula for calculating the amount owed was not in dispute, for this had been set out in Prichard's employment agreement. Yet, the year before, the company had conveniently altered the agreement to allow him full severance even if *he* chose to resign. That change would have huge ramifications. Prichard would ultimately earn $9.58 million in severance when all salary, bonus, pension, and other benefits were included. This would lead to a media frenzy, with much critical commentary both inside and outside the company.

The change of guard was profoundly welcomed at the papers. Cruickshank and Cooke quickly took over the *Star*, helping to right the ship editorially and make their own impressive mark. There were no more fights between ownership and the board. The daunting strategic challenges would remain, but attention was now where it should be—on the business, not the corporate boardroom.

EPILOGUE

It was a moment I had never imagined happening. There in August 2019, in the maple-panelled Torstar boardroom on the fifth floor—once called the publisher's boardroom, whose redesign I had meticulously overseen—the deliberations had turned decidedly sour. The Torstar results, both financial and subscriptional, were downright depressing. The brave projections of a new strategic plan were but a memory, lost in a constant stream of "reforecasts." The once soaring promise of our new investment was now mired in a miasma of Google algorithms, desperately trying to find a new life. The repeated commitments to "bend the curve" of that ever-plummeting advertising trend line had lost any meaning. "Hitting the wall"—the oft-used short form for going out of business—began to creep into conversations and financial projections. We had all agreed this latest strategic plan was our last chance. Not one voting share had been sold by any of the five family owners. That was certainly a signal of commitment to be proud of. But how long could we hold out?

The proverbial last straw came when we were presented with the severance costs for the several thousand loyal employees who would be affected by any wind-up. It would be close to several hundreds of millions of dollars. We simply didn't have those funds. Only the year before, we had carefully and deliberately moved all pension plans to the safe confines of Ontario's college pension plan, called the CAAT Pension Plan. But this new information hit with a profound thud.

The first family director to speak, surprisingly, was Elaine, as committed to the Atkinson Principles as anyone could be, and behind that seemingly calm, soft mannered exterior, a fighter to the core. "I think the time has come to consider a sale," she declared, speaking from notes, to the hushed table. The other family directors were asked to speak. Cam Harvey, Dorothy Strachan (representing the Hindmarsh family), and Martin Thall, in very short order, all agreed. Heads quickly spun to me, now chair and the last to speak. "I agree," I declared, resignedly. The die was cast.

A process began and a carefully chosen cadre of experts was commissioned to guide us through the unimaginable. Almost two dozen potential buyers were quietly contacted, each asked about a possible purchase. There were several nibbles, some intriguing, yet our team remained pessimistic about anything substantive. They would be right. Quietly, I had also pursued several offshore Canadian billionaires, asking if any might want to become "the Jeff Bezos for Canadian newspapering." I had specifically coined that phrase, for, like others in the publishing industry, I had been dazzled by the Amazon honcho's daring bid to buy the *Washington Post* and return it to glory. Could I find someone to do the same? Sadly, no.

The process became mired when, suddenly over the transom, a surprise bid for the entire company floated into the email boxes of Torstar's senior executives. The bidder was Jordan Bitove, youngest son of Toronto's celebrated Bitove clan. His older brother John had earned the city's praise for bringing the Toronto Raptors to town while also spearheading Toronto's much-touted, although losing, Olympic bid in 2008. Jordan had worked on both projects and is an unabashed city booster. He asked to meet me privately. Within the confines of a windowless office cubbyhole we sat down, and all he wanted to talk about was the *Star*. Of course, there were the other components of Torstar. But he was bursting with enthusiasm about the paper he used to deliver as a kid. As was pointed out afterwards, anyone meeting me would have little doubt as to what might capture my fancy. I get that. But Jordan's enthusiasm was infectious. I gave him a copy of *Humanity Above All*, a special celebratory booklet I had personally commissioned, chronicling the *Star*'s 110 years of editorial excellence.

The following day, he arrived to speak to all seven members of the voting trust, whose support—once again—was essential for any sale. On arrival, he told me how he had stayed up very late reading *Humanity Above All* and recited some of his favourite passages. Speaking without notes, but obviously well rehearsed, he then brought that same verve and enthusiasm to his pitch. Foremost in his remarks was his repeated commitment to maintain the Atkinson Principles. He made a point of that—several times. In answer to questions, he also argued forcefully that he and his family had the resources to take the company "to the next level." All voting trustees, to varying degrees, were impressed. At that point, the financial interest of his soon-to-be partner, Paul Rivett, was not clear.

A second group, led by finance industry veteran Neil Selfe, along with the Proud brothers—Matthew and Tyler—of Dye & Durham Corp., then entered the fray. They asked for a meeting with me and, over Zoom, peppered me with questions about our major investment, VerticalScope, a multi-platform media company. Barely mentioned was publishing or the *Star*. They would remedy that omission a day later at a much-improved joint submission to the Torstar board and the voting trust. Former Ontario treasurer Greg Sorbara, designated to oversee editorial in this new venture, gave an impassioned speech about the Atkinson Principles—impressing one and all.

We were left to ponder: Which of these potential buyers should we choose? And how did we get here?

By the time I became board chair in '09, there was no doubt of the severity, if not enormity, of the challenges facing newspapers. The emergence of digital advertising and the mass flight of many advertisers to the internet was an established fact. I used to be very proud as publisher to say you could not successfully advertise in Toronto without the *Star*. Now that was no longer even close to the truth. Facebook and Google were now attracting three quarters of all digital advertising. Print readership was declining annually, and competition on the internet for eyeballs was spiralling upwards. Nor were we alone. These trends were in play everywhere, creating havoc for newspapering across the globe.

Indeed, I was quite shaken in '13 when the Graham family decided to sell its interest in the *Washington Post* to Bezos. Torstar often compared itself to the *Post*, with its comparable family corporate structure and its storied passion for journalism. I studied Don Graham's comments intently, his arguments resonating with a profound clarity. The losses had become too great. The trends were depressingly persistent. The declines had forced unwanted reductions in newsroom staff. As a result, the journalism couldn't be the same. The efforts at innovation had simply not been enough. "So, for the first time in our lives," Graham explained, "we asked ourselves if we thought our small public company was still the best place for the *Post*." Was it not time to hand over to someone with both the resolve *and* the resources to carry on?

Seven years later, his words struck as a prophecy. The question among voting trustees had become just that: With a situation this grim, should we not find someone else with more resources and a new vision to carry on? But what would our fathers, partners, and cousins have thought of selling out? It had taken months, as one would expect, for us to arrive at that fateful board meeting where the final decision was made. But the inexorable crush of bad news had taken its toll. And the relentless reductions in the *Star* newsroom to a third of its peak size had acted as an exclamation mark.

On becoming chair, I still had some optimism. There were plans afoot and a sense of relief that the corporate turmoil was finally over. With the ever-steady David Holland as CEO, we embarked on a three-pronged strategy. First, Torstar sold Harlequin in 2014 to book publishing giant HarperCollins for a hefty $455 million.

Fifteen years after my battle to keep it, Harlequin was seeing a steady and ever decreasing decline in both book sales and earnings as more and more publishers entered the romance fiction world, Amazon being the most ferocious. When the unsolicited offer from HarperCollins came in, there was unanimous agreement that we should accept it. Second, we opted to use part of the proceeds to retire all company debt and the other part to buy VerticalScope, whose prospects then appeared golden. Third, we opted not to go with a paywall but rather to develop, in conjunction with Montreal's *La Presse*, a tablet app called Star Touch, which we hailed as a revolutionary way for readers to get their news. With its dazzling flip pages and cutting-edge design, the app won Apple's award for best new editorial app of the year. But tragically—and after the *Star* had spent tens of millions of dollars—the app never caught on, forcing us to shutter it. We would then install a paywall, like virtually all others. But a precious two years had been lost.

Under Holland's leadership, Torstar also made a daring bid in 2010 to become the biggest newspaper publisher in Canada. With Canwest's debt-ridden chain of eleven large dailies, including the *Ottawa Citizen*, *Montreal Gazette*, and *Edmonton Journal*, along with thirty-five community papers, on the block, Torstar made a $800 million cash offer to buy them all. It would have been a realization of what once had been called "the Southam Dream"—a linking of all major English-speaking dailies across the land. In the new digital era, the thinking was, such a powerful behemoth might be able to win the battle of competing Canadian digital news sites. Sadly, we were outbid by $300 million by a consortium of U.S. hedge funds and unsecured creditors, led by our old nemesis Paul Godfrey. The dream was not to be.

During this period, I also reached out twice to *Globe* owner and billionaire David Thomson to see if the *Globe* and *Star* might find ways to work together, always assuming editorial would be kept strictly distinct. It had taken years for the two papers to finally decide to join distribution forces. Having one truck going down a street delivering two papers always made sense to me. Were there other ways, be it production, technology, or advertising, where we could co-operate and save on cost? Meeting with me in his pristine white boardroom, Thomson was the epitome of charm and open-mindedness. Yet nothing ever emerged from our discussion. It has always been my view that the *Globe*, under the strong urging of Phillip Crawley, would prefer to go it alone, in the hope that it will be the last major paper to survive.

Holland would ultimately retire, and former Rogers executive John Boynton would then enter the scene with promises of rapidly increasing subscriptions and "bending the curve" of advertising decline. A daring three-year strategy was unveiled, and a cadre of new specialists was brought in to "catch up for lost time." The promises were bold, the results less so. By the time the board and voting trust met to discuss the bids for Torstar, the decline in advertising had been relentless and new subscriptions had increased but to nowhere near the levels first promised. The year before, we had put VerticalScope on the market, attracting multiple potential investors committed to paying double-digit multiples. One California giant seemed on the verge of buying when Google unceremoniously changed its algorithms. The results were instantaneous and disastrous. VerticalScope's earnings and unique visitor numbers plunged catastrophically, sending the prospective buyers packing. The company's prospects for the future seemed very dark.

During this time, journalism at the *Star* still provided reminders of past glory. Our relentless and daring unveiling of the foibles and transgressions of former Toronto mayor Rob Ford created headlines around the globe. The fact that these stories continued in the face of advertising and readership boycotts sponsored by the Ford clan, costing the paper tens of thousands of dollars, only reinforced the value of the journalism. And the paper received the coveted Michener Award for its work. One of the reporters on that investigative team, the tenacious and principled Daniel Dale, went on to international fame, first as the paper's Washington correspondent, chronicling the lies of U.S. president Donald Trump, and then at CNN. And there were many other investigations—on everything from tax havens to tainted water on Indigenous reserves, to the unsolved murder of a drug company owner and his wife, to sexual misconduct at the CBC. Finally, there was the constant stream of unrivalled commentary from Ottawa, Queen's Park, and the city.

So the journalistic drive for excellence had not disappeared at the *Star*. But its newsgathering resources had been severely diminished, resulting in a decline obvious to everyone. Much as some family voting members might have wanted the future of the *Star* to be the determining factor in choosing a new owner, we knew as a public company that we would face shareholders' severe criticism, if not lawsuits, if we did not accept the highest bid. Indeed, the threats and counter-threats we received during the bidding process made that abundantly clear. Yet to members of the voting trust—and, not surprisingly, to me in particular—the fate of the *Star* and the Atkinson Principles became of paramount importance. And, unlike directors, trustees were shareholders who could do as they wished with their shares. But any sale required a majority of votes at the trust.

For trustees, the choice became clearer as the process unfolded. The Selfe team interviewed a cadre of senior company executives, all of whom reported they were asked precious few questions about publishing or journalism. This reinforced the intelligence I had gathered that Selfe was a rough-and-tumble takeover specialist for whom the assets of Torstar were his principal interest. My interview with the Selfe team reinforced this view, in sharp contrast to my talks with Bitove. When I did ask Selfe what changes he might make at the *Star*, he replied he wanted the paper to do more in-depth stories "like the *Globe*." His partners, the Proud brothers, admitted they had never had a newspaper subscription. When asked where they got their news, one didn't answer, and the other said "Apple News."

During the process, both Selfe and Bitove phoned me, asking for coverage. Selfe wanted a story planted on Sorbara's decision to take an equity position in his bid—a blatant attempt at self-promotion. Bitove, on the other hand, wondered if we would be interested in publishing an essay by his Black business associate, Wes Hall, on Black Canadians in business during the Black Lives Matter protest. Later, Selfe contacted both Boynton and me asking how Torstar and Postmedia could possibly be brought together, in direct contravention to what he had promised the board. In a previous call, he had also asked that Torstar do an email check to verify if Boynton was "leaking" to Bitove. In another call, he shouted at me with a stream of expletives, warning the paper against naming his partners in a story.

The choice of purchaser was not only clear but stark. Not surprisingly, I made my views known to both the board and voting trustees. But the issue of price remained. It would take a dramatic personal telephone call between Bitove and me, with our lawyers also on the line, for us to reach the needed higher price point at the very last moment. Meetings of both the board and the voting trust were called instantly, with unanimous approvals being registered at each. The press release went out that evening. Selfe later complained he had been prepared to pay even more, starting a legal action to prove his point. But he lost his suit both at submission and on appeal. We had carefully followed all the rules. And the deal was overwhelmingly approved at a necessary Torstar shareholders' meeting.

To say I was relieved would be an understatement. Not only had we increased the bidding price from fifty-two to seventy-four cents a share, I felt assured the *Star* would be in safer hands with Bitove. Upon completion of the sale, the new owner repeated public commitments to uphold the Atkinson Principles, reinforcing my view. And their subsequent expansion of the *Star* newsroom has been further evidence of their dedication to journalism. No director or voting trustee is under any illusion that the new owners could go in an entirely different direction. That is obviously their right and their pre-rogative. But their actions since the sale have indicated otherwise.

What would my father have thought of all this? It was a haunting question that never left me throughout the process. Of course, he would have been sorely and severely disappointed the paper and company he had nurtured to such greatness would flow out of family control. I don't think he ever contemplated that eventuality. At his passing, the pressures facing Torstar were clear. But to sell? He would definitely have wanted us to try everything possible to ensure survival. I felt confident we could say that, indeed, we had tried. That said, I am also confident the ongoing well-being of the *Star*, for which he had worked for forty-five years, would have been determi-native in his idea of our success.

Fellow voting trustees all went through the same painful reckon-ing, and all came to the same conclusion. Preservation of the *Star*, particularly its voice, was critical. If through a sale we could make that more likely, we would be doing justice to our history and com-mitments. Ultimately, that sentiment became paramount.

I also felt that, in making this decision, I was being true to my promise to Bee on his deathbed not to let anyone "ruin the paper." In that regard, neither I nor any other family owner felt we could carry on. It was time for someone else to try.

ACKNOWLEDGEMENTS

This book has been fifteen years in the making, but the inspiration for its form, scope, and emotional range sprang from publishing icon Doug Gibson. I took to him the idea of a book on my father and he countered with the broader concept of a book on a history of the *Star*, my father, myself, and the complex relationship between father and son. His advice rang so true, and after a period of reflection, I adopted it wholeheartedly.

My editor (and publisher) at Signal (an imprint of Penguin Random House Canada), Doug Pepper, provided invaluable insight and commentary that never failed to challenge my writing. It isn't easy to edit an editor, but Doug has the knack. I particularly thank him for the choice of title.

On the early history of the Honderich family, Mennonite historian Lorraine Roth proved invaluable with her insights. The German consul general to Toronto at the time, Sabine Sparwasser, kindly arranged contacts in Kassel, Germany, where I was able to search out documents on my great grandparents. For a sense of life in Baden, Ontario, where my father grew up, Tracy Loch, the ebullient curator of Castle Kilbride could not have been more helpful. So too were Badenites Shirley Koenig, Ernie Ritz, Harold Schmidt, Cathy Young, and hockey legend Howie Meeker. For a true perspective, I couldn't have done without the memories and proddings of my beloved Aunt Ruth Spielbergs and philosopher Uncle Ted Honderich, my father's oldest sister and youngest brother respectively. Finally, thanks to my cousin Cameron Honderich, who farmed the original Honderich homestead on Willow Creek and was a source of invaluable information on the family history.

For my father's high school time in Kitchener, the staff at Kitchener-Waterloo Collegiate Institute graciously opened up the school's archives to me. For his six years at the *Record*, former editor Lynn Haddrall gave me complete access and librarian Johanna Neufeld was tireless in working through hundreds of unbylined stories. The memories of former *Record* journalist Frances Denney Sutton were also invaluable.

For my father's early career at the *Star*, the hidden cache of stories and interviews compiled by reporters Jack Brehl and David Macdonald for the unpublished book, all meticulously organized by Pat Wilson, were a godsend. So too were the insights and memories of Murray Cockburn and Janice Goodman. All reporting on the passage of Ontario's *Charitable Gifts Act* was done by my father, dutifully recorded in an unpublished booklet, most of which I was able to incorporate.

To fully appreciate the scope of Honderich family reporting, I also engaged reporter Gilbert Ndikubayezu to compile a written record of all Honderich bylined stories. This five-volume set tells a story in itself. With regard to the Torstar voting trust, I am particularly thankful to Elaine Berger, Cam Harvey, and Lynne Hindmarsh for their ongoing insights and perspectives. My propensity to keep written records on a surprising host of subjects throughout my career served me well in my research. But thanks must be given to my executive assistants—Sigrid Macfarlane, Sue Wagland, Linda Larsen, and Angela Trunfio—who over the years did their damnedest to keep things in order. I am grateful to them all.

Finally, I am indebted to those who read all or parts of my book, offering corrections, different perceptions, or commentary on events. They include Pedro Barata, Lorraine Campbell, Murray Cockburn, John Ferri, Bob Hepburn, Mary Honderich, Robin Honderich, Kennedy Jawoko, Krishan Mehta, Bill Peterson, Mary Deanne Shears, and Jeremy Smith.

PUBLISHER'S NOTE

The publisher would like to thank Robin Honderich, Mary Deanne Shears, Taras Slawnych, and Jordan Bitove for their invaluable assistance in seeing through this book to publication.

INDEX

Bruser, Bert: as confidant of JH,
218, 263, 277, 286; as *Star* legal
counsel, 218, 234, 273
Bruser, David, 234
Bryant, George, 91
Bryden, John, 178
Burkowski, Stan, 90
Bush, Barbara, 45
Bush, George H.W., 241
Bush, George W., 45

C

Cahill, Jack, 158
Calgary Herald, 113
Cambridge Reporter, 223, 228
Camp, Dalton, 196
Campbell, Bill: *Star* ownership
bid, 70, 72–74, 77–78; on
Torstar board, 66, 67, 70,
74–75, 96
Campbell, Colin, 40
Campbell, Murray, 130
Campbell family *see* Torstar
voting trust
Campion-Smith, Bruce, 255
Canada-U.S. relations: free trade
agreement, 187–189; journalis-
tic differences, 146–151; U.S.
investment in, and economic
nationalism, 117, 124, 154
Canadian Bank of Commerce, 77
Canadian Broadcasting Corpora-
tion (CBC), 82, 86, 147, 317
Canadian Charter of Rights and
Freedoms, 177
Canadian Newspaper
Association, 283

Canadian Press, 113–114, 197, 255,
283
Canadian Women's Army Corps,
33–34
Canadianism, Atkinson Principle,
152
Canwest, 238–239, 259, 273–274, 315
Carter, Jimmy, 144, 149
Carter, Phil, 130
Cavell, Charles, 227–229
Cavell, Paul, 127
CFRB (radio station), 86, 108, 262
Chapman, Geoff, 140
Charitable Gifts Act (1949):
amendments to, 54–55, 72; as
attack on *Star*, 52–58, 65, 70,
80–81; repeal of, 56–57; stipula-
tions of, 50–51
Chemical Corn Bank (New
York), 58, 73
Chrétien, Jean, 128, 141, 237
Chrysler, Lyndsay, 127–128
CHUM (media company), 261
Church of Scientology, 134
Churchill, Mary, 33–34
Churchill, Winston, 33, 157
circulation *see Toronto Star*,
circulation
City Woman (magazine), 164
Clancy, Lou, 140, 216, 235, 254
Clark, Greg, 158
Clark, Joe, 135, 142–143, 191
Clark, Neil, 212–213
Cobb, Chris, 220, 223, 235, 238
Cockburn, Murray: on BH, 170;
on Torstar board, 276, 281; as
Torstar CFO, 167–168, 266

Newman, Peter C.: as editor-in-
chief at *Star*, 117, 154–155, 214;
hiring of, at *Star*, 81, 101
newspaper wars *see also* Black,
Conrad; *Financial Post*;
Toronto Star, editorial/
reporting; with *Metro*,
248–249, 252–257, 273–274;
with *Post*, 220–221, 225–226,
230–234, 238–239, 273–274;
with *Tely*, 80, 89–94, 102–104,
118, 164, 236
Nichols, James, 90
Nielsen, Bob, 100, 152
Nixon, Harry, 52
Nolen, Stephanie, 186
North American Free Trade
Agreement (NAFTA), 147,
187–189
Nyland, Steve, 251–252, 257

O

O'Callaghan, J. Patrick, 113
October Crisis (1970), 154–155
Olive, David, 234
Oliver, Ian, 167
Olympia & York Developments,
138
One Yonge Street, *Star* offices at,
138–139, 162–163
O'Neil, Dottie, 103
Onex, 270
Ontario Law Reform
Commission, 56
Ontario Press Council, 165, 169, 189
Ontario Securities Commission,
181–182

Ontario's Court of Appeal, 217
Order of Canada, JH receives, 285
Osborne, Ron, 306
Oswald, Lee Harvey, 91
Ottawa Citizen: editorial tradition
of, 53, 129–130; JH career at,
124–134, 160; origins of, 129;
ownership of, 315
Ottawa Journal, 53, 129, 130, 164
Ouzounian, Richard, 234

P

Palestine-Israel conflict, media
coverage of, 58, 191–192, 272, 277
Palestine Liberation Organization
(PLO), 191
Palmer, Helen, 222
Parkinson, Roger, 230
Parrish, Wayne, 177–178, 226–228
Pearson, Chas, 133
Pearson, Lester B., 98, 101, 125, 153
Pecaut, David, 215
Péladeau, Pierre Karl, 227–228, 249
Pelletier, Jean, 148
Pennington, Bob, 106
Pentecostal Church, 9–10
Perkins, Dave, 172, 305
Perry, Robert, 159
Picard, André, 186
Pieri, Mike, 148, 149, 222
Pike, Jagoda, 302, 303–308
Port Hope Times, 38
La Prensa, 60, 94
La Presse, 148, 204, 315
Prichard, J. Robert S.: appointed
Torstar CEO, 269–270;
conflicts with JH, 271–282,